OTC Markets in Derivative Instruments

OTC Markets in Derivative Instruments

Nick Cavalla

M

First published in the United Kingdom by
MACMILLAN PUBLISHERS LTD, 1993
Distributed by Globe Book Services Ltd
Brunel Road, Houndmills,
Basingstoke, Hants RG21 2XS, England

ISBN 0-333-58308-6

A catalogue record for this book
is available from The British Library.

While every care has been taken in compiling the information contained in this publication, the publishers and editor accept no responsibility for any errors or omissions.

Typeset and printed in Great Britain

Contents

Contributors

Leon Cane. After qualifying as a chartered accountant in London, Leon Cane read law at Cambridge University and subsequently qualified at the Bar. He is a principal in the Financial Institutions Tax Group of Touche Ross, where his work includes advising on the UK and international tax aspects of derivative instruments. This involves assistance in the development of new products with financial institutions and advising on the implications of existing products for corporate users.

Nick Cavalla. A chartered accountant and MA in mathematics from King's College, Cambridge, Nick Cavalla is currently a management consultant with Touche Ross, specialising in corporate and financial treasury management. His previous employers have included: the futures broker GNI, where he was head of research, and responsible for the interpretation and forecasting of major financial markets, money management in futures and options, and advice on hedge construction and the mathematical and technical aspects of derivative instruments; and County NatWest Investment Management, where, as an assistant director in the quantitative investments section, he managed the fixed income and derivatives dealing operation and the product development group.

Chris Currington is a partner in Arthur Andersen's Financial Markets Division and is a member of the Canadian and Scottish Institute of Chartered Accountants. Chris returned to Arthur Andersen in 1988, after spending 18 months as European Financial Controller for a major American investment bank. He has also been seconded to an international bank and to a major international trading and broking group. The majority of Chris' work is of an advisory nature, including treasury and risk management studies, business reviews and investigations. Chris has directed numerous reviews on the quality of management, financial dealing and treasury control environments for a number of major UK corporates and for a number of international banks based in London. He is a regular speaker at conferences on risk and treasury management and accounting for new financial products. Chris has also written a number of articles on these topics.

Josh Danziger is Senior Quantitative Analyst at GNI. His responsibilities include analysis and advice on hedging techniques and trading strategies using derivative instruments; in particular, he has specialist interests in interest rate options and in the new area of electricity derivatives. Previously, he has worked as a Financial Engineer in the interest rate market for a UK merchant bank. Qualifications include an MA and a PhD from Gonville & Caius College, Cambridge.

Karen Mason graduated from the City University Business School with a degree in Banking and International Finance. Prior to joining BZW Investment Management (BZWIM) she worked for six years in the quantitative team at County NatWest Investment Management, where she headed the team responsible for product development and, subsequently, the management of the fixed income and derivatives team. During this time, she was involved in the development and launch of a number of derivative-based investment strategies, including portfolio insurance and currency dynamic hedging. She joined the quantitative team at BZW Investment Management in 1991 where she provides advice on derivative strategies and is involved in the management of client portfolios.

Andrew Norman. After completing his studies in 1987, Dr Andrew Norman spent three years at County NatWest Investment Management working on quantitative modelling and product development projects for various new fund management products, including asset allocation, dynamic currency hedging and portfolio insurance. In 1990 he moved to Bankers Trust Capital Markets where he has developed analytics for multi-factor derivative products, covering fixed income, foreign exchange and equity markets. He has also worked on risk management advisory assignments for financial institutions.

Recently, he has joined a newly formed group at Bankers Trust in Quantitative Research and Arbitrage, to apply new valuation and hedging techniques to equity and foreign exchange markets, and provide consulting on technical issues. Dr Norman holds degrees in mathematics and statistics from London University and also obtained a PhD in Stochastic Control and Finance from Imperial College. The subject of his doctoral research was an investigation of the effect of transactions costs on the portfolio choices of a utility-maximising agent.

Robert Rountree BA ACA is a Vice President in the Financial Division of JP Morgan in London. Educated at Sedbergh and Lincoln College, Oxford, Robert qualified as a chartered accountant with Touche Ross in 1985. After qualification he spent two years in the financial services audit group of Peat Marwick in Paris, before joining JP Morgan in 1987 to manage the financial accounting area of the bank's London branch. Robert moved to the Swap Financial Control group of JP Morgan Securities Limited in 1990 to supervise implementation of financial controls over the rapidly expanding swap derivative business, and in 1991 took responsibility for managing the support of the New York and Tokyo swap trading areas.

Louise Rowsell is an Associate Director of Mitsubishi Finance International Plc. She joined Mitsubishi in 1990 to set up and develop the Commodity Derivatives operation. This business enhances the related Equity and Interest rate product range provided by the Bank. Louise first entered the commodity markets by joining Phibro Salomon Ltd, London in 1983 where she traded physical non-ferrous and Platinum Group metals. Since that date she has been involved firstly in the trading of energy futures and subsequently energy and metals swaps. In addition to trading activities, Louise also fulfils teaching assignments on Energy and Metals Derivatives as well as being a regular contributor to various financial publications on the subject.

Mike Shilling graduated in 1978 from Oxford University where he studied Politics, Philosophy and Economics. After spending nine years with the British Broadcasting Corporation he joined Record Treasury Management Ltd, part of NP Record plc and one of the world's leading foreign exchange risk management specialists.

He is currently an Associate Director responsible for developing and marketing dynamic hedging and option-based strategies, as well as the on-going management of Record's $4 billion portfolio of risk. Mike contributes regularly to professional journals on such subjects as corporate risk management and currency overlay for institutional investors.

Christopher C. Taylor. After graduating from The City University with an honours degree in Banking and International Finance, Christopher Taylor has gained extensive experience in the field of interest rate and currency exposure management, working for a number of leading international banks. This experience includes: helping to found Midland Bank's financial futures operation; working as a member of Citibank's financial engineering unit, providing the bespoke solutions to exposure management problems; marketing swaps and options for County NatWest working within the bank's Rate Risk Management group. Christopher Taylor has recently joined Barclays de Zoete Wedd as Head of Treasury Sales from Midland Montagu where he was Head of Specialist Derivatives Sales.

Victoria Ward read Modern and Medieval Languages (German and Italian) at Selwyn College, Cambridge. In 1981 she joined Fiamass as a graduate trainee. She moved to Messel Futures Ltd (now part of Shearson Lehman) in 1982 to develop the futures operations, initially in the gilt market. In 1984, she was made a Director of Messel Futures Ltd and moved from gilts to head up Stock Index brokerage. In 1985, Victoria joined Michael Page City, an Executive Search and Recruitment Consultancy, as a Senior Consultant.

Victoria joined the London International Financial Futures Exchange in early 1987 as Market Development Manager, with responsibility for Stock Indices. She then became Director of UK Business Development. Her last post at LIFFE was as Director of Product Development, where she was responsible for monitoring the progress of the market and dealing with the technical issues that arise relating to the contracts already traded, as well as developing a strategy for introducing new products, carrying out appropriate research leading up to the introduction of these products, detailed research and proposals on launching a new contract.

In January 1992 Victoria joined NatWest Capital Markets as Director of Business Development for NatWest Futures. Her role included developing the business strategy for the Futures company in the UK and elsewhere, and in identifying opportunities for NatWest to integrate its services in relation to exchange traded and other derivatives. In June she was promoted and is currently in charge of Global Futures for NatWest.

Mark A. Zurack is a Vice President at Goldman Sachs & Co. in charge of research for all Global Index Products. Throughout his career at Goldman Sachs, Mark has written many reports on strategies using indices and options and futures markets around the world. He joined the firm in November 1983 after working as a consultant at Chase Econometrics/IDC from 1980–83. Mark is a CFA. He received his MBA from Cornell University in 1980, and his BS from the State University of New York at Binghamton in 1978.

Preface

The timing of this publication is perhaps opportune. Around the world, regulatory concern and suspicion about the phenomenal growth in the derivatives markets have recently been voiced, the swaps markets being singled out for particular attention. The implications of the most remarkable and enduring of the financial innovations of the last fifteen years are under intense investigation. Players in the derivatives markets, traditionalists in the 'cash' markets, and regulators, have strong and often opposing opinions regarding the economic value of the newer types of financial instruments. There are many misconceptions fielded in this debate, and it is a responsibility of books of this kind to challenge and correct these. It is hoped that the reader will conclude that in the following chapters these issues have been addressed impartially. Although all of the contributors to this publication have roles within the derivatives markets, and may therefore be characterised as enthusiasts, their contributions are consistently realistic and practical.

Innumerable books have been written on the subject of futures and options. This publication is distinguished in part by its consideration of a wider range of instruments, but more so by its emphasis on the over-the-counter (OTC) markets. For over seven years, the OTC markets have expanded more rapidly than their exchange forebears. The relationship between the two – part competition and part symbiosis – is an interesting one, and is considered carefully in Chapter 7.

Outside of financial institutions, the natural end-users of OTC products are investment managers and corporate treasurers. This book has been aimed especially at these individuals, whose technical knowledge and sophistication in the use of derivative products have lagged well behind comparative awareness in the broking and banking worlds. Although yet more arcane instruments are being developed and marketed, it is inevitable that this gap (essentially, between supply and demand) will be narrowed. This book will have achieved its purpose if it succeeds in both demystifying this particular area of investment and converting a small proportion of an agnostic audience to an appreciation of the interesting applications of derivatives.

Intentionally, the book is not heavily mathematical. It is designed primarily as a qualitative, but objective, survey of an industry which is becoming more heterogeneous as it approaches maturity. I believe that collectively the contributed chapters have largely succeeded in describing the key aspects of the business without being oppressively analytical.

The order of the chapters mirrors the development of the markets: five chapters are devoted to specific markets and constituent products; an ensuing chapter considers the relationship with exchange traded markets; two contributors then deal with the practical applications of the instruments; and the book concludes with the surrounding themes of risk management, taxation, accounting and regulation. As suggested above, regulatory pressures are increasing, and for this reason the subject is alluded to throughout the book as well as being covered in depth in the penultimate chapter.

By way of acknowledgement, I would like to thank all eleven contributors, each of whom has suffered to some degree my importunate requests, editorial changes and comments. I am very grateful to my commissioning editor, Andrea Hartill, for her initial decision to invest me with this editorial responsibility, and for her support throughout the venture. Finally, I must thank the production editor at Macmillan, Penelope Allport, for her speed and efficiency in bringing the book to print.

Nick Cavalla
November, 1992

1: Overview

Nick Cavalla, Touche Ross Management Consultants

It would be well, by way of preface, to attempt to define the terms 'derivative' and 'OTC'.

A 'derivative' instrument is one whose value derives from the price(s) in an underlying primary or 'cash' market. By contrast with equities, derivative instruments have a predetermined finite life at the end of which they expire, and usually involve an exchange of payments which is small by comparison with the notional underlying value of transactions. A confusing variety of instruments is now available, but in essence all are fashioned from two primary building blocks: the forward contract, under which the buyer (long position) and the seller (short position) have symmetrical and opposite exposures to the underlying market; and the option contract, which for the buyer is a right, not an obligation, and so represents a contingent asset. Typically, an option's value at expiry reflects the relationship between the then current underlying market price and a fixed strike price; more complex forms of option exist whose expiry value may depend on other factors, such as the path that the underlying market has followed during the life of the contract, but all options are characterised by an asymmetry of risk and return.

An 'over-the-counter' (OTC) instrument is a contract negotiated between two principals away from an organised exchange, although a broker may act as an intermediary. It is common for the contract to be 'tailored' to meet the precise specifications of one of the counterparties. (A detailed comparison of the characteristics of exchange-traded and OTC markets is contained in Chapter 7.)

The growth in the volume and variety of derivative instruments has been vertiginous. Figures published by the International Swap Dealers Association (ISDA) reveal rises since 1987 of 349 per cent and 342 per cent respectively in the outstanding notional principal of interest rate and currency swaps in all currencies (Figure 1.1); and an eightfold rise since 1985 in US dollar interest rate swaps alone.[1] The markets in other products, such as forward rate agreements (FRAs) and currency options, have not been surveyed with comparable accuracy, but the evidence that is available would suggest that the use of these instruments has also grown substantially. The Bank of International Settlements (BIS) calculates that, as a proportion of the international assets of reporting

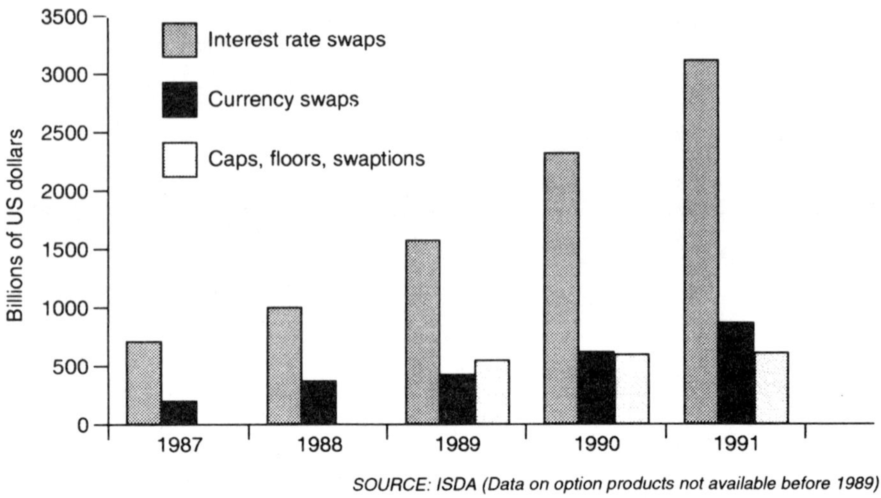

Figure 1.1 Notional Principal Underlying OTC Derivatives

banks, the identifiable underlying notional value of outstanding interest rate and foreign exchange derivatives rose from around 25 per cent at the end of 1986 to nearly 75 per cent by the end of 1990.[2]

These developments are often attributed simply to the increasing internationalisation of companies and investment managers, and the greater volatility of financial markets. In fact, since the volatility of foreign exchange rates has not shown a consistent trend during the last two decades (Figure 1.2), and interest rate volatility has declined since the early 1980s (Figure 1.3), it is clear that the behaviour of market prices cannot in isolation explain the growing use of derivative instruments. The full explanation is more complex, and contains a number of independent elements. The primary intention of this chapter is to identify and describe some of these elements, since this exposition should provide the reader with an insight into the principal OTC markets and products, and, perhaps, a feeling for how they might develop. The chapter concludes with a discussion of some current issues: credit risk, capital adequacy and recent market trends.

REGULATORY AND CREDIT ARBITRAGE AND ACCOUNTING TREATMENT

The origins of the swap market lie in the (mainly sterling/dollar) parallel loans of the 1970s, arranged to bypass foreign exchange controls. As exchange controls were progressively disbanded, the parallel loan became archaic, and the currency swap developed in its place as an off-balance sheet instrument

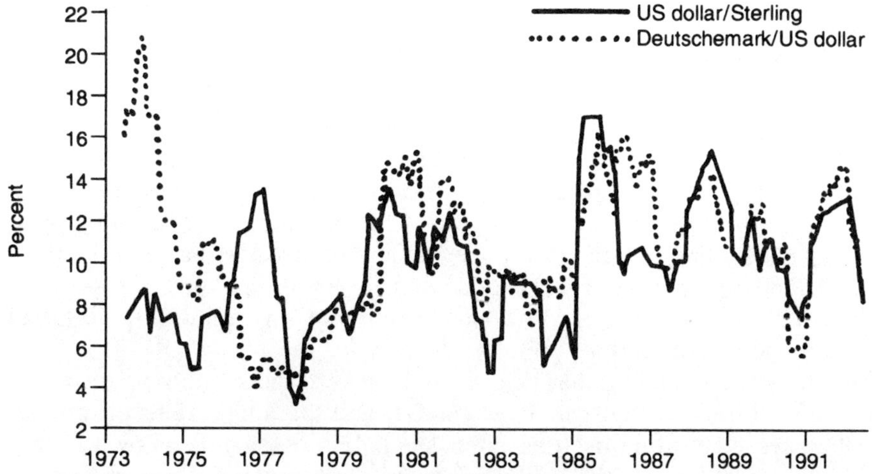

SOURCE OF UNDERLYING DATA: DATASTREAM (Annualised volatility calculated from monthly data)

Figure 1.2 Variability of Foreign Exchange Rates Since 1973

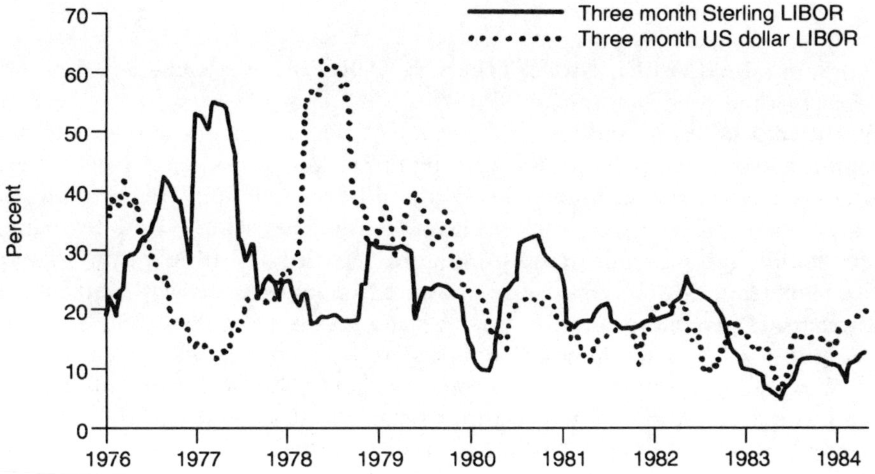

SOURCE OF UNDERLYING DATA: DATASTREAM (Annualised volatility calculated from monthly data)

Figure 1.3 Variability of Interest Rates Since 1976

subject to much reduced credit risks. Later, the market became less motivated by the avoidance of regulatory constraints, and more by the possibility of comparative advantage: where perceptions of credit risk varied between different markets and groups of investors, an institution could reduce its cost of funds by borrowing in the market in which it enjoyed a comparative advantage, and then swapping the proceeds into its preferred currency and interest rate basis. However, this classic explanation of the economic purpose of the swap market is now less complete as the awareness of investors has become more global; and the 'plain vanilla' products in the swap market are now 'commoditised' as instruments for risk management not always linked to new issue or arbitrage activity in the capital markets.

At the same time there has been a growing awareness within financial and other institutions of the scarcity of capital, and the implications of inflating the balance sheet with offsetting assets and liabilities (sharpened by the introduction in 1988 of the BIS capital adequacy guidelines). Traditionally, OTC derivatives have been treated as off-balance sheet transactions, and profit and loss accounted for on an accruals, not mark-to-market basis. For many financial institutions, and some companies, this accounting treatment was seen as attractive, although it is now considered to be less sound. Recent developments in the theory and practice of accounting policy are covered in detail in Chapter 11.

PARALLEL GROWTH IN SECURITIES MARKETS

By the mid-1980s, a significant proportion of new issues in the international capital markets, particularly the Eurobond market, was swap-driven. These issues were often encouraged by credit arbitrage, in that the traditional European retail investor (the 'Belgian dentist') was motivated by name recognition and did not attempt to quantify credit risk with the same rigour as a bank lender. Moreover, Eurobonds are frequently issued with detachable warrants or have more complex pricing structures (e.g. dual currency bonds). The values which different groups of investors place on the option-like elements in these structures may vary, encouraging an additional form of market arbitrage. In addition, certain warrant issues are designed to attract specialised groups of investors for whom a liquid long-term options market is not available.

The trend towards 'structured finance' – which, inevitably, involves the assumption or sale of a derivatives exposure – is a corollary of the growth of the capital markets and the related disintermediation of the banking sector by large international corporate borrowers.

INVESTOR-DRIVEN DEBT ISSUES

Not all exotic debt securities are issued as Eurobonds. For reasons of flexibility and expense, smaller capital issues often take the form of Euro-medium term notes or private bond issues. A trend has emerged for these issues to be driven by the requirements of investors rather than borrowers: an arranging bank designs a security which exploits different investor perceptions, and then encourages a borrower into the transaction with the allure of sub-LIBOR funding. Almost invariably, these securities contain embedded options and for this reason are known familiarly in the capital markets as 'embeddos'. Until recently, the most common of these was the Nikkei-linked bond. An investor in this type of equity-linked security receives an above market yield, but forgoes coupon income or (more usually) principal repayment as the Nikkei 225 index falls. In essence, the investor has sold a Nikkei put option to the issuer in exchange for an initial coupon stream which is higher than that available on straight yen bonds. Since the issuer is unlikely to be willing to assume the Japanese equity market risk indicated by this structure, there is a separate swap contract with the arranging bank which transforms the issuer's combined liability into the form of conventional debt in a desired currency. Usually the arranging bank will then offset its own exposure by selling Nikkei put options to European and US investors. A number of factors contributed to the success of this deal in the late 1980s. Investors had difficulty both in valuing the embedded option and constructing a comparable market exposure for themselves. Japanese buyers may have succumbed to an irrational desire for yield in preference to other forms of return, and the structure exploited the divergent views of Asian and Western investors as to the future direction of the Japanese equity market.

DEREGULATION

It is probable that the relaxation of exchange controls has been the most influential catalyst for the growth in derivatives markets, in which many of the transactions common today would have been impossible in the early 1970s. Additionally, many of the regulatory, legal and tax restrictions relating to the use of derivatives, particularly those faced by pension funds and other institutional investors, have slowly been eased. In the UK, tax changes in the 1990 Finance Act went beyond the removal of uncertainty almost to encourage institutional use of derivatives markets. Permission for the use of derivatives by unit trust managers for the purposes of 'efficient portfolio management' – as defined under the European Community's directive for the regulation of 'Undertakings for Collective Investments in Transferable Securities' – has been similarly beneficial.

By contrast, new regulations in the UK enabling futures and options funds (FOFs) to be sold as unit trusts have so far failed to provoke a meaningful number of launches of new products. This failure has been widely attributed to the incompatibility of the traditional fee structure of unit trusts with the (often high) performance fees charged by futures trading advisers, and the practical difficulty of designing a guarantee, or floor, return – appropriate for many futures-based strategies – within an open-ended fund such as a unit trust. But there is no doubt that the trend towards more permissive regulation regarding the use of derivatives will continue to transform the fund management industry.

QUANTITATIVE INVESTMENT

Until the early 1980s, fund management was dominated by subjective strategies: while there was a widespread understanding of the capital asset pricing model, most portfolio managers would pursue a qualitative process of stock or sector selection. Moreover, international portfolios were relatively rare, and pension fund assets (particularly in the US) were denominated substantially in the same currency as the associated liabilities. Awareness of quantitative investment techniques and the growing internationalisation of portfolios have greatly altered this history.

The application of derivative instruments has naturally followed these trends: swaps, futures and options have been used to modify asset positions to accord with risk management requirements given a performance benchmark or liability profile; and more recently equity index swaps have followed the prevalence of indexation and 'basket' trading techniques. There has been a drive to ensure efficiency in arranging transactions and to reduce costs, both of which objectives are often achieved more easily by employing derivatives strategies in preference to trading in underlying securities. Given the advance in indexation, particularly in pension fund investment, it is perhaps unsurprising that, in both the OTC and exchange-traded markets, the growth in the use of products related to individual stocks has been far slower than that in equity index instruments. Investors have also become more aware and interested in option-based structures, and more sophisticated in the tactical use of derivatives to enhance returns.

Common applications of derivatives with fund management are described in Chapter 8.

TAX EFFICIENCY

Certain debt instruments – for instance, deep discount bonds, dual currency bonds and leasing arrangements – have been particularly effective in exploiting the different tax positions of lenders and borrowers. A derivatives overlay is frequently incorporated, although not always specifically for tax reasons – commonly its purpose is to remove the residual interest rate or foreign exchange risk face by one or more parties to the transaction.

Tax avoidance or minimisation is also an objective of many asset- or investor-driven transactions. Investors are subject to different tax regimes, and increasingly OTC instruments are designed to arbitrage between these different environments. An example is the DAX (German equity) index swap, which enables a foreign investor in the German stock market to avoid a direct exposure to the irrecoverable German withholding tax of 15 per cent on dividends. DAX swaps have attracted interest from managers of index portfolios in the US and Japan, some of whom are prohibited from using futures contracts to achieve the required exposure. In most cases the intermediary financial institution has been able to offer the institutional investor a guaranteed return in excess of the German index by hedging the swap through the purchase of undervalued DAX futures contracts. (This undervaluation has been caused by the unwillingness of domestic German investors to buy futures as an alternative to physical investment – since by so doing they cannot reclaim the tax credit on the implied dividend stream – and the presence of high stock borrowing costs, which have placed a premium value on physical long positions and reduced the gains from index arbitrage.)

NEW PRODUCTS AND 'FINANCIAL ENGINEERING'

The success of the swap market in exploiting the comparative advantage of certain borrowers in particular markets has led to the general use of the term 'financial engineering'. This can be defined as the alteration of an institution's assets and liabilities, or revenue flows, often through the use of derivative instruments, to meet the objectives of economic efficiency, commercial and financial risk reduction (or assumption), or arbitrage.

A simple example might be the arrangement by an aluminium smelter of a loan in which repayments are linked to the London Metal Exchange (LME) aluminium price. In this instance, the lending bank would hedge its commodity exposure using LME contracts. Another example is the 'inverse LIBOR' loan, in which the borrower pays a fixed rate (say 20 per cent) *less* LIBOR, with a floor rate of zero. This funding structure is held to appeal to those companies which face considerable commercial exposure to high interest rates and the economic cycle (e.g. property and construction companies). While the loan appears unusual, its construction is in fact fairly straightforward, being the combination of three elements: a straight floating rate (LIBOR) loan; a fixed/floating interest rate swap (paying fixed) for *twice* the principal amount of the loan; and the sale of an out-of-the-money (LIBOR) interest rate cap (whose strike, in the example given, is 20 per cent).

In many of these types of transactions, the activities of the counterparty bank extend beyond the traditional assumption of price and counterparty credit risk to an involvement in detailed corporate finance or investigative consulting work. Yet banks have generally concluded that they profit most from their derivatives operations by acting as a principal in transactions, not by charging corporate finance or consulting fees. It could be argued that, as a result, there has been a tendency for product development to advance beyond the needs or understanding of the end-user. For instance, in recent years a number of more exotic options have been developed and promoted. The more familiar examples – described in Chapter 4 – are average rate (Asian), look-back, barrier and compound options. For some of these, notably average rate options, there is a genuine demand. But the more arcane and proprietary the instrument, the more probable that it will have been designed without clear regard to the source of investor demand; and therefore the product will add pricing and analytical complexity to the marketplace, but not increase traded volumes or market liquidity. This issue is taken up further in Chapter 7.

In addition, there is a natural and understandable tendency to promote products which take an opportunistic advantage of current market developments. Investors should consider the extent to which a reliable secondary market in these instruments will be available, whether these products will continue to be offered in a few years' time, and even whether they offer genuine benefits now. An interesting example is the differential swap (known also as a 'quanto' or 'cross-indexed basis' swap), under which the investor/borrower receives (say) sterling LIBOR, and pays (say) US dollar LIBOR plus a spread, all payments and receipts being made in sterling on the same notional sterling principal. This swap structure has attracted interest in the early 1990s as a result of the divergent trends in international yield curves: by mid-1992, the US dollar yield curve was steeply positive with short rates at their lowest levels for a generation, while European yield curves were predominantly narrowly inverted and real interest rates at very high levels. In this environment the opportunity to borrow in sterling but pay US dollar short rates (plus a spread) has an obvious appeal – even if the shapes of the yield curves imply that the advantage may disappear or be reversed within several years. The appeal may be deceptive: efficient market theorists would deny that there is any expected benefit from undertaking a differential swap.

OPTION-BASED STRUCTURES

Despite the tendency for banks occasionally to invent exotic options which serve little economic purpose, it is undeniable that the asymmetry of risk and return of the option has proved to be an attractive building block for OTC transactions. Examples in which an option-based return has been successfully packaged and sold to an institutional or retail investment audience include:

- *Guaranteed bonds or funds*, which combine a zero coupon or deep discount security and a call option on an index;
- *Dynamic hedging*, which is the systematic replication of a put option return by progressively buying and selling underlying 'straight' contracts (such as futures or forward agreements). The failure of equity market dynamic hedging, when marketed as 'portfolio insurance', to perform satisfactorily during the 1987 stock market crash has not prevented the application of similar techniques to foreign exchange exposures;
- *Average rate (Asian) options*, whose payoff at expiry relates a strike price to an average underlying market level on a number of predetermined fixing dates. The Asian option is potentially attractive to those companies which face (currency) exposures crystallising over a certain number of days within a period, rather than on a single day;
- *Warrant issues*, either on a stand-alone basis or detachable from an underlying debt issue.

In some cases these products have filled an earlier gap in the catalogue of derivative instruments on offer. For instance, index warrants have enabled longer-term management of financial exposures for which the standard exchange-traded and OTC options available may be unsuitable. Similarly, dynamic currency hedging has provided tailored currency protection at – it is claimed – lower cost than the simple purchase of OTC (or exchange) put options. In some circumstances, the construction of an option return has the attraction – for the intermediary – of obfuscating the issue of valuation. Retail investors, in particular, have paid highly for guaranteed and other option-based products: analysis by Record Treasury Management[3] of a guaranteed equity bond recently issued by a UK building society concludes that the gross margin on the issue was in excess of 4 per cent.

Even banks find difficulty in pricing the most exotic structures. Analytic pricing formulae do not exist for these options, and there is competitive advantage (both real, and in terms of image) to be gained by demonstrating expertise in the development and application of quantitative models and pricing techniques. State-of-the-art proprietary quantitative products, produced by a team of 'rocket scientists', are much in vogue, although in some cases there is doubt about the banks' ability to distribute these products.

RISK MANAGEMENT

The term 'risk management' is probably applied too readily to a variety of distinct management activities and will have different connotations within different companies and market sectors. Financial, commercial and operational risks are diverse in nature and it is not immediately apparent, for instance, why the control of an operational risk – such as the possibility that a key member of staff may leave – should fall under the same management procedure as the control of the interest rate risks attaching to the institution's assets and liabilities.

However, some generalisations can be made concerning financial and market price risks. The first is that the traditional methods of hedging have not always been efficient: for example grossing up the balance sheet with unwanted assets and liabilities to avoid interest rate exposures, or buying commodity price cover through traditional insurance channels. The use of 'cash' markets to alter financial exposures is often more expensive than employing derivatives. A futures overlay is now commonly applied by investment managers to alter asset allocations in preference to the purchase and sale of underlying securities. In addition, the availability of new instruments which can be used to modify or avert financial exposures has encouraged companies to consider these exposures more closely and the conclusion from this analysis does not always accord with earlier preconceptions. As technical knowledge of derivatives within the corporate sector has become more widespread, it is no longer common to encounter the view that financial and commodity price risks must simply be endured.

Before commenting on several issues which may shape future developments, it is worth mentioning briefly one additional factor which has contributed to the use of derivatives markets. Different segments of the financial markets can be seen as offering complementary investment and/or borrowing opportunities, and these segments can often be linked efficiently (and cost effectively) by transactions in derivative instruments. Increasingly, a particular hedge or arbitrage transaction may involve a number of component parts, and the BIS has conjectured that the interaction between different financial markets and products has created a 'considerable degree of pyramiding of transactions in derivatives'.

CREDIT RISK

This book is published during a period of sharp contraction in world economic growth. The economies of the English-speaking countries have suffered particularly, arguably in reaction to an earlier over-extension and a sharp rise in indebtedness within one or more of the private, corporate and government sectors. The increase in debt, combined with historically high levels of real interest rates (most notably in Europe), have led some commentators to fear a 'debt deflation' reminiscent of the 1930s' depression. With rather less rigour, others have connected these developments with the dramatic increase in the notional underlying value of outstanding OTC derivatives positions. It is the view of the editor that this connection displays a lack of understanding of the derivatives markets: there is no reason to believe either that the debtor/creditor relationships implicit in outstanding OTC derivatives transactions are a mirror of those in the general economy, or that net levels of debt are increased by derivatives transactions. Yet there is an undoubted concern among regulators that OTC positions may increase systemic risk within the financial system; and, in the light of background economic developments, the credit risk attaching to both products and counterparties is now considered carefully by many players in the derivatives markets. In the OTC markets there have been two developments: first, innovative attempts have been made to quantify credit risk and, second, products and relationships have been designed which are either more efficient or more secure in their reliance on credit.

It is now commonplace for both companies and financial institutions to mark-to-market derivatives positions for the purposes of risk management, even if an accruals-based approach is still used for financial reporting (e.g. because derivatives are defined always as hedge transactions). Accounting under the accruals method conceals credit risk by failing to record the replacement value of OTC positions. It is also unsafe to conclude that credit risk relates only to those positions which have a positive replacement value: this may be true instantaneously, but this conclusion ignores the dynamic of the exposure. In fact, the credit risk of an OTC portfolio is a variable which depends not only on the innate creditworthiness of counterparty institutions, but also on underlying market prices and volatility, and the time to maturity of the derivative instruments. Within the swaps markets, in particular, much work has been done to model this variable stochastically, and it is probable that as a result banks now have a more sophisticated understanding of the credit risks they face.

There is evidence that in the derivatives markets some banks have lost market share as a consequence of declining credit ratings. This may have encouraged other (predominantly US) institutions to incorporate specialist derivatives subsidiaries with extensive collateral or an insurance guarantee and to arrange a residual relationship with the parent institution which ensures that the subsidiary is awarded a triple-A rating by the credit-rating agencies.

The BIS reports that the weighted average original maturity of new US dollar interest rate swaps fell from 4.1 years to 2.5 years between the first halves of 1987 and 1991. Other market sectors have shown a similar trend, which can be explained in part by the increasing proportion of interbank trading (see below). However, it is plausible to conclude that this contraction in maturities also reflects credit concerns. Additional evidence is provided by the increasing profile of SAFE contracts (synthetic agreement for forward exchange) in the foreign exchange markets, as an alternative to standard forward foreign exchange contracts. There are different types of SAFEs, but all may be regarded as a forward agreement fixing the swap points for a given pair of currencies over a future time period. The agreement does not extend to the physical exchange of the two currencies, and hence, while it is analogous to the more traditional foreign exchange swap, the bank faces less credit and settlement risk. Moreover, most SAFEs are treated as interest rate instruments for the purposes of calculating risk assets under BIS rules, and hence for banks are an efficient use of capital.

One factor which ensures that credit risk is higher than it might otherwise be is the international insecurity regarding (bilateral) netting arrangements. Only in the US, following the 1991 amendment to the Bankruptcy Code, have bilateral netting clauses been proven to be legally binding. Elsewhere, progress has been slower, despite lobbying by ISDA and work undertaken by the supervisory committee of the BIS. Legal opinion would appear to support the view that bilateral netting is enforceable in all of the ten largest Western industrialised countries, but in the absence of watertight arrangements there is always the risk that an administrator/receiver to a bankrupt institution may be able to 'cherry-pick' favourable contracts and renege on others with the same counterparty. Meanwhile, banks and other intermediaries have argued that, as a result of the lack of action by regulators, they are required to maintain an excess of capital to support their derivatives operations.

Anticipating developments in this area, the revised ISDA multi-currency cross-border agreement issued in June 1992 (a copy of which is included in the appendix to this book) contains clauses which facilitate cross-product bilateral netting. Multilateral netting would require an international clearing house and remains a very distant prospect.

REGULATION AND CAPITAL ADEQUACY

In 1988, when the BIS guidelines on capital adequacy were established, it was argued by some participants in the swaps markets that the calculation of the capital required to support derivatives positions (the mechanics of which are described in Chapter 11) would crush the growing market in off-balance sheet instruments. As Figure 1.1 illustrates, these concerns have been proven to be groundless. In part, the intrinsic profitability of swaps operations has encouraged banks to devote capital to these new areas, but the evidence of history is that the current BIS guidelines are not onerous – the favourable risk weighting applied to OECD bank counterparties may even be generous.

However, the 1988 guidelines are now subject to review, and there are clear indications that regulators are beginning to weigh up the implications of the dramatic growth in OTC markets, particularly in respect of the systemic risk to the financial system that may result from the profusion of interconnected payments obligations. Around the world, a number of regulatory bodies and agencies are conducting studies into the derivatives markets. One is being undertaken by the G-30, the international think-tank chaired by Paul Volcker, the erstwhile Chairman of the US Federal Reserve. The BIS is involved in a joint initiative with IOSCO (the International Organisation of Securities Commissions) to extend the BIS capital adequacy guidelines to cover market or price risk. Separately, the EC has already published in draft its capital adequacy directive (CAD), which covers four types of risk including position and counterparty exposures. These important developments are discussed further in Chapter 11.

The outcome and implications of these various initiatives, guidelines and directives remain uncertain, but there is no doubt about the increase in regulatory concern. In January 1992, the president of the New York Federal Reserve, Gerald Corrigan, who also chairs the BIS committee on Banking Supervision, questioned '. . . whether some of the specific purposes for which swaps are being used may be quite at odds with an appropriately conservative view of the purpose of a swap, thereby introducing new elements of risk or distortion into the marketplace.' It was widely believed that Corrigan was referring to 'off-market swaps', under which an up-front premium is paid to support a future stream of fixed rate payments below current market levels. Some swaps dealers admit that off-market transactions are often entered into to pass off a traditional loan arrangement as an interest rate swap. But to judge from other remarks, it would appear that Corrigan's concerns go deeper: 'Given the sheer size of the market, I have to ask myself how it is possible that so many holders of fixed or variable-rate obligations want to shift these obligations from one form to another.'

It is a moot point whether there is justification for this degree of unease. While the traded volumes and outstanding positions in OTC markets have increased far more quickly than comparisions in the cash markets, there is evidence from the futures markets that this trend is supportable: for instance, the ratio of the underlying value of futures transactions to cash transactions in government securities markets has reached 5.4 for France and 3.5 for Germany. Moreover, the settlement risks created by the international foreign exchange markets, in which an average of $1,000 billion is traded each day, dwarf those in the swap and other OTC markets. Nevertheless, the maturities of OTC contracts are far longer, and it may be this that is exercising the minds of regulators.

To date, the few potential crises faced by the derivatives industry – such as the defaults of Drexel Burnham Lambert, British & Commonwealth

Merchant Bank, Bank of New England and DFC in New Zealand – have been defused by sensitive handling, creating only the minimum of turbulence in OTC markets. However, perhaps only in the event of the failure of a significant market player will it be possible to judge with hindsight if the fears of the most ardent regulator were justified.

MARKET TRENDS

As the OTC derivatives markets have grown, the relative importance of US dollar transactions has fallen. At the end of 1987, 79.3 per cent of outstanding interest rate swaps and 88.9 per cent of outstanding currency swaps were denominated in or involved (on one side) the US dollar; by the end of 1991 these proportions had fallen respectively to 49.1 per cent and 72.4 per cent (see Tables 1.1 and 1.2). This decline reflects the progressive easing of regulations and exchange controls outside of the US – particularly in European countries – and the application of risk management techniques pioneered in the US to other parts of the world. Interestingly, the markets in option products – caps, floors and swaptions – remain dominated by US dollar deals. In the late 1980s, the prevalence of equity-related issues by Japanese borrowers in the Eurobond market and the substantial foreign investment of Japanese institutions conspired to cause a marked increase in currency swaps involving the yen. This trend has since reversed, following domestic economic developments in Japan.

Information in ISDA market surveys points also to a steady fall in the proportion of 'end-user' transactions (defined as deals other than those between ISDA members). For instance, outstanding interest rate swaps which involve an end-user now comprise only 56.2 per cent of the total (Table 1.1). The BIS regards this development as evidence of the increased use of swaps for the general purpose of risk management, at the expense of traditional interbank activity. The trend is consistent also with a greater degree of bank trading, possibly encouraged by the 'commoditisation' of the more conventional interest rate products.

A consequence of this 'commoditisation' has been that banks and other players in the OTC derivatives markets have explored new business areas in which greater margins may be obtainable. Some chapters of this book have been commissioned explicitly to cover these relatively new markets: for instance, structured equities (Chapter 2), unusual interest rate options (Chapter 3), energy and other commodity derivatives (Chapter 5) and forward electricity contracts (Chapter 6). There would appear to be no deficiency of imagination among market participants in extending the application of derivatives to market

(Billions of US Dollars)	1987	1988	1989	1990	1991
End-User	476.2	668.9	980.2	1,402.0	1,722.8
– US dollar	379.9	484.3	634.1	779.9	831.0
– Other Currencies	96.3	184.6	346.1	622.1	891.8
Between ISDA Members	206.7	341.3	559.1	909.5	1,342.3
– US dollar	161.6	243.9	377.1	492.8	675.0
– Other Currencies	45.1	97.4	182.0	416.7	667.3
Totals	682.9	1,010.2	1,539.3	2,311.5	3,065.1
– US dollar	541.5	728.2	1,011.2	1,272.7	1,506.0
– Other Currencies	141.4	282.0	528.1	1,038.8	1,559.1
Proportion of US Dollar Transactions	79.3%	72.1%	65.7%	55.1%	49.1%
Proportion of End-User Transactions	69.7%	66.2%	63.7%	60.7%	56.2%

Source: ISDA

Table 1.1 Outstanding Underlying Value of Interest Rate Swaps

(Billions of US Dollars)	1987	1988	1989	1990	1991
End-User	147.3	234.5	323.8	422.5	582.3
– Involving the US dollar	129.2	201.4	257.7	309.0	410.6
– Between Non-US Dollar Currencies	18.1	33.1	66.1	113.5	171.7
Between ISDA Members	35.5	82.3	111.1	155.1	224.9
– Involving the US dollar	33.4	68.1	96.4	119.4	173.6
– Between Non-US Dollar Currencies	2.1	14.2	14.7	35.7	51.3
Totals	182.8	316.8	434.9	577.6	807.2
– Involving the US dollar	162.6	269.5	354.1	428.4	584.2
– Between Non-US Dollar Currencies	20.2	47.3	80.8	149.2	223.0
Proportion Involving the US Dollar	88.9%	85.1%	81.4%	74.2%	72.4%
Proportion of End-User Transactions	80.6%	74.0%	74.5%	73.1%	72.1%

Source: ISDA

Table 1.2 Outstanding Underlying Value of Currency Swaps

price risks which have been historically neglected. Given this, it is perhaps only the zeal of the regulator which will impede further growth in the OTC markets.

References

1. *Market Survey Highlights Year Ended 1991*, ISDA. (A detailed survey was not conducted before 1985.)
2. *International Banking and Financial Market Developments*, BIS, May 1992.
3. *Off The Record*, Record Treasury Management, Summer, 1992.

2: Structured Equities

Mark A. Zurack, Goldman Sachs

INTRODUCTION

Twenty years ago, almost everyone who participated in the stock market bought and sold individual stocks. Today, a fair percentage of equity trading is packaged – that is, portfolios of stocks are bought and sold at once. In addition, exchanges around the world have launched equity products that involve no stock trading: options, stock index futures, stock index options and options on futures.

Physical index funds and listed futures and options contracts help investors meet a range of needs, from buying and selling entire portfolios in one transaction to changing exposure to a broad-based equity index quickly and relatively inexpensively. Yet they have limitations:

- In most futures markets, liquidity is concentrated in contracts that expire in three months or less. Those investors who have longer horizons must bear rollover risk;
- Investors may find that the indices underlying exchange traded contracts do not track their portfolios closely; in such cases, they must bear *tracking risk* if they substitute futures or options positions for stock positions;
- Regulations prevent certain investors from using some or all of the stock index contracts that trade on exchanges around the world;
- In most markets outside the United States the cost of trading baskets of stocks is higher than the cost in the US due to commissions and taxes imposed on stock purchases and sales;
- Holding baskets of foreign stock can be more costly than domestic stock portfolios because of added custody fees and a withholding tax on dividends – although, in some instances, this can be offset by income generated from stock loans.

These limitations have led to the introduction of customised, derivatives-based equity products. The parties to these privately negotiated, OTC contracts are typically corporate or government bond issuers, dealers and institutional investors. In this chapter, these products will be referred to under the broad heading 'structured equities'. Three of the most popular structures will be considered in detail. These are:

OTC options Privately arranged option contracts between two parties who agree on the underlying stock, stock portfolio or index, as well as the strike price, expiry and exercise style.
Equity index swaps Contracts between two counterparties in which an exchange of a stream of payments over a period of time is agreed. One of these payments streams is based on the return of a stock index or stock basket.
Market indexed notes Fixed income securities whose coupons and/or final principal payments are tied to the return on a stock, stock portfolio or stock index.

This short list does not include equity or index warrants. A warrant is a cross between a listed and an OTC option contract. Like listed options, warrants trade on a public secondary market, either an exchange or a dealer screen such as Reuters. However, with warrants, as with OTC options, the investor must look solely to the issuer for payment, not to a clearing house or other centralised intermediary.

This chapter analyses the benefits and risks of structured equities, describes the mechanics of each of these products, and introduces the most common applications in institutional investment. There is a natural bias towards the US, in which these instruments have the highest profile, but for the most part the principles apply to all international equity markets.

BENEFITS OF STRUCTURED EQUITIES

Structured equities can provide a number of advantages to certain investors.

Flexibility

Counterparties can design a structured equity product to meet their needs. The product's terms include underlying stock, portfolio of stocks, or stock index; base currency; date of maturity or expiry; strike price (if any); coupon or dividend payment and frequency; call, put, and other early exit features; interim payment schedule (if any); and exercise style (European, American, other).

Principal Protection

Structured equities can be constructed to provide a known minimum return (or floor) as well as a known percentage of any appreciation in the selected stock index over a one- to five-year horizon. This would be very difficult to accomplish using exchange traded derivatives unless the desired investment horizon and floor match the expiry date and strike price of a listed index option contract. For futures and options contracts there is a chance that a calculated minimum return or appreciation percentage will not be realised; in fact, the floor may be most at risk when its protection is most valuable – during periods of high volatility.

Transaction Costs

For many trading, and even some buy-and-hold, strategies, it costs less to buy and sell securities synthetically than to trade stocks directly. For example, commission costs and taxes to sell a Japanese index and buy a UK index total approximately 120 basis points. These costs would be significantly lower if the trade was done synthetically.

Capital Considerations

OTC options and equity index swaps can return the performance of a market without the requirement to pay for the underlying stocks in full. The underlying cash is typically invested in short-term fixed income instruments. This layered approach may appeal to fixed income managers who believe that they can outperform a standard money market portfolio. If this belief is justified, the combined return of the fixed income portfolio and the synthetic equity position will exceed the return from holding stocks directly.

Currency Protection

Most structured equities can be denominated in the currency of the investor's choice. An investment can be designed which either takes on currency exposure or is fully hedged against it.

Tax, Accounting and Regulation

For some investors in some locations, structured equities receive more favourable tax, accounting, or regulatory treatment than stocks, listed futures, or listed options contracts bought outright. For example, some institutions are prohibited from shorting stocks, but are allowed to trade options. However, since international regulatory and tax regimes are far from consistent, specific legal and tax advice should be sought.

CREDIT AND LIQUIDITY CONSIDERATIONS

Participants in structured transactions must depend on their counterparties for all payments. No clearing corporation stands by to guarantee payment, nor does a structured equity provide the physical ownership of a stock. Even so, the credit risk of a structured equity transaction is no different from that of any corporate obligation. Some dealers are willing to provide or arrange for credit enhancement (at a cost). Financial intermediaries may require that their counterparties provide performance assurance.

Because most transactions are private, structured equities may be less liquid than stocks, futures, or listed options – at least in the US markets. However, it is usually possible to reverse a position with a dealer other than the original counterparty as long as the latter consents.

Legal and tax issues relevant to the location and status of the potential user of these instruments should be considered carefully. A survey of these issues is beyond the scope of this chapter.

THE PRODUCTS

OTC Options

As mentioned earlier, an OTC option is a privately negotiated contract in which the two parties agree to all of the contract's terms. Table 2.1 lists the key characteristics which distinguish listed and OTC options.

The four examples which follow illustrate how portfolio managers might use OTC options to meet certain specific investment requirements for which listed options are not sufficient.

Requirement for a Specific Strike Price and Expiry Date

To construct a fund which guarantees principal at the end of each calendar year and some percentage of any appreciation in the S&P 500 index, the appropriate instrument is a one-year at-the-money call on the S&P 500 expiring on 31 December. Listed options have the limitations of an expiry in mid-December and strike prices that could deviate from the S&P 500 by as much as 12 index points.

Absence of a Listed Option on the Chosen Benchmark

An international investment manager who fears a general decline in equity markets could buy a put option on the FT-Actuaries World Index, denominated in the manager's base currency. Although index puts exist on many of the world's individual country indices, there is no exchange traded market for world indices.

	Listed Options	OTC Options
Listing	Each option is listed on a regulated exchange	Unlisted
Maturities	Typically shorter maturities, although some longer-dated options exist	Can vary between 1 week and 5 years
Trading Procedure	Each exchange has its own mechanisms (e.g. open outcry or computer matching)	Traded OTC by dealers
Settlement	Each exchange has its own settlement and clearing procedures	Negotiated between counterparties
Underlying equity	Dominated by blue chips and major stock indices	Can be based on most stocks, portfolios of stocks and indices
Exercise	Most options can be exercised at any time (American) but some only at expiry (European)	Negotiated between counterparties. Can be American or European, but can also be based on the maximum or average values of the equity during the life of the option. Can also include 'knock-out' features (that is, if the asset reaches a certain price before expiry, the option automatically expires)
Basis of Value	All listed options are based on the absolute performance of a stock or an index	May be based on absolute performance Can also be based on the relative performance of two stocks, a stock and an index, or two indices

Table 2.1 Comparison of the Characteristics of Listed and OTC Options

Desire for an Unusual Exercise Feature

A manager of a Japanese portfolio may believe that the market will either drop sharply or rise quickly and then stabilise. An instrument which reflects this market view is a put option with a 'knock-out' component. This may be structured, for instance, so that if the Nikkei 225 rises by 10 per cent, the put automatically expires. Because the manager is willing to take on the 'knock-out' risk, the put will be cheaper than a conventional option.

Requirement for a Relative Performance Option
A belief that the German market will outperform the French market supports the purchase of a call option on the relative performance of the DAX and CAC-40 indices. The relative performance is calculated by subtracting the total sterling return of the CAC-40 from the sterling return of the DAX. Note that this option can pay off even if the DAX declines, as long as the decline in the CAC-40 is greater.

Equity Index Swaps

An equity index swap, like an interest rate or currency swap, represents a contractual agreement between two parties to exchange cash flows. The cash flows are determined by multiplying a certain principal amount (often referred to as the notional principal) by two rates, at least one of which is tied to the return of an equity index or stock basket. Table 2.2 contains some indicative terms.

The last of these terms raises the issue of credit risk. Swaps do not ordinarily require any exchange of collateral, although either party can request this. This implies that each counterparty must bear the risk of the other not being able to fulfil his swap obligations. However, the credit risk applies only to the swap payments: no principal is ever exchanged. To reduce credit exposure, most swap agreements require that the counterparties calculate and exchange payments periodically before maturity – usually between two and four times a year, but sometimes as often as monthly.

A simple application of an equity swap might be to convert a short-term (LIBOR-based) fixed income portfolio of $100 million into an S&P 500 portfolio. Two possible approaches are to buy S&P 500 futures as an overlay, or to sell the fixed income portfolio and buy physical stocks or an index fund. The alternative is to arrange a swap under which the total return of the S&P 500 is received in exchange for a floating rate payment tied to LIBOR. Swap payments would be on $100 million of notional principal and would be exchanged once a quarter.

Equity return received	S&P 500 (total return)
Floating rate paid	Three-month LIBOR plus 0.125 per cent
Maturity	One year
Notional amount	$100 million
Currency of floating rate and equity payments	US dollar
Frequency of payments	Once a quarter

Table 2.2 Example of Terms for an Equity Index Swap

	Equity Index Swap	Stocks and Bonds	Futures
Settlement	Parties must sign a contract	Physical assets settled	Initial margin required
Price variations	Not marked-to-market	Not marked-to-market	Settled in cash daily
Maturity	Counterparties define the life of the contract	Perpetual or until bond matures	Usually less than three months, and then must be rolled
Tracking risk	Guaranteed index return	Portfolios may not track the index	Futures may be mispriced at the time of the trade
Credit risk	Counterparty credit risk	No credit risk after settlement	Limited credit risk to the broker and clearing house

Table 2.3 Equity Index Swaps, Securities and Futures Contracts

This transaction locks in the full return of the S&P 500 (with no transactions cost) as long as the income generated by the underlying portfolio exceeds the floating rate payment obligations. This implies that if fixed income securities can be identified with a higher yield than the floating rate, the swap strategy will outperform the direct purchase of physical stocks.

In this light, Table 2.3 compares the main investment characteristics of swaps, futures, and physical stocks.

Market Indexed Notes

Market indexed notes (MINEs) are fixed income securities issued by (usually US) corporations, financial institutions, and government agencies. They can be based on a stock, a portfolio of stocks, or a stock market index. The coupon and/or final payment of a MINE depends on the return of the base asset. Although most MINEs are privately placed, some public issues exist.

Many of the MINEs issued to date have three to five-year maturities and either a small coupon or no coupon. They usually offer full return of principal at maturity and participation in any appreciation of the base stock or index. However, it is possible to create MINEs with high coupons which will return the full principal if the market moves in the anticipated direction. In addition, the following characteristics usually apply:

- The longer the MINE's maturity, the higher the coupon and/or the greater the equity participation;
- The higher the prevailing interest rate of the currency of the MINE, the higher the coupon or the equity participation rate;
- The more liquid and less volatile the market, the higher the coupon or the equity participation rate;
- The stronger the creditworthiness of a MINE issuer, the lower the coupon and/or the smaller the equity participation.

In addition to the stock or index on which the MINE is based and the creditworthiness of the issuer, a potential investor will consider the currency in which the MINE's principal value, coupon, and upside appreciation are paid. It is possible for the principal and coupon payments to be paid in one currency and the equity appreciation in another, or for all payments to be made in a single currency.

By way of illustration, suppose that a US investor wants to place \$100 million in the Japanese equity market, as reflected by the FT-Actuaries Japan Index. Suppose further that he wishes to protect this investment against fluctuations in the Japanese stock market and the dollar/yen exchange rate.

The terms of the MINE contained in Table 2.4 serve to meet these requirements.

In this case, because the investor's principal, coupon, and appreciation (upside capture) are all paid in dollars, there is no residual currency risk. Figure 2.1 shows that, if the dollar/yen exchange rate remains constant over the five years, the MINE's return will exceed the return of the FT-Actuaries Japan index in a falling market, and almost match it in a rising market. However, the chart also shows that an index fund will usually outperform the MINE when the yen is strong relative to the dollar.

Issuer	A-rated private issuer
Issue price	100 per cent of the principal amount
Coupon	0.25 per cent (paid annually in dollars)
Maturity	Five years
Market participation	100 per cent of the percentage increase of the index payable in dollars, plus full return of principal
Underlying index	FT-Actuaries Japan Index

Table 2.4 Sample Terms of a MINE Based on the FT-Actuaries Japan Index (For illustrative purposes only: actual market rates will vary)

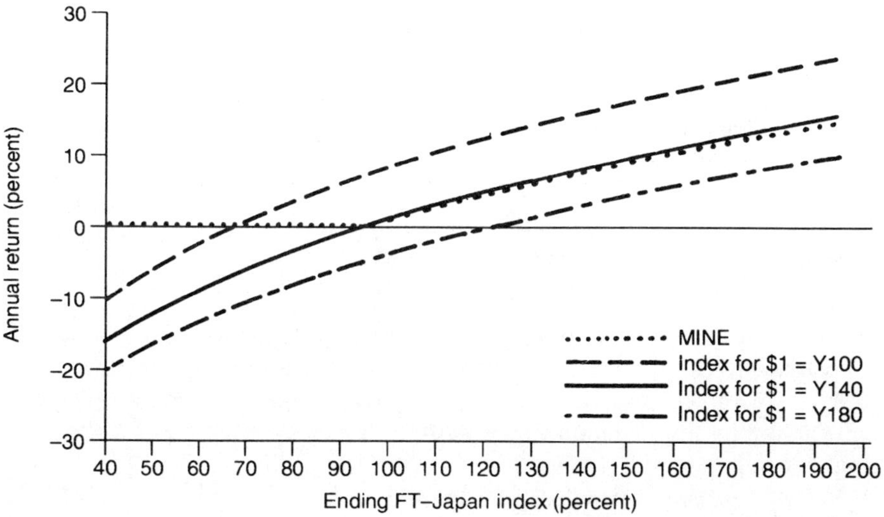

Figure 2.1 Annual Return of FT-Japan Currency Protected Mine and Time Index (for Various Ending Exchange Rate Assumptions; Opening Assumptions: FT-Japan Index 100 per cent; $1 = Y140)

Table 2.5 shows the sensitivity of the MINE's coupon and upside participation rate for varying maturities, two issuer credit ratings (A and AAA), and a range of currency denominations.

Choice of Structure

In certain cases, each of the three products described above can be used to produce identical economic results. For example, to obtain an exposure to the S&P 500 over a five-year period without risking principal, an investor could:

- Buy a five-year zero coupon note and a five-year OTC call on the S&P 500; or
- Buy a portfolio of five-year coupon notes and swap the coupons for the appreciation of the S&P 500; or
- Buy a five-year MINE with a final payment tied to the appreciation of the S&P 500.

The first two strategies offer the greatest flexibility. Both combine derivatives with publicly traded securities, so that either component may be traded separately or the package may be considered as a whole. In contrast, to unwind the MINE an investor must find a counterparty who is willing to take the entire private placement as one security.

Issuer: Corporate
Rating: A*

Maturity	U.S. Treasury Bond Yield	Principal and Coupon in Dollars Appreciation in Yen		All Payments in Dollars	
		Coupon	Upside Participation	Coupon	Upside Participation
5 Years	7.8%	0.50	100	0.25	100
4	7.4%	0.00	98	0.00	94
3	7.2%	0.00	89	0.00	85
2	6.8%	0.00	78	0.00	74

* Private Only.

Issuer: International Bank
Rating: AAA

Maturity	U.S. Treasury Bond Yield	Principal and Coupon in Dollars Appreciation in Yen		All Payments in Dollars	
		Coupon	Upside Participation	Coupon	Upside Participation
5 Years	7.8%	0.10	100	0.00	99
4	7.4%	0.00	94	0.00	90
3	7.2%	0.00	85	0.00	81
2	6.8%	0.00	74	0.00	70

Table 2.5 Sensitivity Analysis: MINE Based on the FT-Actuaries Japan Index

The individual circumstances of the investor will often determine the favoured structure. For instance, an option approach is preferable for those institutions which cannot use the swap market, while the swap may be the superior choice for those investors who do not want to use zero-coupon securities. In some regimes, investors may receive better accounting or regulatory treatment if their bond and equity exposures are attached, as is the case for market indexed notes. The MINE's protection feature allows some investors to treat the total investment as a bond for accounting and regulatory purposes.

STRATEGIES

Structured equity products enable fund managers and corporate treasurers to implement existing strategies more efficiently and to develop new strategies which were once impossible to put into practice. This section describes some techniques which take advantage of the unique properties of these products, under five main headings: index fund management; asset allocation; (equity) portfolio hedging; stock selection; and corporate financial management.

Index Fund Management

Three ways in which an equity index swap or a MINE can be used by index investors are described below.

Unhedged Index Funds
It is conceivable that the returns from combining a short-term fixed income portfolio with an equity swap may exceed the returns from holding stocks.
For example, a US-based fund manager who wants to invest $25 million in an index fund to track the FT-Actuaries Germany Index may either buy a basket of stocks or employ a cash/swap strategy. In the latter case, a contract is negotiated to swap a predetermined LIBOR-based floating rate payment for the US dollar total return of the FT-Actuaries Germany Index, while the underlying cash in the portfolio is managed as a money market fund. Table 2.6 compares the two alternatives.

In some instances, when all transaction costs are considered, the cash/swap strategy will provide a higher return than buying stocks, particularly if the investor is skilful in managing cash.

Currency Hedged Index Funds
If the same US investor wants the German stock exposure, but does not want the foreign exchange risk, he can enter into a swap to make floating rate payments and receive the local return of the German index. If the German market rises 20 per cent, a $25 million investment returns $5 million, regardless of the path of the dollar/deutschemark exchange rate. The only way to create a comparable return pattern would be for the investor to hedge the purchase of the stock index with a forward currency contract. In doing so, however, he takes on two additional risks:

(i) *Rebalancing risk* If the currency hedge generates a positive return, cash must be reinvested into the market. If the hedge loses money, the investor must sell a part of the portfolio to cover losses on the forward contract. The cost of buying and selling securities reduces the return of the currency hedged portfolio.
(ii) *Variable quantity risk* The amount of currency the investor trades in the forward market may not match the value of his portfolio if the stock market moves sharply during the life of the hedge. To reduce that risk, the investor should adjust the amount of the hedge as the market changes. However, the costs or profits of these adjustments are unknown when the hedge is established.

Buy Stocks	**Cash plus Swap**
+ Total return on the index	+ Total return on the index from the swap
– Transaction costs to establish the position	+ Interest income from the money market portfolio
– Custody fees	– Floating rate payment required under the swap
– Cost of rebalancing the portfolio	
+ Income from lending stocks	
+/– Tracking error	

Table 2.6 Two Ways to Obtain the Return on the FT-Actuaries Germany Index

Principal Protected Index Funds
If a portfolio 'floor' value is required at the end of the investment horizon, a bond (i.e. a MINE) could be purchased whose final payment is tied to the value of the German index. If the principal, coupon, and final payment of the bond are in dollars, there is no currency risk. Moreover, the strategy is protected against a decline in the value of the index.

Asset Allocation

This section describes the application of structured equity products to the management of a portfolio's asset mix.

Stock/Bond Total Return Swaps
Typically, portfolio managers shift assets by trading portfolios of stocks and bonds, and occasionally, stock index and Treasury bond futures. Swaps can also be used. For example, to increase US equity exposure by $100 million and decrease dollar duration by $6 million, a portfolio manager can swap the return of a US government bond portfolio with a six-year duration plus a spread for the return of the S&P 500. The notional amount of the swap should equal $100 million. This technique can be especially valuable for investors who own bonds that are difficult to sell.

Country-to-country Swaps
Total return swaps can also be used to shift a portfolio's equity exposure between different countries. For example, instead of selling $50 million of Japanese equities and buying $50 million of UK equities, an equity swap

might be arranged to exchange the return of the FT-A Japan Index in US dollars for the return of the FT-A UK Index in US dollars, on a $50 million notional amount.

For at least three reasons, these country-to-country swaps may be particularly effective for global asset allocation strategies. First, the costs of trading stocks in many foreign markets are high, not only because of taxes on purchases and sales, but also because settlements are often physical rather than electronic. Second, the risk of mispricing of index futures contracts is considerably higher in non-US markets. Finally, the swap structure allows a manager to separate the currency and equity allocation decisions. For example, instead of swapping the US dollar returns of the FT-Actuaries Japan and UK indices, a manager might decide to swap the *local currency* returns.

Options-based Strategies

OTC options can also be used to manage equity exposure. For example, an investor who feels that the stock market is high, but is willing to increase equity exposure should the market decline, can sell out-of-the-money put options to generate premium income. The short put position will be exercised if the market declines below the strike price, but the investor may be comfortable with this risk since he has already planned to increase his equity exposure in a falling market. Since 1987 out-of-the-money (equity) put options have been trading at higher prices than actual market volatility would justify, so that the option writer has been well compensated for taking this risk.

As an indication, if the S&P 500 is at 380, and one-year money market rates at 6.5 per cent, a one-year put with a strike price of 360 could be sold for 12 points. Figure 2.2 illustrates the potential return from combining a long money market and a short put position.

The short put strategy underperforms straight LIBOR if the S&P 500 closes below 347.22 after one year, but it leads to a negative return only if the S&P 500 closes below 322.50.

It is also possible to purchase an option contract that pays the return of the S&P 500 in excess of a bond portfolio over some defined time period. In other words, if the stock market outperforms the bond market, the excess is captured; if it underperforms, the loss is contained to a known premium. Such outperformance options can also be used in global asset allocation decisions. For example, instead of buying an option on the difference between stock and bond market returns, an investment manager might be attracted to the purchase of an option on the difference in returns between German and French equities.

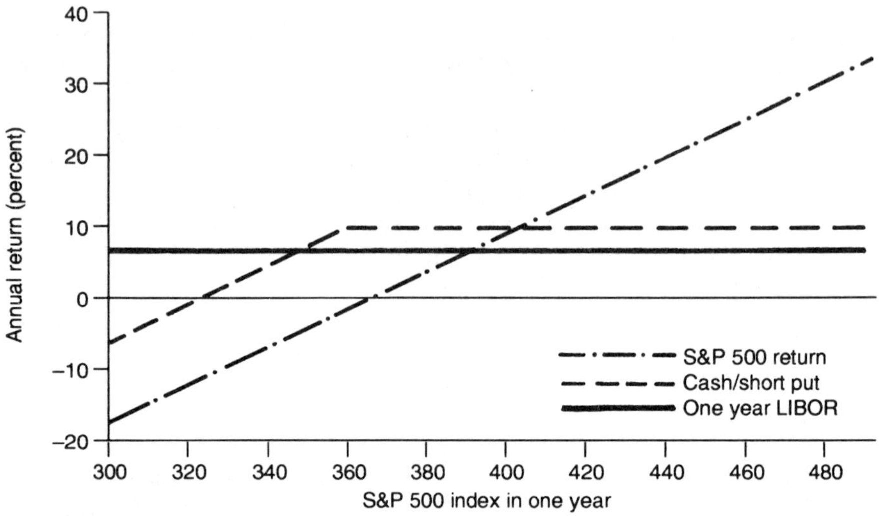

Figure 2.2 Annual Return of a Combined Cash and Short Put Strategy

Hedging Equity Portfolios

Most equity investors use futures, index options and options on futures to hedge the market risk of their equity portfolios. Exchange traded contracts are very effective hedging vehicles for portfolios which track the underlying index, and where the maturity and strike price are consistent with the investment horizon. However, the contracts are limited to a series of defined indices, maturities, strike prices, and exercise provisions. In the OTC market, contracts may be tailored to the investor's requirements. The examples below illustrate the advantage of this flexibility.

Customised Portfolio
The manager of a taxable high yield stock portfolio requires protection against a market decline, but would prefer not to liquidate any of the portfolio because there are large capital gains which would be taxable were they realised. The portfolio bears no resemblance to the S&P 500. The purchase of an OTC put option on the portfolio fully hedges the downside risk without triggering a taxable event, an objective that would not be met with listed index options.

Customised Maturity
An equity mutual fund has enjoyed substantial capital gains in the first nine months of the year. A worst case year end performance can be locked in through the purchase of a put option which matures on 31 December.

Customised Strike Price
In certain cases, it may be necessary that a fund has a guaranteed minimum value on a given future date. This might be achieved by the purchase of a put option in isolation, but an out-of-the-money call might be sold as well to finance the option purchase. In the absence of two listed options whose strike prices and premiums (in conjunction) produce the required floor, the use of OTC options is indicated.

In summary, the OTC options market can offer valuable solutions not available in the listed market. However, it should not be concluded that the exchange traded markets should be eschewed. In the US at least, the exchange contracts are generally more liquid than OTC comparatives, and the listed market is arguably more efficient.

Stock Selection Strategies

Structured equity products can also be used by institutional investors who focus on picking stocks and finding attractive industries and sectors.

Outperformance Options
The belief that one industry or economic sector will outperform another, or that a specific stock within an industry will outperform a comparable stock in the same sector, or group, would support a decision to buy an OTC option that pays the difference between the return of the two stocks or groups of stock. Unlike standard call options, which require an increase in the stock price to pay off, it is possible to profit from an outperformance call option even when the favoured stock or sector falls in price – provided it falls less than the stock or sector disfavoured.

Synthetic Convertibles
It is possible to create a market indexed note that can be converted into a specific stock at maturity at the owner's discretion: hence the name, synthetic convertible. Table 2.7 summarises some typical characteristics of this instrument. The minimum return to the investor is the bond's coupon, in this instance one per cent per year. But at maturity, once the stock price reaches the conversion price, the investor participates in 100 per cent of the price appreciation of the stock.

Synthetic Stocks
The combination of the purchase of an at-the-money call (put) and the sale of an at-the-money put (call) creates the equivalent of a long (short) position in a stock or portfolio of stocks. This strategy may be useful in a number of cases. For instance, some investors may want to sell their stock but cannot

Coupon:	1.00%
Issue Date:	1 April 1993
Maturity Date:	1 April 1998
Price:	Par
Call Protection:	Five-year non-callable
Rating:	A+ (private)
Size:	$25,000,000
Stock Price:	$66.88
Conversion Price:	$79.50
Conversion Ratio:	12.58

Table 2.7 Illustrative Terms of a Synthetic Convertible (Separable Warrants Attached)

(e.g. for tax or regulatory reasons). Alternatively, there may be a need to diversify the economic risk of a large single stock holding, but a disinclination to forego voting rights on that stock. At other times, there may be interest in creating short positions in stocks which are difficult for investors to borrow.

Corporate Financial Management

It is conceivable that structured equities might be used by corporate treasurers to manage the assets and liabilities of their companies. In the event of a stock repurchase programme, costs can be reduced by selling put options on the company's stock. If the stock price rises, the put premium reduces the cost of buying back shares in the open market; and if the stock price falls, the company buys stock through the exercise of the put, resulting in a repurchase consideration equal to the strike price less the premium received.

OTC options have been used to improve the returns on hedge positions which a company has in another company's stock. For example, a company A can sell calls on company B's stock to improve returns if a rise in market price is not expected, and/or buy puts on company B's stock to protect against a decline in price. Neither of these strategies alters the legal consequences and benefits of A's shareholding in B.

3: Interest Rate Products

Andrew Norman, Bankers Trust

INTRODUCTION

This chapter presents some perspectives on the current and prospective range of interest rate derivative products, in addition to some applications and regulatory implications. Amid the growth in innovations which continues from the previous decade, the banking industry of the 1990s will be faced with increased competitive pressures and a tighter regulatory regime; its customers will benefit from an unprecedented array of products offered, but will need to learn how to take maximum advantage of these instruments.

Interest rate markets undoubtably present some of the greatest technical challenges, and attract some of the brightest technical minds of our generation. This has resulted in some very esoteric products. Yet the 'rocket scientist' image is not helpful. All commercial enterprises are faced with interest rate risks and must improve their understanding of them in order to obtain the maximum competitive efficiency from their treasury and risk management functions. At the same time, the producers of financial technology must endeavour to build confidence among their users, and demonstrate how effective financial risk control can be integrated into mainstream corporate financing and even operational decisions through the use of specialised derivative instruments.

With this in mind, the descriptions that follow are intentionally relieved of a heavy mathematical emphasis, more attention being given to applications and possibilities.

It is hoped that this account will serve as a useful adjunct to the many excellent conventional texts already available in this field. It will have succeeded in its purpose if it serves at least partially to demystify this important subject.

TYPES OF PRODUCT AND MARKET

A plethora of interest rate exposure management tools now confronts the hedger and speculator. Recent innovations include hybrids with exchange rates and other security types. Before passing to their applications and uses, some of these instruments are briefly reviewed below.

Basic instruments in the interest rate derivatives market have parallels in other markets. **A forward rate agreement (FRA)** is a contract to enter into a term loan at an agreed rate at a predetermined date in the future. It replaces the old forward-forward contract and has the characteristics of a forward loan agreement.

The swap market has been the source of much innovation over the past decade and many variations are possible. New contract types increase the liquidity of the market and may provide linkages across markets. **Interest rate** and **cross-currency swaps** are contracts between counterparties to exchange the fixed or floating cash flows on loan obligations in the same currency or in different currencies over the life of the loans. The interest is paid on a pre-agreed 'notional principal amount', which in the case of a currency swap is typically exchanged at maturity at the prevailing or starting exchange rate. In a floating-floating or **basis swap**, floating payments on one interest rate index (e.g. the three-month Treasury bill rate) are exchanged for floating payments on another index (e.g. three-month LIBOR) in the same currency. A **differential** or **quanto swap** pays a foreign rate of interest on the principal in the same currency as the principal, allowing investors to benefit from a high interest rate foreign currency without bearing foreign exchange risk. A **variable principal swap** allows the capital outstanding to be repaid or drawn down in a prescribed manner or according to some criterion over the life of the swap. For instance, in Bankers Trust's **Index Principal Swap (IPS)**, principal repayment is amortised at a variable rate linked to LIBOR. Swaps may also be forward-starting.

Caps, floors and collars guarantee agreed constraints on floating interest rates payable over a specified period. In reality they are interest rate options whose payout characteristics take the form of compensatory payments for unpredictable movements in rates over the life of the contract.

Bond and interest rate futures are exchange traded products which provide liquidity in the markets for yields of different maturities.

Swaptions are options to enter into a swap at a prespecified fixed rate at a later date. They may be either European or American in style. They may be issued alone or as part of a callable debt issue. Their pricing characteristics are similar to those of bond options: the holder of a call swaption benefits if interest rates fall, while the holder of a put option benefits if interest rates rise. A **payer swaption** is a variation which confers the right to pay a pre-determined fixed rate and receive floating upon exercise.

Average rate ('Asian') options on interest rates are similar to caps with a strike set equal to the average interest rate occurring over the life of the option, or fixed strike options on the average rate over this period. Their lower volatility makes them cheaper than caps.

Other path-dependent options are also available in the interest rate markets. **Barrier options** extinguish or come into being if the underlying rate breaches a certain level before expiry and are attractive to investors who have particular views on the future behaviour of rates or who desire a reduction in premium.

Two-factor Derivative Products

Often market participants desire a way to hedge against, or obtain exposure to, more than one risk simultaneously, recognising the correlations of these separate risks as well as their volatility. Two-factor derivatives have been devised to meet this demand.

For example, in the interest rate markets **rate spread options** offer plays between different maturity points on the yield curve in the same currency or in different currencies.

The pricing characteristics of these are similar to **options to exchange**, which pay the difference in price between two assets upon exercise, if the first of the asset prices exceeds the other, and **better performance options**, which pay the greater of two asset returns over the period to exercise, if both are positive on exercise. These accommodate bets between assets of the same class, such as two bonds, or assets of different classes, such as a bond and a stock. They are cheaper than options on the maximum price of two assets because the initial asset prices appear in the denominator of the payoff formula.

Another family of options known as **quantos** or **composites** combine asset prices with an exchange rate. A **quanto bond option**[1] is an option struck and priced in domestic currency on the domestic value of a foreign bond at the date of exercise. The pricing takes account of possible correlations between interest rates and exchange rates. Similarly, an **FX strike bond option** is an option expressed in domestic currency on a domestic bond struck in a foreign currency, in which the domestic value of the strike price on the exercise date depends upon the exchange rate on that date.

These products can also incorporate exotic features such as *barriers*, *look-back strikes* and *averages*. It is possible to link a swaption to the price of a commodity such as oil.

The value of all financial contracts is susceptible to interest rate risks. There are two other products that should be classified as two-factor derivatives though they are not generally recognised as such. One is the **equity swap**, an example of an asset swap, in which typically the returns from an equity index are exchanged for a floating interest rate such as LIBOR over a period; the other is the **convertible bond**, in which the redemption of a bond issue is linked to a stock price or stock index, with various other long-dated embedded options. Both of these products are sensitive to interest rates and to the equity price. The 'conversion' features of the issue enhance the appeal to investors who can thereby obtain the better of the stock performance and the coupons.

Prospects and Higher Dimensions

The mathematical pricing and hedging difficulties presented by even two factors are significant, especially when one of the factors is the short rate of interest. It will be some time before all of the major two-factor possibilities are exhausted.

Some three-factor products do exist, and the pricing of higher-dimensional products is analytically tractable in certain special cases, for example the index-tracking basket or geometric option. However, for general payoff structures, computational demands rise steeply with the number of dimensions. For four dimensions or higher, Monte Carlo methods involving repeated simulations of the price path may be the only practical way forward.

RISK AND CAPITAL ADEQUACY REGULATION

Types of Risk

External financial risks may be classified into at least four broad categories: *market*, *credit*, *liquidity* and *basis* risks. Market risks are the potential losses due to adverse movements in asset prices or rates. Credit risks are the potential losses due to a defaulting counterparty, for example on cash inflows from a swap or the final payoff on an option position. Liquidity risk is the risk that there will not be a market for an asset or a funding opportunity when it is required to transact at some time in the future. Basis risk is the risk of a mismatch in a hedged position, for example because the prices of the asset and liability are linked to different market indices. These risks are interconnected through the markets; in particular, credit and liquidity risks appear in the market yields of bonds as spreads over the Treasury or interbank rate.

All of the products described so far are associated with interest rate and basis risks.

The Role of Capital Allocation in the Financial Risk Management of the Firm

All corporates and financial institutions are exposed to financial risks which threaten a firm's ability to meet its liabilities. The aims of risk management within firms are the identification, measurement and control of these risks. The regulatory authorities also attempt to safeguard the financial system as a whole by seeking to establish international standards of prudent financial management and control.

Full elimination of risk would be prohibitively costly and would quash enterprising activity; instead firms will try to ensure first that their risk exposures are within their capacity to absorb losses in the worst likely scenario, and second that the exposures to all risks earn on average an adequate return on a risk-adjusted basis.

Both can be accomplished by the appropriate allocation of risk capital to the business activities of the firm. Risk capital cushions the balance sheet against potential losses and will charge each specific business activity a cost of capital consistent with the risks undertaken. Only viable activities will be able to meet this hurdle. In essence this is just an extension of normal procedures within a firm for the optimal choice of investments. Capital will consist typically of the total equity of the firm and perhaps some subordinated debt.

Regulation

Capital allocation is also the mechanism by which banking regulators can force compliance with prudent standards of risk control. Much effort and debate is currently in progress among governments and central banks to standardise the reporting and measurement of risk for the range of banking products, in preparation for comprehensive international capital regulations.

This process is most advanced in the arena of credit control for basic lending activities and swaps. Capital standards for simple securities, such as bonds and equities, are currently being introduced. Gradually, the regulatory framework will cover the more complex derivative instruments such as mortgage-backed securities, which present special difficulties because of their variety and complex behaviour. However, the same underlying market risks are usually present and this could be the key to simplification.

Credit risk is assessed by measuring exposure to future payments at risk of default and then trying to estimate the probability of default. The latter is modelled by rating agencies through consideration of such factors as the institution's asset and earnings quality, profitability, and balance sheet liquidity.

Exposure measurement itself is concerned with *current* and *potential* exposure to a counterparty. Current exposure is a total present valuation of known expected cash *inflows* from a counterparty, in home currency, and potential exposure is the largest likely enlargement of the current exposure that may result over say a one-year horizon as a result of interest rate and foreign exchange rate movements. Netting of assets and liabilities may be appropriate, especially if there is cancellation of a liability when a counterparty defaults.

For the measurement of current exposures, the Federal Reserve Board and the Bank of England published proposals in the 1980s for a risk-weighting scheme under which the total risk-weighted exposure is a weighted sum of the principals of the assets, such as loans or the receivable side of swaps. For off-balance sheet receivables, the weight includes a credit conversion factor which equates the exposure to a floating rate loan with the same maturity, counterparty and principal. The capital requirement is then stated as a ratio of capital to risk-weighted exposure.

This approach was subsequently adopted by the Bank for International Settlements (BIS) in the 1988 Basle accord. Banks bound by this convention must assign a risk-weighting of 100 per cent to a corporate loan and enough capital to meet at least 8 per cent[2] of the exposure.

The same Basle committee of central bank regulators, the International Organisation of Securities Commissions (IOSCO) and the European Community (EC) are formulating capital adequacy regulations for securities trading, including proposals and directives on capital adequacy for market risk, and have begun to construct a regulatory framework to cover all derivatives and off-balance sheet products. Under particular scrutiny are the capital requirements for swaps, the circumstances in which netting of exposures is appropriate, and the policing of some of the less transparent transaction types. Also of concern to some central bank officers is the proliferation of complex linkages among markets and the increased systemic risk of a global financial disaster.

At the time of writing, the EC had arrived at a capital adequacy directive which allowed subordinated debt in the inclusion of capital, up to 250 per cent of core equity capital, but had set no minimum requirement for investment firms which do not hold clients' money or securities.

The banking and securities industries await the outcome of these developments. For many institutions, the total off-balance sheet positions may be several times the size of the balance sheet itself, and the consequences of heavy capital regulation of derivatives would be profound.

The key to a looser regulatory environment which might still address legitimate concerns over uncontrolled risk positions, is surely a combination of greater transparency and monitoring, especially for some of the most complex instruments, and recognition of the offsetting effects of many risks, by permitting the netting of like with like and the use of a correlation structure among different risks.

Moreover, it may be argued that linkages among markets are a natural feature of an efficient capital market which allows flexible access to fairly-priced capital, investment opportunities and transfers of risks.

Within a portfolio context, risk can be reduced through diversification. Although firms will always want to set appropriate risk-adjusted hurdle rates to each business unit through the allocation of capital, they may nonetheless benefit in capital savings from the presence of low correlations between returns at the portfolio level. To take an extreme example, if the returns on two default-free and otherwise identical assets have a perfect negative correlation, then the capital allocation to the combined position would theoretically be zero (although of course the negative profit business would be closed down in this scenario!). Therefore, in order to assess the capital consumption within a portfolio it is necessary to index all risks in some way and measure correlations of movements. This is easy to do for market price risks such as interest and foreign exchange rates and equity prices, but not for credit, liquidity or basis risks. For instance, changes in interest rates can affect a credit exposure, and an uncovered call option position on an asset is a credit exposure co-mingled with a market exposure.

Hedging of Credit Risk

Unfortunately, there is no exchange traded instrument which can separate credit and market risk (although some OTC products are now appearing). One way to remove the credit exposure of a contract such as a swap is by marking-to-market, the same technique used by futures exchanges for continuous settlement of net liabilities as the value of a contract changes over time. This prevents the build-up of a position that can later default. Such an arrangement can similarly be made between private counterparties by establishing a margin account, but a valuation formula must be agreed in advance. Exchange traded swap futures have emerged (on the CBOT) but have yet to catch on.

Credit protection can also be provided by insurance, usually granted by governments in the form of **loan guarantees** to encourage the financing of international trade or risky projects that are in the public interest. Another (US) variation is **deposit insurance**, provided to protect savers from default and the banking system against 'runs' in times of uncertainty. Fair pricing of such contracts is complicated by many factors including the propensity of managers to take more risk when their liabilities are insured ('moral hazard'). A selection of papers relating to this topic is referenced in the bibliography to this chapter.

Other credit-enhancing measures include **collateralising swaps** (compare with mortgage securities), the formation of highly capitalised derivatives subsidiaries and improved risk management systems.

PRICING CHARACTERISTICS OF INTEREST RATE DERIVATIVES

All interest rate derivatives present special valuation difficulties owing to the complexities of the term structure of interest rates and the fact that the risk-free rate used to discount option payoffs is itself stochastic. Simple analytical approximation methods, adequate for short-dated transactions, are simply not valid for longer-dated transactions, and this problem has been one of the obstacles to the growth in the markets for longer-dated products. Nevertheless, advances in pricing technology are making feasible new types of product for managing longer-term risks, and the markets for these products are expected to grow.

Contingent Claims Theory

Dominant in the field of interest rate derivatives and general asset pricing is *Contingent Claims Theory*, developed from the 1970s onwards. Within a standardised economic framework, most pricing problems can be solved mathematically using a branch of probability theory known as *stochastic calculus* in which the prices of traded assets or interest rates are assumed to follow *diffusion processes*.

The bibliography contains references to some important papers relating to this topic. All derivative prices satisfy a certain *partial differential equation* (see Cox, Ingersoll and Ross) derived from an *equilibrium theory of asset pricing*, which in turn is built upon the intertemporal theory of the representative agent who chooses from among available consumption and investment opportunities to optimise personal utility of ultimate consumption.

The pricing equation can also be arrived at from the *arbitrage theory of asset pricing*, in which it can be shown that in a *complete market*[3] claims can be priced as though all investors are indifferent to risk (see Cox and Ross, 1976; Harrison and Pliska, 1981).

These two approaches are very general. Academic finance theorists expend much effort trying to connect them and examine the equilibria and asset pricing consequences that are consistent with various economic assumptions.

Although any contingent claim dependent on the same set of stochastic variables satisfies the same partial differential equation, the particular payoff structure imposes boundary conditions and most specific pricings require numerical solution, especially those involving interest rates. However, analytical approximations are much in use in the marketplace.

Interest Rate Derivatives

It is possible to apply Black's formula[4] to the pricing of European options on a bond or the fixed side of a swap, using the forward price of the asset to the expiry of the option. The payoff on a call option takes the form of $\max[B - K, 0]$ at expiry, where B is the bond price at expiry.

The term-to-expiry interest rate is used as the risk-free rate in the formula. This method is possibly adequate for options which are very short-dated compared with the underlying bond's maturity, but not for longer-dated contracts, since the Black model formula presupposes that the interest rate and volatilities are constant, neither of which is true for bonds.

Cap payouts take the form of a strip of deferred call payouts of the form $\max[R_i - R_m, 0]$, where R_m is the capped rate and R_i is the actual unknown rate applying to the ith period, usually three months in length. If the forward-forward rates are known for each period, then Black's model can also be used to price these options, treating the forward-forwards as the forward asset price inputs.

Options to exchange may be priced using Margrabe's formula (see bibliography).

The assumption of constant price volatility can be improved upon by making volatility a function of other variables. The option may then be priced, either by binomial methods or by numerical integration of the partial differential equation satisfied by the theoretical option price, over the remaining life of the option. The method can be extended to higher dimensions to accommodate specific assumptions about other stochastic variables, such as *mean reversion* of the short rate of interest and *fat-tailed* price distributions.

Some Models of the Term Structure of Interest Rates

The most sophisticated interest rate models capture the dynamics of the yield curve in a way which is consistent with current market observables such as the prices of zero coupon bonds and volatilities. The resulting stochastic process, which may be multi-dimensional, is used to price claims. The *Heath, Jarrow and Morton* model reflects shift patterns that the curve may take, such as parallel movements, twists and bends.

A large family of models takes the short rate of interest as stochastic state variable, for example Cox, Ingersoll and Ross (CIR), Ho and Lee, Vasicek, Black, Derman and Toy, and Hull and White (HW). CIR incorporates mean reversion of the short rate and has a square-root volatility assumption, one useful effect of which is to prevent model rates becoming negative. HW also incorporates mean reversion and a term-dependent volatility function which can be fitted to market data so as to preclude arbitrage.

Binomial or numerical integration techniques are used to price securities from these stochastic processes. These models require considerable computing resources but are necessary for longer-dated obligations, such as swaps and bond options.

A Contingent Claims Approach to the Pricing of Credit Risk

The market price of a credit exposure to a particular corporation is reflected in the corporate spread over Treasury yields of its own bond issues and in the ratings supplied by ratings agencies. The plain swap deal to be described below is a simple credit arbitrage. Whether or not the credit premium of the weaker credit's floating rate is a fair price for the default risk, the fact remains that the stronger-credit institution and the intermediating bank are exposed to the weaker credit which supplies the floating rate payments for the structure. This is the real price of the deal.

An uncovered short call option position on a traded stock could become a major credit hazard to a counterparty as the potential losses are unlimited. Notice though that in this example, market risk and credit risk are interconnected. This relationship allows partial hedging of the credit exposure using the underlying asset and also gives a clue as to a possible alternative method of pricing credit risk using options theory.

Conventional assessments of credit risk involve large-scale modelling of the company's assets and liabilities, comparisons with other companies in a universe, relevant macroeconomic variables and examinations of default rates under various scenarios.

There is, however, an alternative approach which argues that all factors governing the default probability for a particular company act through the total asset value, for the default will begin if this falls below the value of total fixed rate liabilities outstanding, and the distribution to the bondholders will then depend on both the recoverable asset value and their priority ordering. Thus, for a simple company with one bond issue that liquidates at maturity, the bond pays $\min(D,V)$, where D = debt principal, V = recoverable asset value.

In this way, corporate bonds can be viewed as contingent claims on both the term rate of interest and the total asset value of the company. Alternatively, the difference in value between the actual debt and a default-free equivalent, that is the price of a loan guarantee, has the same value as a put option on the assets of the company struck at the face value of the debt. (See, for example, Merton, 1974, 1977, in the references.) This model was first applied to the pricing of US Federal Deposit Insurance and to the investigation of the effects of loan guarantees on industrial investment (see for example Sosin, Selby, Franks and Karki).

It will be noted that this theory has been in existence for nearly two decades, but that there is no evidence as yet of its widespread application to the pricing of credits. One difficulty lies in the modelling of a real-world capital structure in default, since the relationship between the outcome and observable variables that could be used for pricing is in practice neither simple nor unique, and the analytical credit pricing models are critically dependent upon these assumptions. Moreover, a study by Jones, Mason, and Rosenfeld was pessimistic in its outlook for this field.

An accurate determination of total asset value for a corporation is not generally observable, although for a financial institution or natural resources producer a reasonably accurate total mark-to-market of assets and liabilities ought to be possible on a continuing basis.

There has, however, been an upsurge of academic interest recently, particularly in the light of the regulatory developments described earlier. An exhaustive review is beyond the scope of this book, but the bibliography contains references to new papers by Jarrow and Turnbull, and Hull and White. The new approaches model observable proxies for credit risk such as credit spread. For instance, Jarrow and Turnbull apply their earlier term structure technology to the dynamics of credit spreads and express defaultable debt as default-free debt denominated in a risky foreign currency. Hull and White, on the other hand, have shown how to apply the theory of two-factor barrier options to the pricing of vulnerable options and other derivatives. In cases where default is known to be associated with the extremes of other market prices, they have shown how to obtain upper and lower limits due to credit risk on the prices of derivatives. These are promising innovations and further papers are eagerly awaited by practitioners. One final paper should be mentioned, by Ramaswamy and Sundaresan.

APPLICATIONS OF INTEREST RATE DERIVATIVES

Corporate Asset and Liability Management

An industrial corporation will make profits through optimised resource allocation among available production opportunities and by minimisation of costs, including funding and material costs and financial risks.

All interest rate derivatives, such as swaps, bond and interest rate options and futures, have applications within financial exposure management, both as instruments for taking bets on interest rate differential movements and for hedging and arbitrage. Non-financial institutions may be concerned merely with the complete elimination of incidental financial risks unconnected with the business activity. Many large corporates, however, have active treasury operations seeking to lower the cost of funds through the active trading and arbitrage of money market instruments and derivatives.

Historically, there have been three principal uses for interest rate swaps: first, as a liability management tool allowing corporate treasurers to hedge and arbitrage interest rate risk and also take exposures on interest rate views; second, as a vehicle which allows access to fixed rate funds at favourable rates for corporates that find direct bond issues expensive or impossible; and third, as a means of reducing borrowing costs. Many new corporate bond issues are linked to a swap from the outset.

More recently, interest rate swaps have found applications on the asset side, examples being the conversion of investment income flows to match a liability or to improve returns or liquidity. The income flows may come from fixed or floating rate instruments or from other security types; equity swaps exchange the returns on stocks for a floating rate payment stream such as LIBOR.

Typically, corporations with a high credit rating have a greater comparative advantage in borrowing costs over lower-rated institutions in fixed rate markets than in floating rate markets. A highly rated institution wishing to borrow floating rate funds can sometimes obtain cheaper rates than are available in the open market by sharing some of its cost advantage in the fixed rate market with a lower credit counterparty and/or an arranging institution. An interest rate swap is a structure that permits this.

The textbook example of a 'plain vanilla' interest rate swap consists of companies A and B whose direct financing costs in the fixed and floating rate markets are:

	Fixed	**Floating**
Company A	10%	LIBOR + 0.8%
Company B	9%	LIBOR + 0.2%

Suppose in fact that A wishes to borrow fixed rate funds, while B wishes to borrow floating rate on the same principal amount as A. If they do so directly, A pays 10 per cent and B LIBOR + 0.2 per cent; together they pay LIBOR + 10.2 per cent. If instead A takes a floating rate loan for LIBOR + 0.8 per cent, and B takes a fixed rate loan for 9 per cent, then their combined funding cost would be only LIBOR + 9.8 per cent. The saving of 40 basis points can then be distributed among the parties in the form of reductions in their normal funding costs, in either fixed or floating rates, including the fees of a financial intermediary which arranges the deal. Conventionally the interbank floating flows are expressed as six-month LIBOR, while any adjustments to the rates are made on the fixed side.

Interest rate options such as caps, floors and collars offer partial hedging or exposure to anticipated interest rate behaviour. Swaptions offer similar possibilities and may be used to hedge caps. They also have tax planning applications.

Financial Institutions and Funds Management

The asset and liability management problem confronting the institutional fund manager is generally the converse of that confronting the corporate treasurer: the liabilities are already set by the obligations of the fund – for example, pensions or insurance benefits – and the assets have to be chosen to meet them. The liabilities are typically presented to the fund manager in the form of an investment benchmark such as a market index or the aggregate performance of a peer group. Interest rate derivatives have a part to play in a fixed income portfolio management strategy to adjust exposures to different maturities and also to effect asset allocation switches from bonds to other asset classes such as equities (e.g. an equity swap). Moreover, remembering that returns from all assets held over the long term are subject to interest rate risk, these securities are relevant to all portions of a multi-asset portfolio, not just the fixed income portion. However, attention will be confined to the fixed income portfolio for the remainder of this section.

Applications of interest rate instruments to the matching of the exposures to be described below are also valid in fund management, especially in so-called *passive* funds, in which the fund manager is tightly constrained to match assets to liabilities according to some criterion.

In a *dedicated* bond portfolio, fixed income securities are selected so as to match future payments to coupons and principal exactly by amount and maturity. Of course, the manager has little flexibility in such a fund. In an *immunised* fund, on the other hand, the total portfolio is constructed so as to neutralise the overall exposure of either assets, or assets less liabilities, to particular interest rate movements. The rebalancing of such a fund requires small adjustments to the overall exposures to make as small as possible the first and second derivatives of the current market value of assets less liabilities with respect to rates (viz. duration and convexity). An *indexed* fund seeks to replicate the performance of a benchmark index by matching risk exposures rather than specific payments or securities. Such funds exploit the assertion of the capital asset pricing model, that like risks attract like rewards, and the correlation structure among security returns, to replicate the behaviour of an index with a small subset of its constituents.

A more typical fixed income manager attempts to beat a benchmark return by actively trading assets, and will require liquid instruments to adjust exposures to particular maturities. Exchange traded interest rate futures have low transactions costs and are highly liquid instruments suitable for this purpose. Bond options, caps and floors allow upside exposure to favoured assets and rates while limiting the downside to the cost of the premium.

Other basic applications of interest rate derivatives in fixed income fund management include the use of bond options to take levered exposures and covered writing according to the investor's views on interest rates. Covered writing benefits the fund immediately by the receipt of premium income while ensuring that the fund can meet the option liability in the event of exercise by surrendering the security. Option positions may be combined to structure different payout characteristics. For example, a straddle profits the buyer if the underlying asset price is in a predetermined range at expiry. Other possibilities include 'buy-write' strategies with a zero up-front premium.

A cross-currency swap may be used to convert the returns on foreign fixed income assets back into domestic currency, removing foreign exchange risks, and asset swaps may be used to effect asset allocation changes between, say, a fixed income and other markets, and sometimes to enhance returns.

Multi-dimensional asset allocator options, such as best performance options, can also be applied to interest rates.

Banks

Commercial banks face particular problems in financial risk management. A large loan book will pose issues of credit quality, liquidity, and various funding risks. A typical funding strategy might be to match-fund the loan book by maturity, taking the spread over the cost of funds charged to borrowers as profit. Failure to do this will result in significant exposures to different parts of the interest rate curve – so-called *gap-risk*. A common occurrence of this is a maturity mismatch produced by long-term loan assets being financed by short-term money. The exposure in such cases may be seen as a set of spread risks between pairs of interest rates of differing maturities. A movement of the spread in the adverse direction may be hedged using the rate spread options described earlier.

Liquidity constraints may also lead to basis risks between matched floating payments whose reset formulae are dependent on differing market indices. Interest rate swaps or options may be used to improve the matching of assets to liabilities. In a basis swap this is achieved by exchanging a set of floating payments on one basis for a set of another. Spread options or swaptions also have a role to play in the hedging of interest rate basis risks.

Securities (especially bond) trading operations may have rapidly changing interest rate exposures which are difficult to track or to match. In these circumstances, it is better to measure, for example by duration, exposure to different parts of the yield curve, then to hedge the resultant exposures in aggregate, using some of the instruments that have been described. The portfolio approach also allows the trader to take controlled exposures to market risks.

SOME EXAMPLES

The following simple examples illustrate some of the applications of the products described above.

1) Rate Spread Options

Suppose an investor wishes to receive on a US dollar 100 million principal the spread between US dollar LIBOR and French franc PIBOR rates, over a six-month period, to be paid in dollars, believing that the spread will widen. Suppose that currently, LIBOR = PIBOR + 10 basis points.

A suitable strategy would be to purchase a call spread option on the rates, at a strike price of 0.1 per cent (i.e. at-the-money). The payback to the holder of the option at the end of the six-month period (182 days) would be:

$$\$100\text{m} \times \max[\text{LIBOR} - \text{PIBOR} - 0.1, 0] \times 182/(100 \times 360),$$

assuming that the rates are expressed as annualised percentages (on an actual/360 days basis).

2) FX Strike Swap Option

The treasurer of a UK-based car producer wants the option to raise five-year sterling finance of £50 million in one year's time, to increase production for export to Germany if the deutschemark strengthens against the pound.

One possibility would be to buy a put swaption with a strike price denominated in deutschemarks. If the option is exercised, there will be a double benefit from a capped cost of (sterling) funds and a bonus from the exchange rate:

	£ 5-year swap	**FX rate (DM/£)**	**Strike**
Current:	90	2.60	DM 2.40
Expected:	85	2.40	

If the expected scenario occurs, the benefit from the put options with a strike price of DM 2.40 will be:

$$£555{,}555.55 \times \max[90 \times 2.60/2.40 - 85, 0] = £6.9 \text{ million}$$

(In this example, the 'price' of the swap should be seen as the value of its fixed side i.e. the bond issue price. The sterling value of the option's strike price depends upon the exchange rate on the date of exercise (DM 2.40). The option is initially struck at-the-money. The principal amount of the option is equated to the required issue value – £50 million – at the prevailing swap price viz. £555,555.55 = 50,000,000/90.)

3) Better Performance Bond Options

In a flat yield curve environment, a fixed income fund manager wants to receive over a one-month horizon on a principal of Yen 100bn the better of two investments, one at the long end, the other at the short end of the Treasury yield curve.

	3 month T-bills	20 year notes
Current prices	98.50	93.00
Final prices	99.00	95.00

The three-month bill will be a two-month instrument at the option's expiry. The result from holding a better performance option would be:

$$\text{Yen100bn} \times \max[(99-98.5)/98.5,(95-93)/93,0] = \text{Yen } 2.15 \text{ bn}$$

The bonds themselves do not have to be Yen-denominated.

4) Contingent financing

A North Sea oil producer purchases the option to enter into a swap 18 months hence for £400 million as part of a financing for drilling operations, provided that the price of oil is then above US dollars 30 per barrel.

The payback will be identical to that from a put swaption if the oil price criterion is met on expiration (compare example 2 with a fixed exchange rate).

ACKNOWLEDGEMENTS

Discussions with the following colleagues at Bankers Trust are gratefully acknowledged: Peter Freund, Jim Gatheral, Don Goldman, Charles Hayes, Francois Jourdain, Nona Liang, Michele McCarthy, Lorna Ness, Gerson Riddy, Ariel Salama and Peter Udale. Thanks also to Ron Liesching of Pareto Partners and to Marc Hotimsky of CSFB for helpful comments on an earlier draft.

Additionally, in the section on capital adequacy, I have drawn heavily, with the authors' kind permission, on the concepts set forth by Dan Mudge and Nona Liang of Bankers Trust in their article on integrated risk capital.

Finally, I would like to thank Nick Cavalla for editorial guidance.

Notes

1. Unfortunately, this terminology is not universally agreed.
2. Local requirements may be more stringent.
3. A complete market is one in which the payoffs to all contingent claims can be replicated using the basic instruments of the market. In such a market, the pricing of assets is such as to preclude arbitrage opportunities.
4. Black's formula can be viewed as a re-expression of the Black and Scholes model in terms of the forward price.

BIBLIOGRAPHY

F. Black, 'The Pricing of Commodity Contracts', *J. of Financial Economics*, **3**, 1976.

F. Black and M. Scholes, 'The Pricing of Options and Corporate Liabilities', *J. of Political Economy*, **81**, 1973.

J.C. Cox, J.E. Ingersoll and S.A. Ross, 'An Intertemporal General Equilibrium Model of Asset Prices', *Econometrica*, **53**(2), 1985.

J.C. Cox, J.E. Ingersoll and S.A. Ross, 'A Theory of the Term Structure of Interest Rates', *Econometrica*, **53**(2), 1985.

J.C. Cox and S.A. Ross, 'The Valuation of Options for Alternative Stochastic Processes', *J. of Financial Economics*, **3** 1976.

D. Duffie, *Securities Markets*, Academic Press, 1988.

Federal Reserve Board and the Bank of England, 'Agreed Proposal of the United States Federal Banking Supervisory Authorities and the Bank of England on Primary Capital and Adequacy Assessment', January 1987.

Federal Reserve Board, 'Treatment of Interest Rate and Exchange Rate Contracts in the Risk Asset Ratio', March 1987.

Federal Reserve Board, 'Potential Credit Exposure on Interest Rate and Foreign Exchange Related Instruments', March 1987.

J.M. Harrison and S.R. Pliska, 'Martingales and Stochastic Integrals in the Theory of Continuous Trading', *Stochastic Processes and Their Applications*, **11**, 1981.

D. Heath, R. Jarrow and A. Morton, 'Bond Pricing and the Term Structure of Interest Rates: A New Methodology for Contingent Claims Valuation', Working Paper, Cornell University, 1989.

J. Hull, *Options, Futures, and other Derivatives Securities*, Prentice-Hall, 1989.

J. Hull and A. White, 'Pricing Interest Rate Derivative Securities', Working Paper, University of Toronto, 1990.

J. Hull and A. White, 'The Impact of Default Risk on the Prices of Options and other Derivative Securities', *Preprint*, University of Toronto, 1991, (Revised 1992).

R.A. Jarrow, 'Pricing Options on Financial Securities Subject to Credit Risk', Working Paper, Cornell University, June 1991.

R.A. Jarrow and S.M. Turnbull, 'Pricing Options on Financial Securities Subject to Credit Risk', *Preprint*, Cornell University, 1990, (Revised 1992).

R.A. Jarrow and S.M. Turnbull, 'A Unified Approach for Pricing Contingent Claims On Multiple Term Structures', *Preprint*, Cornell University, 1991, (Revised 1992).

R.A. Jarrow and S.M. Turnbull, 'Interest Rate Risk Management in the Presence of Default Risk', *Preprint*, Cornell University, 1992.

R.A. Jarrow and S.M. Turnbull, 'The Pricing and Hedging of Options on Financial Securities Subject to Credit Risk: The Discrete Time Case', *Preprint*, Cornell University, 1992.

H. Johnson, 'Options on the Maximum and Minimum of Several Assets', *J. of Financial and Quantitative Analysis*, **22**, 1987.

E.P. Jones and S.P. Mason, 'Valuation of Loan Guarantees', *Journal of Banking and Finance*, **4**, 1980.

E.P. Jones, S.P. Mason and E. Rosenfeld, 'Contingent Claims Analysis of Corporate Capital Structures: an Empirical Investigation', *Journal of Finance*, **XXXIX**(3), July 1984.

D. Kim and A.M. Santomero, 'Risk in Banking and Capital Regulation', *Journal of Finance*, **XLIII** (5), December 1988.

R. Layard-Leisching, 'Swap fever', *Euromoney*, Supplement, January 1986.

A.J. Marcus and I.S. Shaked, 'The Valuation of FDIC Deposit Insurance Using Option-Pricing Estimates', *Journal of Money, Credit and Banking*, **16**(4), November 1984.

W. Margrabe, 'The Value of an Option to Exchange One Asset for Another', *J. of Finance*, **XXXIII**(1), 1978.

R.C. Merton, 'On the Pricing of Corporate Debt: The Risk Structure of Interest Rates', *Journal of Finance*, **29**(2), May 1974.
R.C. Merton, 'An Analytic Derivation of the Cost of Deposit Insurance and Loan Guarantees', *Journal of Banking and Finance*, **1**, January 1977.
R.C. Merton, *Continuous-Time Finance*, Blackwell, 1990.
D. Mudge and N. Liang, 'Integrated Circuit', *RISK*, September 1991.
K. Ramaswamy, S. Sundaresan, 'The Valuation of Floating Rate Instruments', *J. of Financial Economics*, **17**, 1986.
M.J.P. Selby, J.R. Franks and J.P. Karki, 'Loan Guarantees, Wealth Transfers and Incentives to Invest', *Journal of Industrial Economics*, **XXXVII**, September 1988, 1.
W.F. Sharpe, 'Bank Capital Adequacy, Deposit Insurance and Security Values' *Journal of Financial and Quantitative Analysis*, Proceedings Issue, November 1978.
H.B. Sosin, 'On the Valuation of Federal Loan Guarantees to Corporations', *Journal of Finance*, **XXXV**(5), December 1980.
R.M. Stulz, 'Options on the Minimum or Maximum of Two Risky Assets', *J. of Financial Economics*, **10**, 1982.

4: Foreign Exchange Products

Christopher C. Taylor, Barclays de Zoete Wedd

INTRODUCTION

Three largely unrelated factors combined in the early 1980s to create an environment that favoured the development of an OTC market in foreign exchange options.

The first was a period of intense market volatility, as currency values moved sharply upwards and downwards in response to economic uncertainties and uncoordinated monetary policies. This created a pressing need within the corporate sector for a means of limiting the risks involved in international trade, which was expanding rapidly as a proportion of GDP in the major industrial countries.

A second influence was the corporate trend towards centralised treasury operations, to achieve economies of scale and increased financial control. As the head of this new department, the group treasurer was expected not only to guarantee liquidity, but also to safeguard the company from the financial risks associated with changing currency and interest rate values.

The third, and perhaps least acknowledged, factor was the advent of the personal computer. This technological advance facilitated the pricing and management of option positions; and also provided necessary accounting and portfolio management support.

At the time, banks were beginning to understand that the value of corporate foreign exchange and money market business could not be measured solely in terms of 'bottom line' earnings, but should also be viewed in terms of an enhanced overall relationship. With this in mind, many banks constructed corporate dealing divisions to 'sell' treasury services to their corporate customer base. An overriding desire to satisfy perceived corporate demand spurred the banks into a new phase of development, during which they invested heavily in resources to create OTC alternatives to existing exchange traded risk management instruments.

The scene was therefore set for the widespread development of foreign exchange OTC markets in options and other derivative instruments. There was a need and a will to provide the service, and there was a focal point – the treasurer – to whom attention could be directed.

Early Experiences in Running Options Books

In the United Kingdom, the volatility of sterling encouraged unprecedented interest in options that could be tailored to match a company's foreign exchange exposures. In the early 1980s, sterling depreciated with ever increasing and alarming speed against the US dollar only to bounce back unexpectedly from close to parity to $1.30, and then move quickly to $1.50. In a spirit of one-upmanship, a handful of banks started to offer a service in currency options during this period.

Their experience was not favourable. Large sums were lost by certain banks as they grappled with the theory and practice of running options portfolios. There was little liquidity in the fledgling interbank market, which habitually dried up in times of extreme volatility (when market makers most needed it). To compound these problems, some early models used to price options were faulty. Moreover, some players simply ignored pricing models and traded options using techniques more suited to the spot market.

This period of volatility frustrated the orderly development of the foreign exchange options market, and tempered corporate demand for a product which was regarded as 'too expensive' – a result of high levels of volatility, poor market liquidity and the perceived requirement of the banks for a large 'safety margin'.

A number of major international banks did not re-emerge as option market makers for five or six years after the financial losses of the 1983/84 period, and indeed some have yet to re-establish a significant presence to this day.

The Management Perspective

From a management and control standpoint, the advent of the options market marked a major departure from established procedures. Hitherto, the bank treasurer or treasury manager understood every aspect of the business taking place in the dealing room, and usually had practical experience of trading foreign exchange or money market instruments. With options, he had to take on trust the integrity of output from a complex computer model and the ability of a 'rocket scientist' to relate option theory to an unpredictable, fast moving foreign exchange market.

More often than not, those selected to set up and manage options departments were erstwhile foreign exchange traders who had succeeded through their ability to make money by risk-taking. This set of skills was not necessarily compatible with the disciplines required to run an options business. In fact, the ideal candidate in those early days was someone who could successfully identify and limit risk.

THE DEVELOPMENT OF DERIVATIVES

Today the market is mature. There is widespread understanding of the instruments and their application within the corporate and financial sectors, and there is a vigorously traded interbank market. The presence of the latter enables banks to trade, rather than merely to write options, and manage portfolio risks for a sustained period of time. 'Volatility' is now traded in very much the same way as any other financial commodity.

After participants had become comfortable with book running, and confident that a position could be 'turned' into a market, options specialists began the process of refining the instrument: developing by-products or derivatives of standard options.

In fact, although corporate demand catalysed the development of the OTC options market, in reality there was very little corporate business transacted in the early 1980s. There was, however, widespread discussion of the mechanics of options. Understandably, attention focused upon cost. How was the option premium determined?; why was it 'so high'?; and was it, as banks claimed, 'fair value'?

Two distinct phases of development can be identified. The first was characterised by the creation of imaginative strategies designed to reduce perceived premium costs. The second involved the refinement of the option itself, and the creation of new forms of derivative instrument.

PHASE ONE: STRATEGY-DRIVEN INSTRUMENTS

Deferred Premium Options

The first reaction of many companies was to ask for the option premium to be tailored more to their general methods of making payment. It was not, and still is not, common practice for goods or services to be paid for in advance. Interest is generally incurred or earned at the end of a loan or depositing period, and similarly the impact of an exchange rate – whether fixed forward or exchanged spot – is felt when the translation actually takes place. The fact that the option premium had to be paid 'up front' made this payment both highly visible and a less convenient alternative to the established methods of corporate payment. For these reasons, it is unsurprising that the first option variant involved a deferred premium.

The Boston Option or Break Forward

To state the obvious, the simplest way to defer a premium is to delay payment from inception of the deal to maturity. In essence, this amounts to a loan of the premium for the period of the option. However, this method of deferral is not favoured by the majority of companies, since it increases the actual premium paid by the interest charged for the loan and still fails to overcome the problem of premium visibility.

The Boston option, otherwise known as a break forward, makes the deferral more convenient and less transparent by factoring the premium into an actual exchange of currencies. This mechanism combines the purchase of an option with a forward foreign exchange contract, resulting in an 'off market' forward contract that may be unwound.

Example
Assume that a UK-based company has to make a payment of US$10m in three months' time. The current spot exchange rate is $1.53, and the three-month forward rate is $1.52.

The treasurer expects sterling to rise against the US dollar over the next three months, but also wishes to hedge against an unfavourable movement. He decides to embark upon an option strategy with deferred premium payment.
He could proceed as follows.

Strategy
Step 1 Take out a forward contract to buy $10m for sterling in three months.
Step 2 Purchase a European style sterling call/US dollar put option for $10m with a strike price of $1.52 expiring in three months. The option premium is 2.17 per cent of the US dollar amount (3.21 cents).

Since a deferred premium is desired, the premium cost is factored into the exchange rate of the forward contract (in practice this will include an adjustment for the interest accruing from the deferral). Hence the company will be obliged to buy $10m at an exchange rate of $1.4871, not the prevailing forward rate of $1.52. The rate of $1.4871 is calculated as the strike of $1.52 less the premium expressed in cents per pound, adjusted to take account of the three-month deferral period. Interest charged on this 'premium loan' will be at market rates plus any relevant loan margin.

Outcome
After three months, if sterling is weaker than $1.52 then the company will simply buy $10m through the forward exchange contract and let the option lapse.

If, on the other hand, sterling is stronger than $1.52, the company will exercise the option to buy sterling and sell US dollars at $1.52. This will effectively net out the purchase of dollars at $1.4871 made under the forward contract, the difference between $1.52 and $1.4871 being the deferred premium. The company will then be able to purchase $10m at the more favourable spot exchange rate.

As can be seen, this mechanism is extremely cumbersome in practice. In addition, identifying the premium in the form of cents per pound, as opposed to a flat percentage of the principal, makes the cost look higher and so less attractive – even though it is not explicit from the contract. An out-of-the-money variant of this instrument exists (the original break forward) which entails an involved process of buying and selling a total of three options.

Collar Options: Cylinders and Range Forwards

The preoccupation of corporate buyers with premium cost was the major driving force behind the development by banks of strategies involving no premium outlay. In 1985, Citibank launched the zero cost 'cylinder option', a product closely followed by Salomon's 'range forward'. Today these products are known generically as collar options. By writing an option, a company may relinquish the potential to profit from part of any favourable exchange rate movement but earn enough premium to offset the cost of an option purchased as a hedge. Essentially collar options ensure a maximum and minimum exchange rate that can be applied to a defined exposure.

Example
A company expects to receive US$50m in six months' time. When received, these funds will be translated into sterling. The current spot exchange rate is $1.72 and the six-month outright forward is $1.70.

While believing that sterling is overvalued, and that rates will move favourably over the next six months, the treasurer would like to safeguard a 'worst case' exchange rate of $1.75. This requirement favours the purchase of an option, but the company does not wish to pay a premium.

Strategy
The company employs a zero cost option strategy, purchasing a $1.75 six-month European style sterling call/US dollar put option and selling a $1.66 six-month European style sterling put/US dollar call option.

These options are chosen to be European style since they relate to an actual underlying transaction. As this strategy involves the writing of an option, it is important that there is no risk of early exercise against the company before the funds are in hand, i.e. in six months' time.

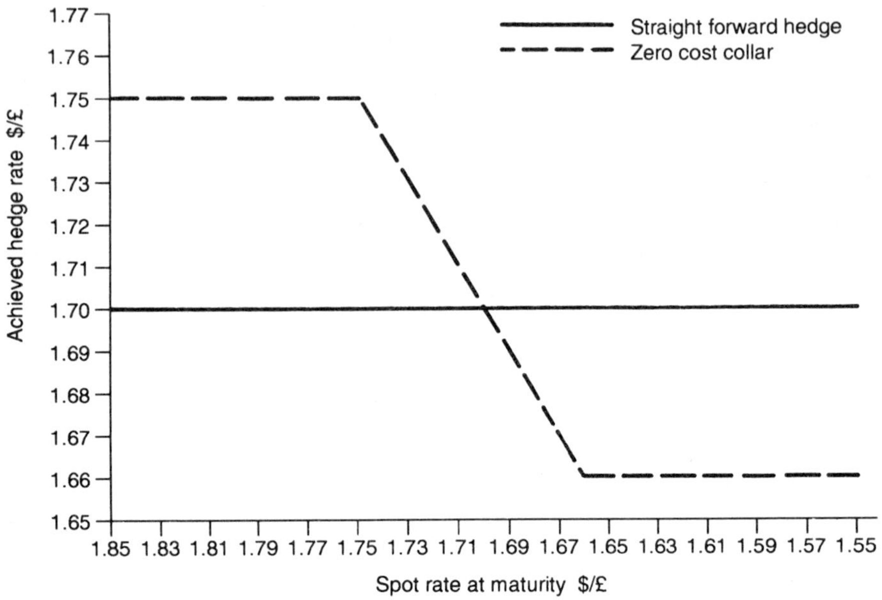

Figure 4.1 *The Zero Cost Collar*

Outcome
At maturity there are three possible outcomes.

1. If the exchange rate is anywhere between $1.75 and $1.66, the company will sell $50m at the prevailing spot exchange rate.
2. If the US dollar has depreciated beyond $1.75, then the company will exercise its right to sell dollars for sterling at $1.75.
3. If sterling has fallen beneath $1.66, then the option written by the company will be exercised, obliging it to sell $50m at $1.66.

The possible outcomes are illustrated graphically in Figure 4.1.

Collar options may be structured to conform to the perceived risks and rewards of a particular exposure. For zero cost collars, the purchased option will always be out-of-the-money to allow for a 'reasonable' differential between the purchased and written option strike prices. The collar bands may be moved outwards and inwards depending upon the level of protection selected. At one extreme, a strategy based on a deep out-of-the-money option will resemble an open position, the level of protection being negligible and little upside being forfeited. Conversely, if a high level of protection is obtained by buying an option struck close-to-the-money, the collar will involve the simultaneous

Spot = 1.72	Forward = 1.70	Period: three months
Option purchased	Option sold	Premium
Exchange rate	Exchange rate (rounded to nearest cent)	
1.71	1.69	zero cost
1.75	1.66	zero cost
1.78	1.63	zero cost
1.85	1.57	zero cost

Table 4.1 Possible Collar Options

sale of a valuable option. The strategy will show a risk/reward payoff similar to that of a straight forward contract. Table 4.1 demonstrates the type of trade-offs associated with zero cost strategies.

Collar strategies need not of course be zero cost. In fact, a strategy should be selected with regard to the desired payoff, not the desired level of premium payment.

Strike price selection is straightforward, provided two simple questions are addressed:

1. What level of protection is desired? This will dictate the strike price of the purchased option. It is probable that any view about currency direction will also have a bearing upon this decision.
2. How far is the currency expected to move favourably? Specifying a rate will determine the level at which an option should be written.

There is a compelling logic to this approach: why retain any potential to benefit from a movement beyond a particular market level if this level is considered unlikely to be reached? It may arguably be more sensible to 'trade this in' for a reduced overall option cost.

Participating Forwards

A participating forward is a variation on the zero cost theme. Rather than establishing maximum and minimum rates around the current forward quotation, the participating forward provides 100 per cent cover against an adverse exchange rate movement beyond a predefined level and the ability to share (or participate) in a fixed percentage of all favourable movements. The degree of participation is determined by the strike price selected.

Example
Assume that the current six-month (sterling/US dollar) forward rate is \$1.50, and a six-month European style \$1.54 sterling call/US dollar put option costs 2.5 per cent.

A sterling put/US dollar call option written at this strike price would earn 5 per cent. This means that, by purchasing a call at $1.54 and simultaneously writing a put option at the same strike, a net premium of 2.5 per cent would be received. This position would resemble an 'off market' forward contract. Five per cent is twice the premium that needs to be earned to offset the cost of the purchased option. Therefore, in order to earn the exact sum required, it is only necessary to write an option for half the amount being hedged. By doing this, a hedge is created against a rise in the value of sterling above $1.54 for the total exposure, and an option written that obliges the company to sell dollars and buy sterling at $1.54 for half the exposure. On the remaining 50 per cent the company will be free to transact at the prevailing exchange rate, so long as the rate is below $1.54. In summary, for no premium outlay the company will have entered into a participating forward transaction with 50 per cent participation.

The participating forward is an attractive, neatly packaged instrument, but it does have an element that is easily overlooked: the company is obliged to undertake a future transaction at a rate not equal to the current forward rate, but at a less attractive level ($1.54, in the above example).

PHASE TWO: NEW FORMS OF OPTION DERIVATIVES

By the late 1980s, option specialists had developed the expertise to manipulate the variables and change the payoff characteristics of the basic currency option. This, coupled with continuing advancement in personal computer software, has enabled the construction of more complex option-based derivatives.

Of these, there are six instruments which merit detailed explanation:

(1) Average rate (Asian) options.
(2) Barrier options: drop-in, drop-out and knock-out.
(3) Compound options.
(4) Dual currency options.
(5) Look-back, hindsight, and max/min options.
(6) Options on swap points.

These are now considered in turn. Each has a potential commercial logic, but some are enjoying more widespread use than others.

Average Rate Options

Description

An average rate option (ARO), sometimes referred to as an Asian option, enables its purchaser to hedge the average exchange rate over a specified period of time rather than a single spot exchange rate at maturity. The average rate is calculated on the basis of a given fixing frequency at a set time of day, these details being mutually agreed between buyer and seller at the outset of the transaction. The ARO is cash settled at maturity, there is no physical exercise involved.

Uses of AROs

The ARO is a genuine hedging instrument, with clear application to companies facing a constant and regular flow of funds in a foreign currency, or having to make regular overseas payments. By using an option settled against an average exchange rate, payments or receipts for an entire year may be hedged with reference to a single specified budget rate.

AROs are not generally used by market profesionals as a mechanism for taking speculative positions.

Example

A French exporter wins a contract that generates a cash flow of US$1m on the last day of each month for the next year. The original contract was based upon the expectation that the receipts would be sold at an exchange rate no worse than FFr5.64.

Strategy

The company wishes to guarantee a 'worst case' exchange rate, but feels that the spot rate will appreciate. A decision is made to retain 'upside' potential through the use of an ARO with a strike price of FFr5.64, agreeing fixings on the last day of each month at 3 pm, for a total of $12m. The premium for this option is 1.15 per cent of the US dollar amount.

Outcome

At the end of each month the company will sell $1m spot. At maturity, if the average of the twelve fixings is worse than FFr5.64 the writer of the option will compensate the company with an amount equal to the difference between the average rate and the strike price applied to the notional principal amount.

If the average of the twelve fixings is better than FFr5.64, no settlement will take place and the option will lapse worthless.

Pricing an ARO

The valuation of an ARO may be examined by comparing it with the purchase of an equivalent strip of European options.

An ARO will always cost less than an equivalent option strip. This is because the payoff of an ARO is far more predictable. Logically, the distribution of final spot prices for each standard option is wider than the possible distribution of the average. As the maturity of the ARO is approached, the outcome becomes more certain. While it is not possible to generalise as to the percentage saving that one should expect from an ARO, usually the premium is between 65 and 90 per cent of a standard option strip (for strike prices which are not deep in- or out-of-the-money). The strip is a function of volatilities and forward rates for twelve different maturities. Hence the price is dependent, inter alia, on the shape of both the volatility and forward rate curves, and not just a single level.

The fixing dates need not be exactly consistent. In fact it is possible to price an ARO which is based upon a weighted average. Naturally this will materially affect the price. If the fixings are biased towards the latter part of the ARO's life, the option will be more expensive since it shares more characteristics with a European style option.

Hedging

The delta of an ARO always approaches zero at expiry, even if it is in-the-money. There are two reasons for this:

(1) It is cash settled.
(2) As the expiry approaches, the certainty of the final value becomes greater. Hence the spot hedge required is relatively small, and the position's sensitivity to the spot exchange is reduced.

Expanding upon this second point, it is easy to see that most of the gamma (i.e. delta variability) risk associated with an ARO is at the start of its life, and this falls in steps as each fixing is made. This characteristic contrasts with a standard European option, for which the gamma risk can increase near maturity if the spot exchange rate is close to the strike level. Since most of the risk of an ARO reflects the early stages of its life, the volatility of this shorter period is given greater emphasis in pricing the instrument than the volatility of the entire period.

Average Strike Option

A variation on the ARO is the average strike option. The strike price of this instrument is set at maturity rather than at the start of the deal, and is derived by taking the average exchange rate over the period on the basis of agreed fixing intervals. The spot rate at expiry is then compared with the strike price and a cash settlement made if necessary. Average strike options are most commonly used to hedge profits translation exposure arising from certain accounting conventions.

Barrier Options: Drop-in and Drop-out

A drop-out option is identical to a European style currency option except that the option is cancelled (drops out) if the exchange rate reaches a predetermined level.

Since a drop-out option can never pay out more than a standard European option, but can disappear before expiry, it will always be cheaper. The proximity of the chosen drop out level to the spot rate at inception of the deal will influence the premium cost of the option. Usually the drop out level is set some distance away from the current spot level in the direction that would make the underlying option further out-of-the-money.

Use of Drop-out Options

Drop-out options are used for both hedging and trading purposes. Primarily the instrument appeals to professionals who are able to execute spot and forward deals with ease, since it is important to act in a timely fashion should the option drop out to avoid being 'whipsawed'. It is advisable for non-professionals to leave an order to transact a forward contract should the option drop out. The instrument lends itself readily to trading strategies formed around 'chart points' or key exchange rate levels; and to hedging strategies tied to the achievement of set target exchange rates.

Options professionals buy and sell drop-out options speculatively. The instrument provides a way of trading a market at a lower initial cost than through the purchase of a standard option. Writing a drop-out option enables a trader to receive premium income in exchange for the assumption of a risk which may quickly disappear if his view as to market direction proves to be correct.

Hedging with Drop-out Options

Example

A German exporter has a budget US dollar/deutschemark rate of DM1.62. However, since the start of the financial year the exchange rate has moved adversely, with the current spot rate being DM1.57. The treasurer believes that the rate will improve but feels compelled to obtain protection against the effect of a further depreciation in the US dollar on receipts due in three months' time.

Strategy

The company decides to buy a three-month DM1.57 US dollar put/deutschemark call option with a drop out level of DM1.62. This would cost 1.28 per cent of the US dollar amount, compared with 1.55 per cent for a standard DM1.57 strike European option.

Outcome
If the exchange rate remains below DM1.62 throughout the three-month period, the option will remain in place and may be exercised. If at any time the dollar rises above DM1.62, the option will drop out. This will give the company the opportunity to lock in the more favourable rate via a forward contract.

Evidencing and Referencing the Rate

The option drops out if the exchange rate trades at the prearranged level. Therefore, it is important that both parties to the transaction agree an acceptable reference mechanism to prove that this level has been reached. Buyers of drop-out options should be vigilant in this regard, since the writer will necessarily trade at this level in order to terminate his hedge. In the event that the market moves close to, but not through, the drop-out level, it is possible for the writer to cause the option to drop out merely by trading at the hedging level.

Cost Advantage of Drop-out Options

The sole reason for the purchase of a drop-out option is to reduce the cost of cover. The proximity of the drop-out level to the prevailing spot exchange rate will directly influence the size of the premium payable. The closer the drop-out level to the current rate, the lower the premium. Table 4.2 illustrates the premium payable on a three-month US dollar put/deutschemark call (as per the above example), given a variety of drop-out levels.

Pricing and Hedging Drop-out Options

A drop-out option only has value when the market is below the drop-out level for a put, or above this level for a call (i.e. it has not dropped out); in addition, as the spot rate moves away from the drop-out level it becomes increasingly less likely that the option will drop out and so its price approaches that of a European option.

Between the drop-out level and the strike price, drop-out options have a low gamma, the delta remaining relatively constant over a wide range of spot values. In fact, because of opposing factors a change in volatility has little effect upon the overall shape of a drop-out pricing curve. Higher volatility means that the probability of larger exchange rate movements increases, and so that the option could expire more deeply in-the-money. In isolation this

Option Specification		Drop-out Level	Premium (%) Bid	Offer
US$ Put/DM Call		1.58	0.39	0.42
Strike	1.57	1.60	0.93	0.97
Fwd	+220	1.65	1.46	1.50
Spot	1.57	1.67	1.50	1.54
Expiry	3 months	1.70	1.51	1.55
Volatility	10.8/11.0	Standard Option	1.51	1.55

Premiums are expressed as a flat percentage of the underlying dollar amount.

Table 4.2 Illustrative Premiums of Drop-out Options

would increase the option's price, but higher volatility also increases the chance that the option will drop out.

A drop-out option is not an easy instrument to hedge. The major problem for the option writer is controlling the delta risk, since the spot rate may hover around the drop-out level at any time (or any number of times for that matter) during the life of the option. At such times, the risk manager will have to decide whether to be fully hedged or fully unhedged. This problem is compounded by the fact that the hedge may be comprised of forward contracts rather than spot transactions, and hence changing interest rate differentials will have an impact.

Drop-in Options

A drop-in option is identical to a European style option, except that it does not exist until the exchange rate breaches a predetermined drop in level. As such, it is the opposite of a drop-out option. In fact, a drop-in option is equivalent to the simultaneous purchase of a European option and sale of a drop-out option. Appropriately, drop-in options cost less than European options.

The major use of drop-in options is in trading strategies which anticipate a major movement in the exchange rate (buying a drop-in option), or little movement in the exchange rate (selling a drop-in option).

Compound Options

A compound option is an option on an option, giving its buyer the right to buy an underlying option at a fixed premium. An additional initial premium is payable for this right. If the compound option is exercised, then the agreed (second) premium will be paid and the buyer of the compound option will own the underlying option.

A degree of caution should be exercised when applying the terms 'put' and 'call' to these options, since the terminology does not relate to the component currencies of the deal, but instead to the sale or purchase of the underlying option. Accordingly, a put gives its buyer the right to sell the underlying option, and a call the right to buy the underlying option. It should also be noted that the 'strike price' of the compound option is not a given exchange rate, but the second premium, and is payable upon exercise.

Uses of Compound Options

It is widely believed that the compound option is primarily used by companies wishing to hedge contingent exposures such as tender-to-contract risks or bids for overseas companies. In theory this should be the major application, but in practice it is not the case. The initial premium is considered too high by tenderers with a low success ratio; and the combined premia (exceeding that of an equivalent standard European option) is considered to be excessive by those with a high success ratio. In addition, contingent risks can be hedged more economically through proprietary tender-to-contract schemes which are offered by intermediaries running an insurance, rather than an options, portfolio.

The most common use of the compound option is in leveraged trading strategies. An attractive feature of the instrument is that, for only a modest initial premium outlay, it is geared to a large underlying principal amount. The option price can increase by many multiples of a relatively small percentage movement in the spot rate, rewarding its buyer substantially if the view about market direction proves to be correct.

Compound options offer traders a wide range of different payoff patterns. Three variables influence the shape of the payoff: the nature of the transaction (buy/sell); the type of compound option (call/put); and the type of underlying option (call/put). Hence eight ($=2^3$) strategies are immediately apparent, even before the selection of the particular exchange rate and strike price.

Pricing and Hedging

Compound option pricing models operate in very much the same way as traditional option pricing models, but to reduce risk the hedger may choose to trade in the underlying option rather than delta hedging in the spot market. It is relatively straightforward to calculate the percentage of the underlying option required to generate the correct delta hedge and conveniently, this method of hedging covers some of the gamma (delta variability) and vega (volatility) risks. The only disadvantage of this technique is that the bid/offer spreads incurred when buying and selling options are wider than those in the spot market, so hedging costs are increased.

Dual Currency Options

On occasions companies have the opportunity to source goods or raw materials from two different countries. In these circumstances, it can be useful to hedge the exchange rate of both countries, so that the choice of which source to use may be maintained. At a later date it will then be possible to decide upon the most economical course of action given both the local prices of the underlying goods and the hedged exchange rates.

A dual currency option provides this desired hedge. It allows its purchaser to buy two European style currency options with fixed strike rates and maturities and a common call (or put) currency. However, only one of these options may be exercised at expiry.

The premium payable for this option will be less than the sum of two equivalent separate options, the magnitude of the difference depending largely upon the correlation between the two currency pairs. The higher the correlation, the lower the dual currency premium.

Uses of Dual Currency Options

Sadly, the dual currency option is a good example of a customer-driven development that has no real customer demand: a solution looking for a problem. While academics and consultants often identify hidden, embedded options or advantageous choices implicit in corporate transactions, these opportunities are rarely exploited. Banks now have the ability to develop bespoke option instruments such as the dual currency option, but often their development follows from a belief that a commercial need exists, rather than an actual request. However 'textbook' the exposure appears, these instruments often remain on the shelf.

To date the only identifiable applications of the dual currency option have been in driving warrant issues, and as an enhancement to bond issues. The potential uses are more interesting, and may be exploited in the future. The instrument should be highly relevant to institutional fund managers who swap from one currency into another following movements in relative yields and/or perceived changes in currency trends. As a speculative tool, this instrument provides an attractive way to take a position on the movement of two currencies against a single base currency.

Pricing Comparison

The following example provides an indication of the relative premium cost of a dual currency option and two equivalent separate options.

Example
A dual currency option which combines a US dollar call/deutschemark put and a US dollar call/French franc put, both with a maturity of six months and struck at-the-money (spot), costs 4.87 per cent of the US dollar amount.

In comparison, the individual (European) options cost respectively 3.92 per cent (US dollar/deutschemark) and 4.17 per cent (US dollar/French franc), for a total of 8.09 per cent of the dollar amount.

Look-back, Hindsight, and Max/Min Options

A common lament of dealers is that 'you can't job backwards'. The look-back option goes a little way to remedying this state of affairs.

In most respects, a look-back option is identical to an ordinary European style option: it has a fixed maturity, specified put and call currencies and a stated amount. The obvious difference is that the strike price of a look-back option is unknown until maturity, and it is set at that time at the most advantageous spot rate (for the buyer) experienced over the life of the deal. This exchange rate is obtained from a reference source agreed at the outset of the transaction. This may be a real time source (24 hours) or a daily update (fix), and the choice may affect the pricing.

During the life of a look-back option, the reference fixings are recorded. At expiry the option's strike price is set, and exercise takes place in the same way as for a standard European option. A look-back option is obviously more likely to be exercised than a standard European option, and if the last fixing is on the last day the option will always be exercised (since it must expire in-the-money). This implies that the instrument is more valuable than a standard option, and as a result the premium payable for a look-back is somewhat higher than for an equivalent European option. Table 4.3 provides some indicative premium costs.

There is a little utilised variant of the standard look-back option known as the fixed strike look-back. For this option, a strike rate is set at inception, and subsequently compared with the maximum or minimum exchange rate experienced over the life of the option.

Uses
In similarity to the dual currency option, this instrument has more potential applications than uses to which it has been put. Few companies have ever used look-back options and equally few traders have taken advantage of them. Part of the lack of appeal must relate to the large premium cost. A criticism levelled at bought option strategies (which is difficult to refute) is that the approach constitutes a 'bet' that the rate will move favourably. Underlying this argument is the fact that there is no premium payment required for a

US dollar/ sterling	Maturity	Look back	Standard European	Volatility	Forward
Spot $1.7750	3 months	3.41	2.02	10.25	−288
	6 months	4.52	2.84	10.60	−530
	9 months	5.40	3.55	11.00	−735

Premiums are expressed as percentages of the dollar amount.

Table 4.3 Standard European and Look-back Premiums

forward contract. Of course, it is naive to consider the opportunity loss which may be associated with a forward contract as anything other than an actual cost. Nevertheless, uneasiness about premium payments and the value of the protection purchased is probably the major reason for the lack of corporate application of look-back options. From a trading perspective, the look-back option is an ideal instrument to speculate on an increase in market volatility, or a forthcoming large shift in relative currency values.

Options on Swap Points

A forward contract to exchange two currencies is simply a combination of the prevailing spot exchange rate and the interest differential for the relevant period. When deciding how to hedge an exposure, few people pay significant attention to the forward element of the transaction (as indicated by the 'swap points'). Usually, strategies are formed on the basis of expectations of how the spot exchange rate will move within the period of the hedge.

An option on forward swap points enables these two elements to be treated separately (if required) and action on each to be taken independently. The purchaser of an option on forward points pays a premium to secure the right to deal at a stated number of forward swap points on a date in the future for a specified maturity. For instance, a three-month option may be purchased which secures the forward points which will apply to a six-month forward taken out in three months' time.

Uses

This instrument is used chiefly by companies with long horizons for payments or receipts which are opportunistic in their hedging, choosing to 'lock in' attractive interest rate differentials when presented and then wait for an advantageous spot exchange level to combine the transaction into a forward contract.

As familiarity with this type of product increases, it is likely that the instrument will enjoy more widespread application. Investment managers, for whom relative yields are as important as absolute exchange rates levels, may become enthusiastic buyers.

Pricing and Hedging
To price and hedge these options is relatively straightforward. The instrument is in reality a combination of two interest rate options. Accordingly, interest rate futures and bonds denominated in the different currencies are the appropriate hedging media.

Other Derivatives

In addition to the instruments described above, there are a number of interesting foreign exchange derivatives which are less well known. Several of these are outlined below.

Contingent Options
A contingent option is identical to a standard European option except that the premium is only payable if the option is exercised. If the option is not at- or in-the-money at expiry, no premium payment is necessary. The premium of the contingent option is typically at least twice the size of an equivalent European option.

Chooser Options
A chooser option is equivalent to a bought straddle position, giving its buyer the right to choose between exercising a put or a call option on the underlying currency.

Binary, Bet Options
A binary or bet option allows its purchaser either to define the required payoff at expiry or to specify a premium payment. In turn, the writer of the bet option will specify the required premium or the potential payoff respectively. The options are cash settled and derive their name from their similarity to a simple bet, the buyer being informed how much he must advance in order to have the opportunity to 'win' a given sum of money.

Pay as You Go, Instalment Options
As the two different names suggest, this instrument is equivalent to a European style option for which the premium is paid in instalments at equal intervals of time over the life of the transaction. If at any stage the buyer of the option decides that he does not wish to continue with the option, then he can cease paying future instalments and the option is automatically cancelled. This instrument offers its buyer the opportunity to ratchet down the level of protection by buying further pay-as-you-go options if the market moves favourably. Options purchased previously may be abandoned for no further premium. This eases the dilemma of whether to continue to hold an option that is becoming further and further out-of-the-money, or whether to sell it.

FUTURE DEVELOPMENTS

The derivatives markets will undoubtedly grow in size and diversity of product range. This growth is likely to take three different forms.

Development of New Derivatives

Because derivative risk managers are now so comfortable with the management and manipulation of the various factors which influence an option's price, there is likely to be a greater willingness to provide highly engineered 'one-off' instruments.

Although bespoke solutions have been offered in the past, option specialists have usually sought the comfort of a diversified portfolio, i.e. they have packaged a solution and attempted to sell it as a stand alone instrument in an effort to spread their risks more evenly.

Application of Techniques to Other Commodities

The techniques discussed in this chaper can be readily applied to commodities other than foreign exchange. There is, for example, no reason why an airline could not hedge its fuel costs with a drop-out kerosene option, and similarly an aircraft manufacturer might wish to hedge production costs with an average rate aluminium option. These techniques are quickly becoming established in the equity derivatives market where their use can only increase over time.

Synthetic Options and Option Replication Techniques

Over the last few years there has been growing interest from the corporate and investment sectors in dynamic hedging techniques and the application of currency overlays. This trend is likely to continue, since it is logical when addressing multi-currency risks, or strategic business risks of a long-term nature, to embark upon a flexible hedge under which costs are minimised and spread over the life of the exposure.

Dynamic hedging involves the systematic adjustment of a hedge position in response to market movements. No currency forecasting is involved. The size of each hedge adjustment will be determined by predetermined trading rules designed to meet desired objectives. This technique essentially creates an option-like return, but with no explicit premium payment. The premium cost is incurred in the form of transaction losses which follow from the hedge adjustments. Quite simply you write yourself an option.

Currency overlays apply similar trading rules, but extend this concept further by covering a number of currencies simultaneously. The intention is to exploit the economies obtainable by partially hedging a portfolio comprised of related currencies.

CONCLUSION

Since the first faltering steps in the early 1980s to create an OTC currency options market, the nature of corporate and institutional demand has continually shaped the development of the market. Those who need to cover, or wish to assume, foreign exchange risks, now have an impressive array of derivative instruments at their disposal. As investment managers begin to regard foreign exchange as a separate 'asset class', further market growth and product diversity appear to be guaranteed.

To the outsider, the options market can appear complex. But, on closer examination, it becomes apparent that most of the newer derivatives are manipulated option-like constructions which alter one or more of the standard components:

- By limiting the upside potential, the cost may be reduced (e.g. drop-out, drop-in, bet and Asian collar, participating options);
- Increasing upside potential necessitates a higher premium (e.g. look-back, dual currency and chooser options);
- The premium of an option on a different benchmark will reflect the behaviour of that benchmark (e.g. Asian and compound options);
- Altering the payment convention will affect the total premium payable (e.g. contingent instalment boston options).

The applications of these instruments is most likely to be more straightforward than the calculation and management of their price and risks.

5: Commodity Derivatives

Louise Rowsell, Mitsubishi Finance International

INTRODUCTION

> Suppose the supply of oils was cornered by some rival soap maker who might temporarily acquire control of the market for palm oil. A few shillings per ton on the price of raw vegetable oil and what would become of my plans for the future of Lever Brothers?
>
> Lord Leverhulme 1851–1925 (William Lever), *Men of Stress*, Harley Williams

Just before the turn of the century, a soap manufacturer from Bolton, William Lever, leased at a nominal rent one million acres of land from the Belgian government in the Congo Basin. Twenty-five years later, after a personal investment of one million pounds, the land was to pass into his possession. Ownership enabled Lever to build his own palm plantations to produce palm oil, the essential raw ingredient in the manufacture of soap.

With this bold move, Lever secured both the supply and, more importantly, the price of palm oil. He was then able to concentrate his attentions on increasing the sales of his product and the efficiency of its manufacture. Today, Unilever has a market capitalisation in excess of £7 billion, and is of a size comparable to companies such as Ford Motors and Texaco. Vegetable oil remains a key ingredient in many of the company's products.

Like William Lever, modern-day financial managers in companies across the world are preoccupied with the risks associated with the reliance on the availability and prices of commodities vital to their businesses. These risks increase in line with the proportion of overall manufacturing costs represented by the costs of raw materials. Managing commodity price risk can be of paramount importance in industries where margins are narrow.

This principle is, of course, relevant not only to costs but also to revenues. A producing company, or indeed country, may rely on the value of a single raw material for its income; and it is not uncommon for the price of a commodity to fall beneath its (overall) cost of production, in which event every ton of output represents a loss to the producer.

The success of any company, large or small, hinges on the maintenance of a positive margin between receipts and payments. An adverse shift in the relative prices of inputs and outputs can upset this balance, and result in a severe decline in profitability. Categories of cost and revenue are numerous, and the sensitivity of net profit to individual price movements will depend on a number of variables, including the relative elasticity of different components of the profit and loss account. Many of these components are within the control of the company, and indeed it is the responsibility and skill of management to influence these. However, there are other factors which will inevitably be contingent on external events. Usually, these include the prices of raw materials, foreign exchange and interest rates.

William Lever was fortunate to be able to secure a monopoly of supply of the key commodity that he required. Moreover, at that time Lever enjoyed the benefit of scant foreign competition in his own domestic market. Exchange rate fluctuations were unlikely, therefore, to undermine the competitiveness of Lever Brothers. In addition, interest rates, a major cause of uncertainty for the modern corporate treasurer, were low and stable. Today, these risks are more pervasive, and their management is more complex. Advances in communication and transport have created highly competitive international markets, in which currency fluctuations can have a dramatic impact. British Coal, in its battle for survival, must compete with the attractive US dollar denominated price of coal imported from former Eastern Bloc countries. It is no longer insulated from a world market, or the movement in the sterling/dollar exchange rate.

It is vital for management to form an understanding of the extent to which it can, and indeed needs to, exercise positive control over the contingent aspects of the company's performance. Traditionally, market valuation of companies has been heavily influenced by historical results. But an annual record of assets and liabilities is no more than a 'snapshot' of the continuous dynamic relationship between the costs of running a company and the value of its sales. Creative management must explore beyond the financial reporting structure and the historical price relationships in preceding years. Only by developing sophisticated risk management models may a company be able to assess with some accuracy both its current value and the impact of contingent events on future profitability.

These risk models will focus on two major issues. Firstly, an analysis of the timing and extent of future commodity flows; and secondly, the present value of these flows. The latter exercise requires knowledge of the forward values of these commodities in the relevant currency(ies). A clear understanding of the present value of future flows will enable a company both to determine the risks to which it is exposed, and to consider the steps required to limit price risks or take full advantage of investment opportunities.

Techniques for modelling the long-term forward prices for commodities have been undertaken by financial institutions as the basis for pricing commodity swaps. The commodity swap is a recent and powerful financial innovation which enables a company not only to value a stream of future commodity assets and liabilities, but also to 'lock in' to a current forward price structure.

Reduced to its parts, the swap equates to a series of individual forward contracts. The nature and mechanics of the instrument are described in detail later in this chapter.

The expertise of large institutions in recognising interest rate and currency risk is now relatively advanced, and the use of related risk management instruments is widespread. However, the understanding and measurement of commodity price exposures is less sophisticated. Unfortunately, these exposures – over which management may feel it has little control – can occasionally have a far greater impact on corporate profitability than any efforts made by management to improve operational efficiency. A familiar example is the airline industry, which faced, during the Gulf War in 1990–91, a threefold increase in jet fuel prices and a sharp downturn in passenger numbers. These events led to a period of sharp retrenchment: a number of airlines closed or merged, and most major carriers reduced the size of their workforces.

Faced with a serious and adverse movement in those costs which are contingent on external factors, the management response is often to focus on those areas over which control can be exercised. It is conceivable that these efforts in reducing inefficiency may subsequently enable a company both to survive a downturn and take advantage of a future recovery. Enrique Castelli, the former president of Venalum, has said that: 'the decline in aluminium prices is good for Venezuela, since it will force the sector to get into shape' (*Financial Times*, 6 February 1992).

However, for those companies which operate efficiently, but on low margins, a failure to protect against unexpected price movements can have disastrous consequences. It must also be recognised that, in certain cases, commodity price risk may be more pernicious than interest or foreign exchange rate variability.

While commodities futures contracts predate financial futures by over a century, these instruments have traditionally been structured as hedge tools for the short-term commodity trader or merchant. The maturities of the forward contracts in metals traded on the London Metal Exchange were designed to mirror the journey time from producing to consuming areas. Although the maturities of some futures contracts have been extended, the majority are still not able to offer ideal hedging solutions to the long-term producer or consumer. As a result, it is only more recently in many markets that companies with significant exposures have been able to consider integrated risk management strategies. With some notable exceptions, it is the financial institutions, rather than the commodities houses, which have developed the modern (OTC) commodity risk management tools to accommodate the broader scope of the corporate user.

The benefits of these new instruments are not limited, however, to corporate treasurers or those responsible for the purchase or sale of commodity raw materials. There is potentially a wide variety of applications, including: commodity dependent project financing; protection of the bad debt risk associated with a portfolio of loans to commodity dependent companies or countries; hedging of long-term fixed price commodity supply contracts both in the underlying commodity and in related commodities (for instance, in the electricity industry); the management of indirect commodity price risk; and as an alternative to a commodity related equity portfolio to obtain long-term commodity price exposure.

The last of these applications raises an interesting issue. The commodity exposures integral to the trading performance of certain companies may on occasions be inconsistent with both the perceptions and strategic requirements of institutional investors in these companies. For instance, the purchase of a basket of oil stocks has traditionally been perceived by investors as a way to benefit from favourable movements in the price of oil. The following analyst's report, which appeared in the *Financial Times* of 7 September 1991, is illustrative of this view:

> Oil shares started to rally . . . on the back of firming crude oil prices and positive analysts' comments which estimated that crude could rise to $24 per barrel by the end of the year . . . if uncertainties over supply continue.

The simple investor perception may not always be justified by events. A range of oil companies will have very different exposures to crude oil price movements, depending on, *inter alia*, their equity production, refining capacity, the tax regimes under which they operate, their exploration success and costs of extraction, as well as the efficiency of management and the extent of business diversification.

Figure 5.1 shows the relative performance (in terms of earnings per share) of five major oil companies over the last five years, and the oil price history for the same period. It is clear that, in general, the relationship of earnings performance to the oil price has been at best erratic. In theory, the price of any of these stocks should reflect a multiple of the current value of future cash flows based partly on a more or less subjective assessment of company performance, and, more critically, on the current cost or value of forward commodity price flows. However, if an investor requires a pure long-term investment linked to the oil price, it may well be more appropriate to make use of a derivative instrument which is so linked. Commodity swaps may be tailored to the investor's requirements, and obviate an exposure to the myriad of variables intrinsic to an oil company's performance which may be impossible to evaluate.

These derivative instruments have been developed in order to accommodate very specific commodity price exposures. Companies may use them to offset an opposite risk profile implicit in the business of the company, while an investor may see the product as a means of taking more precise control over the price behaviour of his portfolio. Commodity risk management is of obvious

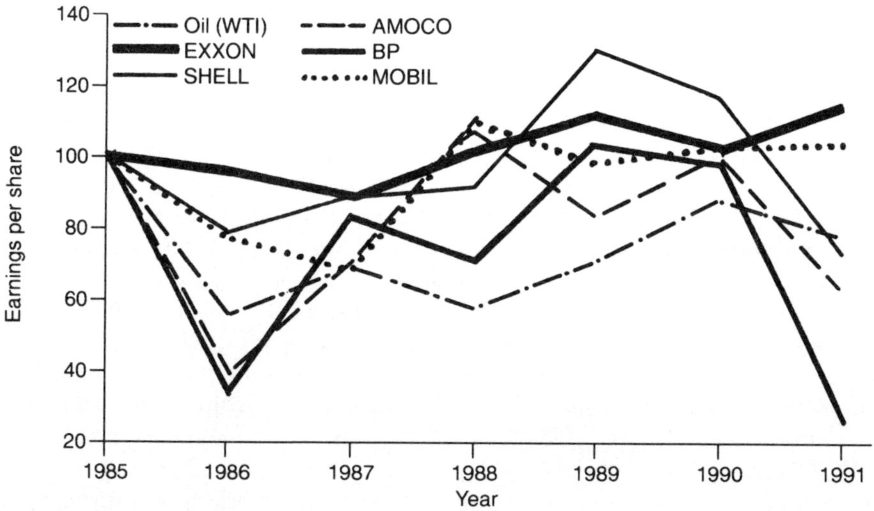

Figure 5.1 Earnings Performance of Major Oil Companies and the Oil Price (1985 = 100)

relevance to governments whose national income may be influenced markedly by the fluctuating price of commodities. At the microeconomic level, all companies have, in varying degrees, an exposure to the prices of raw materials or commodity assets. Since companies face these commodity price risks, so too must the bankers and shareholders of these institutions.

Hence this chapter is directed at a wide audience which includes corporate treasurers, purchasing managers, commercial bank lenders, corporate and project financiers, equity analysts and fund managers. The following section illustrates the nature of the risks which these various parties face. A later section outlines the commercial and financial approaches to these risks, and the chapter concludes by explaining the structure and pricing of commodity swaps.

Financial and commodity price risks should be considered jointly. Their management is not a mechanical role, but is a continuing and dynamic process, in which the risk manager may be able to take advantage of market fluctuations to lock in attractive values for future payments flows. At a minimum, the process should seek – through the purchase of disaster insurance, or by other means – to ensure the company's survival in the event of unexpected price movements.

THE NATURE OF COMMODITY PRICE RISK

Throughout the 1980s, deregulation of the world's financial markets and an acceleration in international trade led to far more volatile patterns of interest rate and currency movement than had been seen in earlier decades. This volatility was, in part, the catalyst for a revolution in financial risk management techniques. Hedging of foreign exchange became routine amongst large companies involved in international trade; and arguably the interest rate swap was the most successful financial instrument of the last decade. Yet in comparison very little was being done to manage the greater volatility in the price of raw materials. Commodity price volatility has always existed, and, if anything, has risen over the last twenty years as a result of increasing trade flows and international competition. Table 5.1 suggests that commodity price risk may have always exceeded foreign exchange risk.

In Europe, the Exchange Rate Mechanism has encouraged greater stability of exchange rates and a convergence of interest rates. Although turbulence in the foreign exchange markets in September 1992 brought realignments and instability, it appears likely that the long-term aim of European governments to maintain a framework to promote a convergence of individual economies remains. If this aim is indeed attainable, then the attendant benefits should be more stable European interest rates and the eventual introduction of a single currency. However, it does not seem likely that commodity prices will become less volatile or more predictable, and, in a more competitive world, the ability to control these risks will become increasingly important.

Countries

The most damaging effects of commodity price fluctuations are to be found in the lesser developed countries. In a large number of these countries, income is derived from the production of a single commodity, or a small range of commodities. These countries are prone to balance-of-payments crises and chronic levels of indebtedness, as their shifting export income fails to meet the cost of goods imported from the industrialised world. In contrast, the industrialised countries are largely insulated from declines in the prices of commodities, even when significant producers: these economies are diversified and the deflationary impact is lessened by the benefit to the domestic consumer from reduced costs.

In a study performed by the World Bank it is reported that, in aggregate, commodities account for 42 per cent of developing country exports, but only 25 per cent of industrial country exports. Dependence on commodity exports is highest in Africa, Oceania and South Central America. In 14 out of 27 countries in the last of these regions, commodity exports represented more

	Commodities								Commodity Index	Currencies		
	Crude Oil	**Cocoa**	**Coffee**	**Sugar**	**Copper**	**Gold**	**Platinum**	**Silver**	**CRB Index**	**JPY/USD**	**GBP/USD**	**DEM/USD**
1985	20.6	14.0	27.6	68.2	16.9	11.5	21.1	12.0	5.7	6.7	11.2	12.0
1986	60.7	24.3	39.4	57.8	13.5	18.0	33.5	23.9	9.0	12.8	12.1	9.4
1987	28.4	18.5	31.6	40.7	30.8	13.5	23.4	42.6	10.2	14.0	12.4	12.0
1988	30.5	27.1	25.1	63.3	50.4	12.9	26.4	24.9	12.4	12.3	13.1	10.9
1989	35.3	31.0	39.0	38.7	35.1	12.7	20.4	18.4	8.1	12.1	11.0	12.2
1990	48.7	42.0	26.9	35.3	26.9	16.1	16.8	18.1	8.6	12.4	12.0	8.7
1991	46.2	30.4	18.5	41.2	16.7	10.4	17.2	23.8	9.3	8.6	11.5	12.6
Average 1985-91	38.6	26.8	29.7	49.3	27.2	13.6	22.7	23.4	9.1	11.3	11.9	11.1

(All figures are annualised volatilities expressed in percentages)

Table 5.1 Comparison of Historical Volatilities of Selected Commodities and Exchange Rates.

than 50 per cent of total exports. Moreover, these countries are usually found to be dependent on a very small number of primary commodities. Nowhere is this narrow dependence more critical than in the oil producing countries of the Middle East, where oil exports often account for more than 90 per cent of total income. As a result, the oil price and each country's OPEC quota are probably the two numbers which influence most markedly the country's wealth.

Oil is not only an alternative to cash, but also a strategic weapon. Many Middle Eastern countries spend up to 50 per cent of their oil export income on defence, a percentage which is unlikely to be sustainable in the long term. Dr Mana Saeed Al-Otaiba, (Petroleum and Mineral Resources Minister, Abu Dhabi), has remarked in *Essays on Petroleum*, Croom Helm, 1982:

> In the case of the oil exporting countries, it is not only future revenues that are at stake, but statehood and nationhood and their very survival, because many of the OPEC countries are completely dependent on one national reserve – oil.

Otaiba does not only believe that a stable (supply/demand) solution must be found which guarantees the purchasing power of oil revenues. This purchasing power will depend also on foreign exchange values: a weak dollar against other major currencies will have a major impact on the value of oil income. Between 1985 and 1987, a consistent deterioration in the international value of the US dollar accentuated the difficulties faced by the OPEC nations after the 1985–6 oil price collapse. The deflationary impact of this price collapse was severe. A BIS report published in 1986–7 concluded that, in fourteen major oil exporting countries, the ratio of debt service costs to exports deteriorated in this period (despite the predominance of US dollar denominated debt), and that in 1986 alone the combined surplus from oil trade fell by $18 billion. A continuing period of depreciation in the US dollar from 1986 to 1992, most particularly against the deutschemark, has reduced the value of oil in DM to prices not even experienced even at the lows of 1986. Indeed, in real terms, prices in DM at the beginning of 1992 were the lowest seen in 20 years. These prices equated to those experienced before the first oil shock following the Yom Kippur War, when spot prices were trading at more than $20 per barrel.

The adverse impact of falling prices on the producing countries is not felt solely in revenue terms: a lack of control over commodity prices frustrates long-term strategic planning. Indeed, even rising prices can create problems, as Otaiba recognised:

> When oil prices started to increase in the early 1970s, the member countries (of OPEC), were all caught by surprise, and consequently no economic plans were ready to absorb the available financial resources.

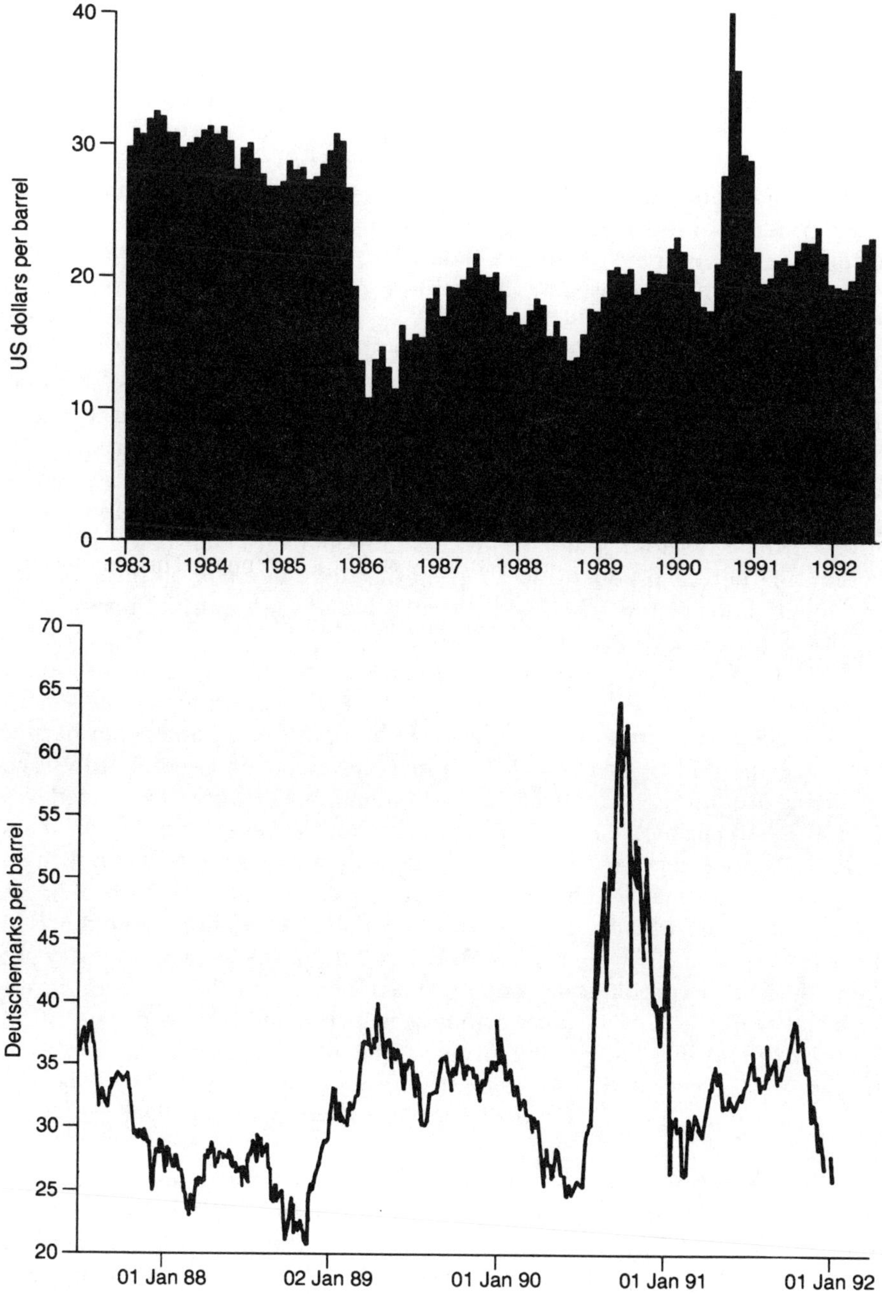

Figure 5.2 History of Oil Prices since 1983 (NYMEX WTI First Month Futures (a) US$ (b) DM)

SOURCE: DATASTREAM

Companies

In many ways, the problems faced by companies are no different, except in scale, from those of the developing countries. The impact of commodity price movements on a company, like a country, will be based on the proportion of total income represented by commodity revenues or input costs. Manufacturers which produce or use very large quantities of single commodities such as the fertiliser, glass and petrochemicals industries, will have more exposure than a company which purchases or sells a more diverse range of raw materials. However, most importantly, it is the company which is unable to pass on additional costs to its customers which will be most at risk.

For independent upstream oil companies, the only way to pass on these risks is to hedge. In terms of the value of their upstream assets and the costs of debt, these companies face problems similar to those of sovereign producers. After a rise in earnings during the invasion of Kuwait and the subsequent Gulf War of 1990–91, the profitability of oil companies slumped as oil prices retreated. Those companies with a predominant downstream business were hit harder, as product prices lagged the surge in crude oil prices in the first few months of the crisis, and refining margins fell away in response to the developing world recession.

By way of example, British Petroleum announced, in response to a deterioration in profitability after the Gulf War, that the company had more recently been structured to take advantage of a price of oil at $25 per barrel. Yet since the end of the Gulf War, prices have remained stubbornly low, averaging around $21 per barrel. In the first half of 1992, prices averaged less than $20, $10 per barrel below the peak six-month average nearly two years earlier. A price recovery to levels which will prove acceptable to British Petroleum still remains a distant prospect.

Of course, the consumer faces opposite risks. A relatively unpublicised decline in profitability has been suffered by the petrochemical industry. In this industry, the problem has been a sharp increase in the prices of petrochemical feedstock, particularly naphtha, which could not be passed on in the price of ethylene, the refined product. The impact of this collapse in gross margin was exacerbated by a general fall in world demand. The 1990–91 results shown in Table 5.2 for the major European petrochemical producers reflect this.

It is interesting to look more closely at the results of the industrial products division of ICI. Profitability from the petrochemicals and plastics division fell from £417m in 1989 to £103m the following year. In fact, over the past five years the results of this division have closely shadowed the petrochemical margins from the naphtha feedstock. ICI chairman Sir Denys Henderson underlined the problem in the 1990 annual report:

	1990	1991	% change
ICI (£m)	733	507	−31.0
Bayer (DM m)	2010	1945	− 3.2
BASF (DM m)	1736	1552	−10.6
Hoescht (DM m)	1816	1411	−22.4

Table 5.2 Profitability of the Petrochemical Industry

> This year, profit margins in the petrochemicals and plastics business were seriously squeezed as new capacity, growing competition and, in some sectors, falling demand made it difficult to compensate for rising costs. The invasion of Kuwait and the consequent volatility of oil prices exacerbated these problems.

Between 1990 and 1992 crude oil prices have oscillated from $15 to $42 per barrel, and refining margins (dependent on yield) from breakeven to $9 per barrel. Unsurprisingly, nearly all consumers and producers in oil-related industries have suffered erratic movements in profitability throughout this period.

There is a similar picture in the non-ferrous and precious metals industry. In 1991 and 1992, aluminium stocks from the former Soviet Union were shipped in extremely large quantities to the West to raise much needed foreign exchange. Aluminium exports to Europe from the Soviet Union, which produces 2.5 million tons per annum, doubled from 1990 to 1991. Prices on the London Metal Exchange fell from a peak of over $2000 per ton in 1990 to almost $1000 per ton in late 1991 – their lowest level ever in real terms. At such prices, it was suggested that half the aluminium industry was losing money. All of the major Western smelters, including Alcan, Reynolds and Austria Metall, responded with large cuts in production.

Aside from falling aluminium prices, the smelters are also very sensitive to the price of energy. Approximately fifteen megawatt hours of electricity are required for the production of one ton of metal. As a result, rising oil prices have historically precipitated a rise in aluminium prices. However, an accompaniment of rising energy prices has often been a downturn in world economic activity, which in turn impacts on the demand for aluminium. After a brief hike in prices during the Gulf War period, prices subsequently responded to a combination of oversupply and lack of demand. In such an environment it seems that even a sharp increase in oil prices would fail to revive prices of aluminium, serving only to increase costs to smelters and further reduce profitability.

While producers of non-ferrous metals and oil related products have endured mixed fortunes over the past decade, gold producers have experienced a consistently weak market. Nowhere has this been felt more acutely than in the South African mining community. Profit margins in the industry have been slashed by the combination of falling gold revenues and persistent double-digit cost inflation.

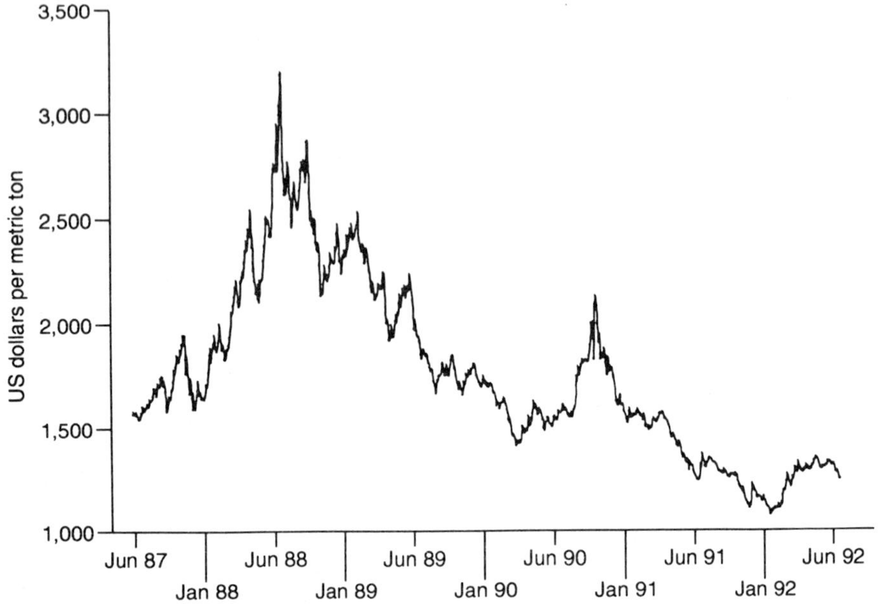

Figure 5.3 London Metal Exchange Aluminium Price (Three Months Forward)
SOURCE: DATASTREAM

The impact of adverse commodity price movements may be felt not only in a decline in profitability, but also in the availability and cost of finance. In the first quarter of 1992, after a series of poor results in the oil industry caused by weak oil and gas prices, low refining margins, cuts in book value of reserves and the investment required to fulfil the (US) Clean Air Act regulations of 1995, 23 per cent of the oil companies rated by Standard and Poors were downgraded and a further 19 per cent were on watch for downgrading. Inevitably this served to increase the cost of raising funds in the capital markets at a most unpropitious time for these companies.

Investors

The shareholders of a company whose profits are directly or indirectly affected by the movement in commodity prices will themselves be exposed to the commodity price through dividend receipts and the movement in the share price. The exposure is, of course, dependent on the relative importance to the company of the individual commodity, either as an asset or a raw material.

The RTZ Corporation is a major international natural resources group. The company has interests in a wide range of metals including aluminium, copper, gold, iron ore, lead, silver, tin and zinc. Despite this, the fortunes

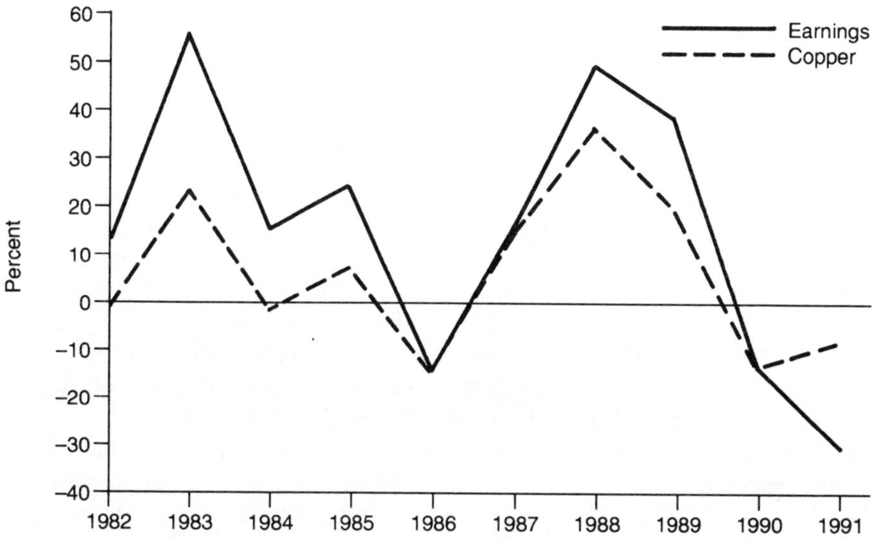

Figure 5.4 RTZ – Annual Change in Earnings and the Copper Price

of RTZ are very closely tied to those of copper. Operating profits fell from £866m in 1989 to £667m in 1990, and further to £360m in 1991. The company's chairman, Sir Derek Birkin, noted that:

> A deteriorating trend in prices was the main problem for metals in 1991. . . . Prices of non-ferrous metals were 17 per cent and 34 per cent lower on average than in 1990 and 1989 respectively.

Yet Figure 5.4, which shows the operating profits of RTZ and the assessed value of its copper production over a ten year period, suggests that profits appear to be linked almost exclusively to the US dollar price of copper.

The closeness of this link may be exceptional. But a large number of major industrial companies are to varying degrees directly or indirectly exposed to commodity price movements. Shareholders will wish to identify, and invest in, those companies, which, apart form general commercial competence, show consistent expertise in taking advantage of business cycles to lock in commodity asset values and raw material costs. Nevertheless, as mentioned above, if a pure commodity play is desired, a direct commodity price investment may prove to be more appropriate.

Financial Institutions

In addition to countries, companies and their shareholders, financial institutions will also face vicarious risks from the commodity price movements suffered by their customers. It has been roughly estimated that commercial banks have an indirect commodity exposure, through their loan portfolios to developing countries, in the region of US$100 billion. As noted earlier, due to the very large dependence of many of these countries on single commodities, heavy price falls can lead to a serious deterioration in the quality of the loan assets. Banks encounter commodity risks when financing new projects which are commodity related; aside from the interest rate risks implicit in the funding structure, new smelting, power or mining projects all involve commodity risk which can threaten their viability. Beyond fixing financing costs, it may be equally if not more important to lock in the costs of raw materials and value of products which will be consumed or produced by the venture. Indeed the valuation of the cash flows indicated by the current forward structure of commodity prices should dictate the viability of such a project.

By way of illustration, during the latter half of the last decade there were an increasing number of prospective projects, both in the Middle East and elsewhere, to develop new aluminium smelting capacity, taking advantage of local cheap energy. However, these projects had very long lead times, and as the aluminium price declined, many plans were shelved. In an industry in which the price of the refined product is notoriously erratic, any assurance of profitability must depend upon locking in as far as possible in advance the future sales proceeds from the projected production.

Although interest rate and foreign exchange risk management instruments have been used widely in such projects, particularly during the era of highly leveraged transactions in the late 1980s, decisions to hedge the future commodity receipts or payments streams are still uncommon. But the banking community is becoming more aware of the instruments available to hedge such exposures, and an increasing number of banks are looking to provide such mechanisms to hedge commodity price risk, both as self-protection and to preserve the commercial viability of the prospective new business.

Individuals

Due to the wide spread of commodities to which the consumer is exposed, the effects of price movements are rarely as severe as on producing countries or companies. Over the last decade, the consumer has enjoyed a continuing decline in commodity prices. Figure 5.5 illustrates the movement over this period in the Commodity Research Bureau index, a weighted index of metals, energy and food and fibre prices.

However, the inflationary trends in the 1970s, exacerbated by the two energy price shocks, had a knock-on effect on the broad range of commodities. In this inflationary period short-term interest rates rose to extremely high levels. Both the higher prices for commodities at a retail level, and higher

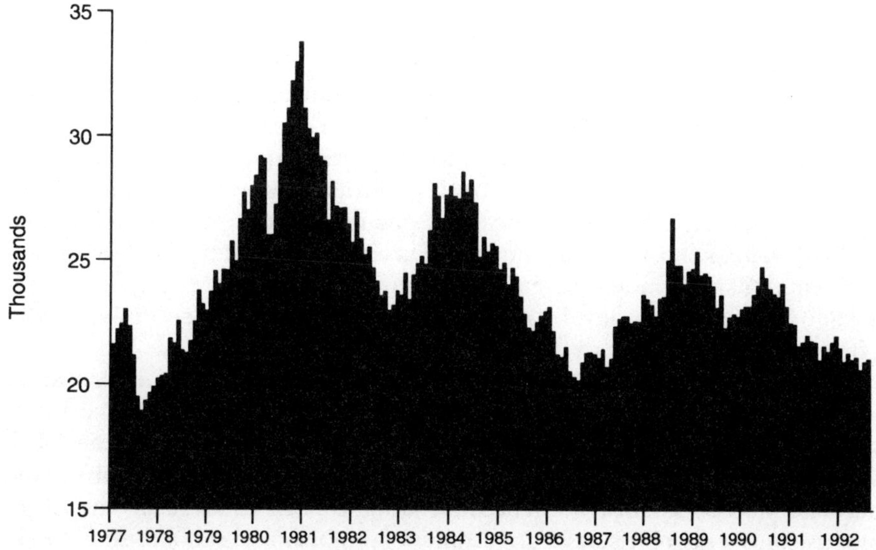

Figure 5.5 CRB Index (Monthly since 1977)

financing costs, were extremely damaging throughout the Western world, reducing the stock of savings and fostering a period of deteriorating industrial relations.

Although in the past decade there has been a general trend towards lower energy prices, the short experience of the Gulf War, which caused a sharp increase, not only in oil, but in other commodity prices, should not be forgotten. The existence of instruments which enable companies and their customers to protect themselves from the effects of dramatic price moves is of clear benefit. Indeed, the wholesale management of price risk should in theory reduce volatility in markets. When supply concerns are felt, as in the period after the invasion of Kuwait, consumers will be less concerned to purchase large quantities of inventory to ensure supply if they are covered by hedge contracts. In the aftermath of the Gulf War, there was a large over-supply of oil in tank, since supply shortages were not in fact experienced, and the 150 per cent increase in oil prices was not justified by events.

RISK MANAGEMENT

Historic Attempts at Price and Supply Management

In his introduction to "Commodity Risk Management and Finance" (Oxford University Press, 1991), Theophilos Priovolos has identified three broad classes of commercial structures that have been employed in an attempt to stabilise or compensate for commodity price movements. The first, which might be labelled 'self-insurance', includes reserve management and domestic stabilisation schemes, and diversification programmes. The second consists of third party insurance techniques such as exchange traded futures and commodity linked bonds, loans and notes. The final group covers price management schemes, international commodity agreements and compensatory financial schemes such as those managed by the European Community. In addition to these, nationalised industries in many countries may ensure price stability, but not necessarily at a level comparable to the competitive cost of supply in a free market.

International commodity agreements between producer and consumer nations are unlikely to be successful for all time. One example is the International Coffee Organisation. Another is the Tin Restriction Scheme. The latter was established in 1931 in an attempt to control the supply of tin to the market and so stabilise prices. The International Tin Council, as it was subsequently known, comprised 22 government members and ran a 'buffer stock' until 1985. However, unable to finance the purchase of an ever-increasing excess supply of tin, the Council defaulted, leading to an immediate collapse in the tin price and, eventually, restoration of a free market in the metal.

Self-regulating producer bodies have usually fared no better. OPEC has had a mixed history in its 'regulation' of the oil exports of its members. A noteworthy exception to this has been the diamond market, in which the existence of a single dominant wholesale buyer and distributor in de Beers has enabled the flow of the product to be effectively controlled, and its price stabilised successfully.

Financial Solutions

Of the methods available for the management of commodity risk, financial third party solutions are the most flexible. There is a bewildering array of instruments available, but usually any given structure may be dissected into some collection of basic building blocks. While the precise mechanics of the various instruments will differ, every financial solution may be considered as either a one- or a two-way contract for differences. In the latter case, the buyer and seller fix a price for a notional forward delivery and a settlement date(s). On the maturity date the buyer will take delivery and pay for the commodity at the pre-agreed price, or make a settlement with the seller for the difference between the fixed price and the then current market value of the commodity.

Futures, forwards and swaps are examples of instruments which fall broadly into the description of two-way contracts for differences, while options, caps and floors may be described as 'one-way' contracts for difference. Futures, and some options contracts, are traded on organised exchanges where the exchange (or clearing house) acts as financial intermediary; these instruments are, by necessity, standardised. Other instruments are principal-to-principal OTC transactions, and may have a single or multiple settlement dates. Commodity bonds, loans, notes and warrants are securitised instruments in which one- or two-way contracts for differences have been embedded which will determine the payoff of the instrument.

The first forward contracts in commodities are difficult to trace, but a form of rice contract may date from more than five hundred years ago. Other contracts in spices and tulips are better documented. Varieties of commodity futures markets have existed in their current form in various locations across the world for more than a century. The first forward market in oil was informally established during the oil rush of the early 1870s in Titusville, Pennsylvania. The delivery and payment periods were spot, within ten days (regular) and within a specified period of time (futures). Settlement was either by physical delivery and payment at the agreed fixed price, or by cash payment of the difference in price between the 'regular' contract then trading and the fixed price agreed in the contract. This contract appears very close in structure to the swap contracts of today, which are themselves contracts for differences with multiple settlement periods. Futures markets in metals and grain have an equally long history.

Today, by far the most liquid international commodity future is based on West Texas Intermediate (WTI) crude oil, and is listed on the New York Mercantile Exchange (NYMEX). This contract trades an average of 100,000 contracts per day, which, in terms of notional underlying oil, represents substantially more than the daily world production of crude. The vast majority of trading takes place in the first three contract months, although the longest maturities (in which there is little liquidity) have recently been increased to a maximum of three years.

An analysis of the NYMEX trades reveals that only a very small proportion – less than 5 per cent – is transacted by the producers. Although this ratio may differ in other markets, the evidence of both exchange volumes and the economic performance of producers serves to indicate that only a small proportion of the world's total commodity production is hedged using futures contracts. An absence of long-term contracts and adequate liquidity has in part discouraged producers, and indeed large consumers, from using futures contracts as an integrated component of risk management. A further problem is the standardised characteristics of the futures contract, which permits flexibility only in the number of contracts which are bought or sold. Other factors, such as the specific characteristics of the deliverable commodity, currency, delivery points and settlement date are unchangeable except within narrow bands. In the oil markets, the wide range of specifications and delivery points for crude oil leads to problems when using the standardised futures contract. This is emphasised by the fact that WTI accounts for less than 2 per cent of world crude oil production. In addition to these issues, exchange regulations require that the trader must provide or receive margins, to cover both an initial stake for each contract and any daily mark-to-market profits or losses on outstanding contracts. Any or all of these constraints may prove frustrating for an institution which may well require a method for hedging long-term commodity price risk.

It is arguable that the ideal risk management instruments will take the form of contracts for differences, settled in cash, but have the possibility of longer maturities than are common in exchange traded vehicles, be traded in a liquid market, have a range of possible underlying specifications and be capable of settlement in currencies other than the US dollar.

These requirements are, at least in major part, met by the commodity swap structure. In this instrument, the financial intermediary prices a tailor-made series of forward contracts for differences for each hedger. The hedger is offered a single 'fixed price' at which he will notionally buy or sell for agreed future delivery dates. Cash settlement will comprise the product of the difference between the fixed price and the price of an agreed index, and a predetermined quantity of the commodity for the relevant period. Commodity swaps enable the user to fix a series of inherently variable future commodity payments or receipts for up to ten years at a single price, in the commodity and currency most closely relating to the projected exposure. As hedging instruments, swaps have obvious applications for the governments of producing countries, as well as for companies and financial institutions.

In the light of the volatility of commodity prices, and the breadth of institutions which face some form of exposure, it is perhaps surprising that financial institutions were not quicker to develop OTC products to manage commodity price risk. One explanation is that the role of the wholesale purchaser and distributor of commodities was historically the preserve of the large trading houses; financial institutions had little or no involvement in the trade of physical commodities other than gold, and their connection to commodities was limited to the financing of cargoes or the issuing of letters of credit to commodity trading houses.

The nature of the commodity futures markets was seen as inherently speculative by the more risk-averse elements of the banking community. Admittedly, banks had become highly experienced in the development of financial risk management products, and had clear skills in advising and distributing to a corporate customer base. But the commodity trading houses, who lacked these abilities, had a near monopoly of knowledge of the physical commodity markets. It is perhaps because of these reasons that the development of a tool for the management of commodity price risk analogous to the interest rate swap was very slow.

The first commodity swap was probably executed by Chase Manhattan, in the second half of 1986. This contract was based on WTI, and was arranged to enable an airline to secure oil price costs in line with its budget for the forthcoming financial year. The first few swaps were substantially limited to oil, and maturities were relatively short, rarely exceeding one year. Since then, considerable progress has been made, both in the range of underlying commodities on which contracts are available and in the variety of specifications.

As the swap 'contracts for differences' offered the equivalent of a series of tailored, off-exchange futures, so caps and floors, which were developed alongside swaps, represented the options equivalents. These contracts have become far more complex, and more flexible, than exchange traded commodity options. In recent years, the most popular instrument for both consumers and producers has been the 'Asian' or average price option, under which the payoff is based on the difference (if positive), between the average of the floating price and the fixed or 'strike' price for each settlement period.

Although by comparison with the interest rate swaps market, the commodity derivatives market is still in its infancy, in the last two years there has been a significant number of new entrants. Some of these have been financial institutions, while others are trading houses, and typically each set fulfils a different market role. In general, the principal strength of the trading houses lies in their familiarity with a large range of different underlying commodities, and their niche is to match the products they offer against existing commodity books. Usually, the structures of these products will tend to be relatively standardised and their maturities relatively short. By contrast, the strength of the financial institutions lies in their ability to construct products which will address a range of risks, including interest rate and currency risk. Experience in the pricing of more complex financial instruments has been invaluable in this new area. In addition to a depth of technical expertise, the balance sheet of some banks has permitted distribution of longer-term and sizeable contracts.

Regulation was one of the original hurdles to the fledgling commodity swap industry. Under the US Commodity Exchange Act, futures contracts may lawfully be entered into only on a regulated exchange. However, in July 1989 the Commodity Futures Trading Commission (CFTC) issued a 'safe harbour agreement' for those swap transactions which satisfied a stated set of criteria. These criteria distinguished the forward, non-standard characteristics of a swap arranged between two principal counterparties and the standardized futures contracts protected by exchange guarantees. The safe harbour agreement opened up the US market in commodity swaps. Previously contracts had been executed through institutions in the UK, where regulation was more permissive: in the UK the focus is to control and regulate the parties to financial transactions with no implied focus on the protection of the exclusive right of the exchanges to conduct futures business. The regulatory position in other countries, notably Japan, remains to be clarified.

Following the safe harbour agreement, US banks have moved swiftly to gain an understanding of the workings of the physical commodity markets, in order that they may both advise and price structures for their clients, and successfully measure and manage risk on their own books. Trading houses, although very experienced in the physical commodity markets, have needed to develop technical and marketing competence in order to offer an advisory and distribution capability to clients, and to structure financial instruments. It is the challenge of the providers of these instruments to recognise and understand the needs of those companies whose business could be enhanced by the use of commodity derivatives, and to advise them correctly in the initial education process before the instruments can become accepted as part of the risk management strategy of the company.

In most cases, the aim of the corporate treasurer is to convert fluctuating commodity revenues or costs into fixed future flows on the best possible terms (having regard to the portfolio interaction of commodity and other financial risks). However, the ability to fix now the price of a series of variable flows as far forward as ten years opens up other opportunities:

- Project financing in the mining or oil exploration businesses, where the movement in a commodity's price is vital to the success of the venture;
- Enhancement of existing business by offering fixed price contracts to customers;
- Objective valuation of future corporate cash flows to provide a better understanding of the (stock) valuation of commodity producers;
- Translation of floating commodity cash flows into fixed flows in a specific currency for use in long-term countertrade agreements;
- Improvement in corporate planning and budgeting, and working capital management;
- Design of attractive investment instruments whose value does not hinge on peripheral, stock-specific factors;
- Anticipatory hedging and speculation for both consumers and producers at attractive points in the price cycle, without the requirement to purchase or deliver physical material;
- Preparation of more objective company valuations and profit forecasts to support credit appraisal and corporate finance activities undertaken by banks.

THE STRUCTURE AND PRICING OF COMMODITY DERIVATIVES

Background to Two-way Contracts for Differences

In order to measure the effects of commodity price risk on the profitability of a company, it is necessary first to project forward the future commodity

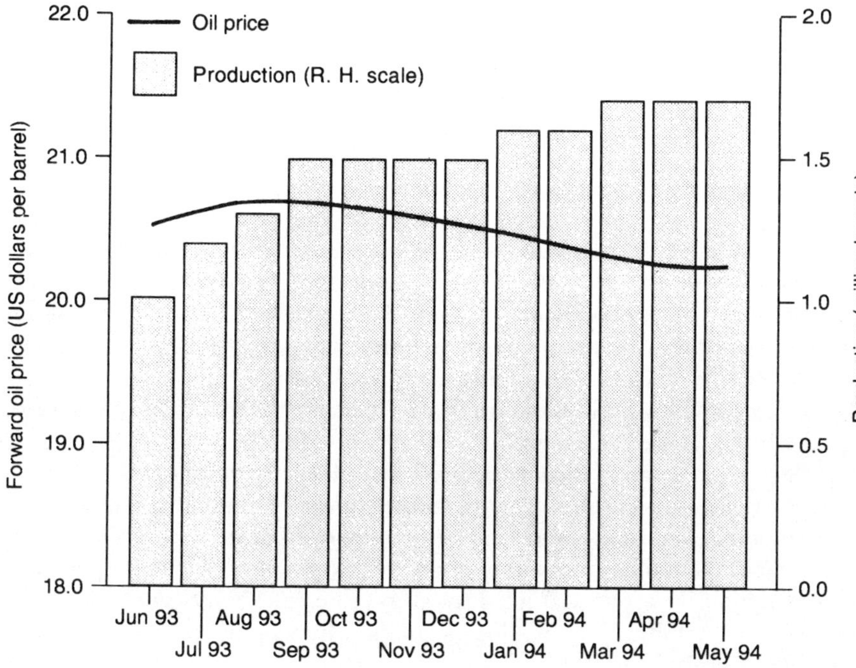

Figure 5.6 Illustrative Future Oil Production and the Forward Oil Market

sales and/or purchases. The length of this projection will reflect the period forward for which the company may reasonably wish to plan, and this will vary between different companies.

Figure 5.6 illustrates the expected future production of an oil producer, and associated oil prices.

In theory, a company's value should be equal to a multiple of the sum of the present values of all future net cash flows (not taking into consideration capital, exploration or other costs). For an oil producer, the (US dollar) value of the future production will equal the product of the total barrels sold in each period and the forward price of the relevant oil grade deliverable in that period, reduced to a present value at an appropriate discount rate. If no action is taken, these cash flows will vary with the movement in the forward oil price curve.

In order to lock in the value, or cost, of these future flows, an offsetting contract must be negotiated whose (mark-to-market) value fluctuates in direct opposition to the net present value of the budgeted flows. A perfect match will enable the company to lock in a known sales or purchase price for the commodity which reflects the commodity's forward price structure implicit at the time of the hedge.

The two-way contract for differences, or commodity swap, is an agreement to pay or receive the net difference between a fixed price (agreed in advance) and a floating 'index' price of the commodity.

Calculation of the Fixed Price for a Commodity Swap

In order to calculate this single fixed price for a series of future cash flows, each cash flow must be discounted back to spot using the risk-free (US dollar) zero coupon rate for the relevant maturity. The single fixed price for the series of future cash flows will equate to an 'annuity' weighted to reflect the appropriate quantity of commodity applicable to each period.

Table 5.3 provides an illustration of the fixed (or swap) price calculation, using the same figures as Figure 5.6.

The 'fair' swap price is the quotient of the total present value of future oil production (= production in barrels × futures price × discount factor, summed over all months) and the total discounted number of barrels (= production × discount factor, summed over all months). The top half of Table 5.3 performs these calculations to arrive at a fixed (or swap) price of $20.497 per barrel. The lower half of the table 'proves' this calculation by valuing an 'annuity' comprising the variable monthly production at the fixed price of $20.497 per barrel: the identical net present value of future oil production of $353.838 is obtained.

Swaps in Alternative Currencies

In many cases, the hedger may require that the forward commodity cash flows be fixed in local currency. However, most commodities are denominated in US dollars. Hence, in addition to a standard commodity swap, the hedger must open a series of foreign exchange contracts, either to sell (if long the commodity), or buy (if short the commodity), US dollars against the domestic currency. The maturities of these contracts should coincide with the fixing dates of the swap.

But there are reasons why a non-financial institution may not wish to execute this form of currency hedge. Firstly, the required foreign exchange contracts must be settled by price differences (as with the swap), rather than by actual delivery of currency. Secondly, the settlement of the foreign exchange hedge position must take place at the same time as the commodity hedge to avoid potential funding of hedge losses. More importantly, the very large number of contracts which must be opened, if all of the swap fixing dates are to be covered, could prove inefficient to monitor and expensive in terms of implicit transaction costs. A possibly cheaper alternative is to request a swap quotation

Swap Price Calculation

Spot May-93	Notional Cash Flow Date											
	Jun-93	**Jul-93**	**Aug-93**	**Sep-93**	**Oct-93**	**Nov-93**	**Dec-93**	**Jan-94**	**Feb-94**	**Mar-94**	**Apr-94**	**May-94**
US$ Zero Coupon Rate	0.0440	0.0440	0.0460	0.0480	0.0490	0.0500	0.0510	0.0520	0.0530	0.0547	0.0562	0.0590
Futures Price	20.55	20.68	20.72	20.70	20.65	20.58	20.54	20.46	20.39	20.33	20.27	20.24
Present Value	20.4724	24.6324	26.6230	30.5490	30.3431	30.1008	29.9034	31.6171	31.3501	33.0351	32.7465	32.4659
Future Barrels	1.0	1.2	1.3	1.5	1.5	1.5	1.5	1.6	1.6	1.7	1.7	1.7
Discounted Barrels	0.9962	1.1911	1.2849	1.4758	1.4694	1.4626	1.4559	1.5453	1.5375	1.6249	1.6155	1.6040

Total Discounted Barrels: 17.2632
Total Present Value Oil: 353.838

$$\frac{\text{Present Value Oil}}{\text{Discounted Barrels}} = \$20.4966 = \text{Swap Price or Annuity}$$

Proof

Spot May-93	Notional Cash Flow Date											
	Jun-93	**Jul-93**	**Aug-93**	**Sep-93**	**Oct-93**	**Nov-93**	**Dec-93**	**Jan-94**	**Feb-94**	**Mar-94**	**Apr-94**	**May-94**
Annuity/Swap price	20.4966	20.4966	20.4966	20.4966	20.4966	20.4966	20.4966	20.4966	20.4966	20.4966	20.4966	20.4966
Future Barrels	1.0	1.2	1.3	1.5	1.5	1.5	1.5	1.6	1.6	1.7	1.7	1.7
Weighted	20.4966	24.5959	26.6456	30.7449	30.7449	30.7449	30.7449	32.7946	32.7946	32.8442	32.8442	34.8442
US$ Zero Coupon Rate	0.0440	0.0440	0.0460	0.0480	0.0490	0.0500	0.0510	0.0520	0.0530	0.0547	0.0562	0.0590
Present Value	20.4193	24.4139	26.3360	30.2489	30.1177	29.9788	29.8403	31.6737	31.5141	33.3058	33.1126	32.8776

Total Present Value Oil: 353.838

Table 5.3 Calculation and Proof of Fixed Swap Price

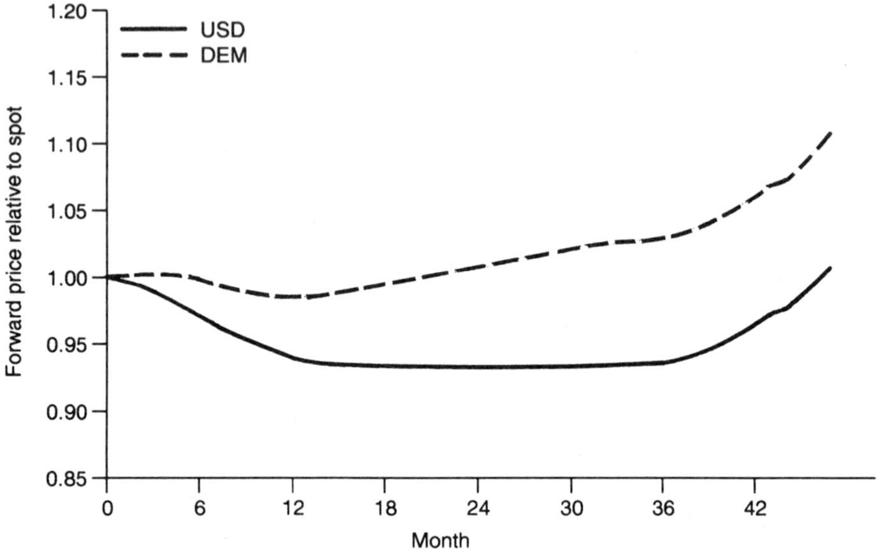

Figure 5.7 Illustrative Forward Oil Curves (Relative to Spot, Measured in US Dollars and Deutschemarks)

in the required currency from the financial intermediary. Usually, it will be more efficient for this intermediary to provide the foreign currency hedge.

It is often sensible for a company exposed to commodity prices to monitor the forward value of their asset or liabilities not only in US dollars, but also in domestic currency. Relative interest rate differentials can often lead to more appealing fixed rate quotations in one currency rather than another. Figure 5.7 provides an illustration of this.

Variable Components of the Swap Contract

In advance of each contract, both counterparties must agree the variable components of the swap agreement. For an oil swap, these will include:

- The total notional number of barrels under the contract;
- The beginning and end dates of each calculation period after which a settlement is made reflecting the difference between the fixed and floating prices;
- The dates in each period which will be used in the calculation of the (average) floating price;
- The number of barrels relating to each calculation date;

- The published index which will represent the floating price;
- The date(s) on which price difference payments are due.

The possibility of variation in these terms permits the swap user great flexibility to match his own physical exposures and contractual arrangements.

Depth of the Swap Market

Swaps may now be executed on a wide range of commodity indices. These include a variety of crude oils, refined products, petrochemicals, natural gas (in the US market), non-ferrous metals, precious metals and some foodstuffs. Transaction sizes are limited in part by application of counterparty credit exposure limits. For any given swap, credit exposure is calculated as a function, *inter alia*, of the volatility of the index and the maturity of the contract. The majority of swaps have maturities of less than one year, particularly if based on the less common indices. Exceptionally, swaps may be executed with original maturities of seven years or longer.

If a futures market exists for the commodity, then a mathematical calculation of the 'fair price' of the swap is relatively straightforward. However, in many cases, the longest maturity traded on the exchange may be less than one year, and in other cases no futures market exists. In addition to this, the simple calculation of the 'fair price' does not take into account various intrinsic costs and risks to the trader, which must be embedded in the swap's bid–offer spread.

The swap trader must find solutions to the following issues:

- The generation of a synthetic futures strip which extends the visible futures curve;
- The generation of a notional futures strip from a futures curve in a related commodity;
- An assessment of the implicit costs involved in hedging a particular derivative, including slippage, brokerage costs, financing of futures margin, calendar spread risk, basis and credit risks.

These issues are discussed in turn below.

Generation of a Synthetic Futures Strip from the Visible Futures Curve

In many ways the pricing of forward contracts in commodities is no different from that in bond or equity markets. The traditional relationship of the futures price to the spot price (the contango, or forward premium) is a function of the financing and storage costs of the cash commodity to the delivery and payment date. The forward premium cannot exceed this amount without an arbitrage (risk-free) profit becoming available, and this should quickly push the price relationship back into line. For equity and bond futures, coupon or dividend payments receivable by the holder of the asset reduce the financing costs; there is also a (weaker) reverse arbitrage which constrains the amount by which a forward premium (or discount) can lie below its fair value. This lower arbitrage boundary does not exist in the commodity markets, other than in the gold market. But in the commodity markets there is one further element which influences the spot–futures relationship. For industrial commodities, which are raw materials in the fabrication of manufactured products, availability can be crucial, and consumers will often be prepared to pay a premium for this immediate supply. Particularly in times of uncertainty of supply, this will cause the spot and shorter-term futures contracts to gain considerable premiums to the more distant months.

The following term structures for oil futures (Figure 5.8) have been taken at the start of each of the past six years, and illustrate the changing shape of forward oil prices.

The premium payable for availability is commonly referred to as 'convenience yield'. This value itself has a term structure, which reflects the diminishing risk premium attached to longer delivery dates. The measurement of convenience yield, and, more importantly, its term structure beyond the visible futures curve, is the key to the determination of any long-term futures price. Currently, there are no standard models for the extension of the convenience yield term structure, although it is the subject of much proprietary research. Once a synthetic 'strip' of futures prices beyond the visible curve has been calculated, then theoretically any swap structure may be priced.

Generation of a Futures Strip from a Futures Curve in a Related Commodity

Due to the very large variety and different grades of physical commodities, and the standardised nature of futures markets, companies will be exposed to the prices of many commodities in which no futures market is available. This is particularly important in the case of the oil market, where there is a plethora of grades of crude oil. To price the swap, a synthetic strip of futures prices must again be constructed. First, the swap trader will attempt to isolate the commodity in which a futures market is available which bears the closest relationship to the index required. He will then analyse the historical correlation between the two commodities to simulate a futures curve. In the case of oil products, a price seasonality is often visible. In such cases the forward curve will display both upward and downward slopes, which must be taken into consideration, particularly for short-term swaps of less than one year.

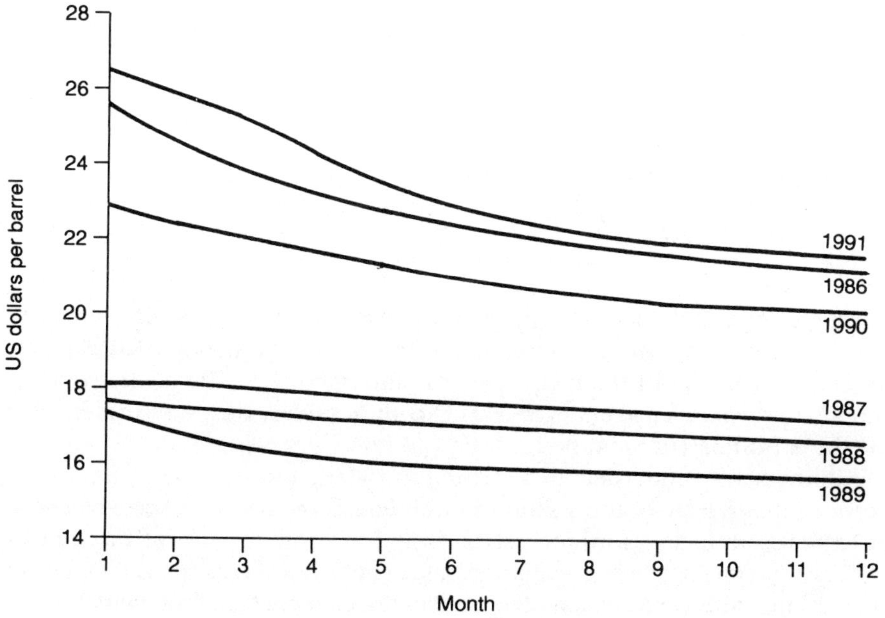

Figure 5.8 Illustrative Term Structures of Oil Futures (NYMEX WTI, taken as at 2 January in Each Year)

Implicit Hedging Costs and Risks

The first, and most complex task of the swap trader is to generate a forward strip of futures prices out to maturities that cover the needs of the client. The creation of such a 'curve' is based on an understanding of the behaviour of the 'premium' or 'convenience yield' which is often displayed in the value of the contracts for shorter term maturity in industrial commodity markets. These markets exhibit a term structure in which the availability premium increases exponentially with proximity to delivery. Following the generation of the synthetic futures curve, the calculation of the 'fair' swap price for any given structure will be relatively straightforward. However, the fixed price quoted by the swap trader should incorporate not only the trader's profit, but also a spread which reflects the various hedging costs and risks. The size of this spread will be a function of a number of factors including into which of the following three categories the swap falls.

(1) *Swaps Inside the Futures Curve*
For swaps whose notional underlying principal represents only a small proportion of the daily volume of the representative futures market, and for which

the floating price for the swap is indeed the futures contract, the hedging risks are limited to:

- Slippage of the futures prices after the swap is arranged, but before the hedge has been placed;
- Slippage in the management of a dynamic hedge position;
- The cost of financing (negative) exchange variation margins;
- Brokerage costs;
- Credit risk.

For larger swaps, the risk of slippage may increase, due to the relatively poor liquidity in futures contracts whose maturities exceed six months. The slippage in the management of the hedge position throughout the life of the contract can also prove expensive. As the OTC contract fixes, the swap trader must lift the offsetting (futures) hedge.

Although less important in short-dated swaps, the dynamic relationship between forward and futures contracts will require the hedge to be re-balanced in response to changes in interest rates and the convergence of the futures contracts to spot. The mark-to-market value of a forward contract is the present value of the difference between the fixed contracted price and the market price for the same commodity on a matching delivery date. By contrast, the mark-to-market profits or losses of a futures contract are paid immediately in the form of variation margin. As a result, in order to hedge a series of forward contracts with futures, the size of the futures equivalent hedge must be discounted by the zero coupon rate which applies to the fixing date of each forward contract.

On rare occasions, exactly matching counterparties may be found, so that the swap trader acts purely as a financial intermediary; in this event the spread will reflect only credit risk and profit.

(2) *Swaps Beyond the Futures Curve*

There are additional and complex risks associated with the hedging of forward commodity positions which extend beyond the visible futures curve. Even after a synthetic futures curve has been generated to calculate the 'fair' price of the swap, the problem of hedging these long-term positions will remain.

Unless an offsetting position has been found in the OTC market in the form of another swap, or series of swaps, the trader must offset the position in the closest maturity available. This will usually result in 'stacking' long-term futures contracts, and leave the trader with a series of long or short calendar spread positions: in effect, a series of positions sensitive to the underlying value of the commodity, interest rates and 'convenience yield'. If the trader were to manage this futures hedge as far as its maturity, then the actual 'price' achieved from the hedge of that part of the exposure which initially lay beyond the last maturity of the futures market will be the combination of the forward or 'swap price' achieved on the initial hedge up to the last futures maturity and the net 'rollover' costs or gains from the stacked contracts. This price may well diverge from the theoretical price identified at inception from the synthetic futures curve.

In practice, the trader is unlikely to use futures to hedge the swap to maturity, but will attempt to offset the position risk earlier with offsetting swaps. Until a more transparent and generally accepted method has been developed to price long-term swaps, it is likely that projected rollover cost, rather than an understanding of the term structure of convenience yield, will dictate the pricing of these long-term instruments.

(3) *Swaps on Commodities with No Futures Market*

The hedging risks inherent in these contracts will include the risks described in (1), and perhaps (2), above. In addition, there is the risk associated with hedging forward contracts in one commodity with futures contracts in another commodity. Ideally, a swap trader will run two-way books in a variety of non-exchange traded commodities and, assuming a good flow of business, his risk may be contained. However, it is probable that, on the immediate execution of the swap contract, he must use the futures market to hedge the outright market level, particularly in times of high volatility. The trader then incurs the potential risk that the relationship between the commodity contracted in

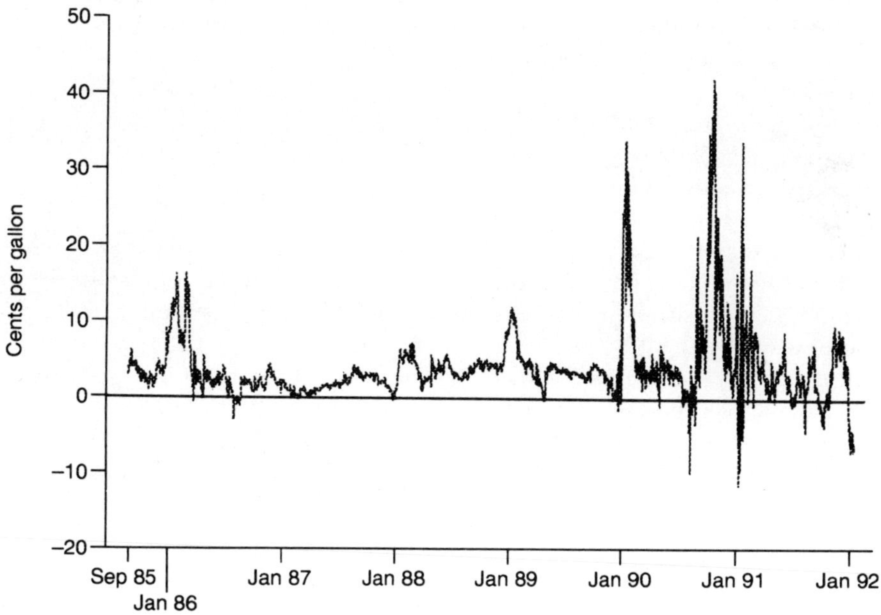

Figure 5.9 Heating Oil/Jet Fuel Oil Spread History (Heating Oil: NYMEX First Month Futures; Jet Fuel Oil: f.o.b. New York Barges)

the swap, and the futures contract employed as a hedge, will change either generally or at any point on the (futures) curve.

In the oil market, the spread relationships between the various grades and delivery areas of crudes and products can be highly erratic. Prior to the Gulf War, the reliable and steady relationship between heating oil deliverable in New York Harbour – traded on NYMEX – and a range of jet fuel prices, provided a reliable hedge mechanism for the swap trader. Yet, as Figure 5.9 illustrates, this relationship became dislocated during the Gulf War, with expensive consequences for some traders.

Documentation

Usually the legal documentation covering commodity swaps has reflected the status of the intermediaries. Contracts issued by financial institutions were based predominantly on the format developed for the interest rate and currency swap markets, while those issued by commodity traders and oil companies often reflected the more concise documentation commonly used in these businesses. However, as the market has developed, a more standardised approach has been taken. A committee drawn from a large number of representative organisations is currently working on the production of a standard commodity swap master agreement, which will be designed to cover a wide range of different commodity indices.

6: The Forward Market in Electricity

Josh Danziger, GNI Limited

INTRODUCTION

The construction of the electricity market prior to the privatisation of the UK industry gave rise to an open market in physical electricity, known as the *pool*. It also gave rise to a completely new type of commodity risk for generators, suppliers and users of electricity: electricity price risk. Electricity prices in the pool are highly volatile: typically they average around £20/MWh, but sometimes fall to below £10/MWh and on occasion rise to above £300/MWh.

In response to this volatility, trading in OTC electricity derivatives has developed to allow electricity traders to hedge pool price risks. In particular, generators and regional electricity companies (RECs) regularly trade electricity derivatives, known as 'contracts for differences' (CFDs), between themselves. The CFD market is large: about 80 per cent of current electricity consumption, equivalent to around £5 billion per annum, is covered by these contracts. Yet, although pool price volatility has attracted considerable public interest, so far little attention has focused on CFD trading. This is perhaps surprising, since a single CFD may fix a price for several years of electricity, while pool prices only cover individual half-hours. As a result, CFD trading may have far more significance than pool prices.

CFDs are now supplemented by another type of derivative, the Electricity Forward Agreement (EFA). EFAs provide a standard framework for trading and hedging pool prices, particularly for short-term trades. Through the involvement of an EFA broker and a network of price screens, EFA trading is much more transparent than CFD trading, and it is open to any company that wishes to participate.

The UK electricity derivatives markets are still new – indeed, the pool itself started only in 1990 – and there is the potential for substantial development and growth. This chapter contains an introduction to the pool mechanism, describes the current state of the derivatives markets, and discusses electricity price behaviour.

THE UK ELECTRICITY INDUSTRY

Structure of the Industry

The decision to privatise the UK electricity industry led to a number of changes. The twelve area boards of England and Wales were set up as individual companies, known as regional electricity companies (RECs). The RECs run the local distribution networks for their region, and also act as electricity suppliers. Conventional generation capacity is divided between two generators, National Power and PowerGen, while nuclear generation remains in public ownership in the form of Nuclear Electric (the generating company) and BNFL (the reprocessing company). The National Grid Company (NGC), owned by the RECs, has been set up to run the grid.

In addition, in England and Wales a market for physical electricity, known as the pool, was established. This market is central to the operation of the industry. Generators sell all of their output into the pool, while suppliers (and wholesale industrial consumers, if they wish) buy from the pool. The pool itself does not have a physical existence: it is simply the set of procedures and rules which are used to determine the market price of electricity for each half-hour of the day, and to select which generating sets are to be operated. However, the pool may be regarded as the market which corresponds to the physical structure of the national grid, and it is also operated by NGC.

A key feature of the privatisation was the distinction drawn between natural monopoly businesses, such as distribution or retail supply, and areas where competition is feasible, such as generation or wholesale supply. The theory is that natural monopoly businesses should be subject to fairly strict regulation from OFFER, the regulatory body, while market forces should be allowed to operate in other areas. Thus, the pool price for wholesale electricity is set by market competition between generators acting through the pool. The pool is essentially open to anyone who wishes to join: new independent generators can sell their output through the pool, while industrial consumers are able to purchase electricity direct from the pool. Of course, consumers are not compelled to join the pool, and can buy from whichever supplier offers them the best deal.

The position is different in Scotland, where two vertically integrated companies – Scottish Power and Scottish Hydro – were privatised, each acting as a generator, distributor and supplier. In this chapter, the principal focus is on pool prices in England and Wales.

Generation and Demand

Electricity demand naturally varies considerably between different times of the day, between weekdays and weekends, between one season and another,

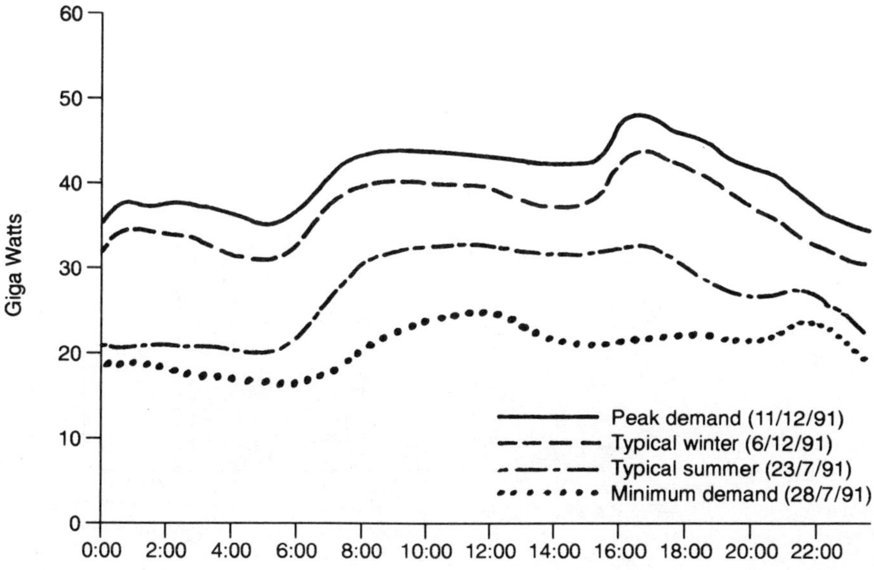

Figure 6.1 Pool Demand Profiles (GW)

and so forth. Moreover, factors such as the weather, and the general level of economic activity, have an effect. Around 5.00–5.30 pm on some days in the winter, National Grid demand may peak at nearly 50 GW (1 GW = 1,000 MW), while on some summer days peak demand may be only half of this. Minimum demand is typically 30 per cent less than peak. Figure 6.1 illustrates some typical demand profiles.

Generation capacity currently exceeds 60 GW, leaving a 25 per cent plant margin against peak demand. Figure 6.2 shows the constituents of this capacity, in terms of both the types of plant and the companies which own the plant. Generation plant is supplemented both by imported electricity and by a certain limited amount of storage capacity. There are interconnectors linking the National Grid both to Scotland (850 MW, to be upgraded to 1,600 MW) and across the channel to France (2,000 MW). Although both interconnectors can be operated in either direction, in practice England is nearly always an importer of electricity. There are pumped storage sites at Dinorwig and Ffestiniog (2,088 MW combined capacity), which are operated as an independent business by NGC. Off-peak, cheap electricity is used to pump water uphill from one reservoir to a higher one; at peak times, the water is allowed to run back down through a turbine, driving a generator, and so producing electricity. NGC Pumped Storage buys electricity from the pool and sells to it; it also offers reserve capacity to the system.

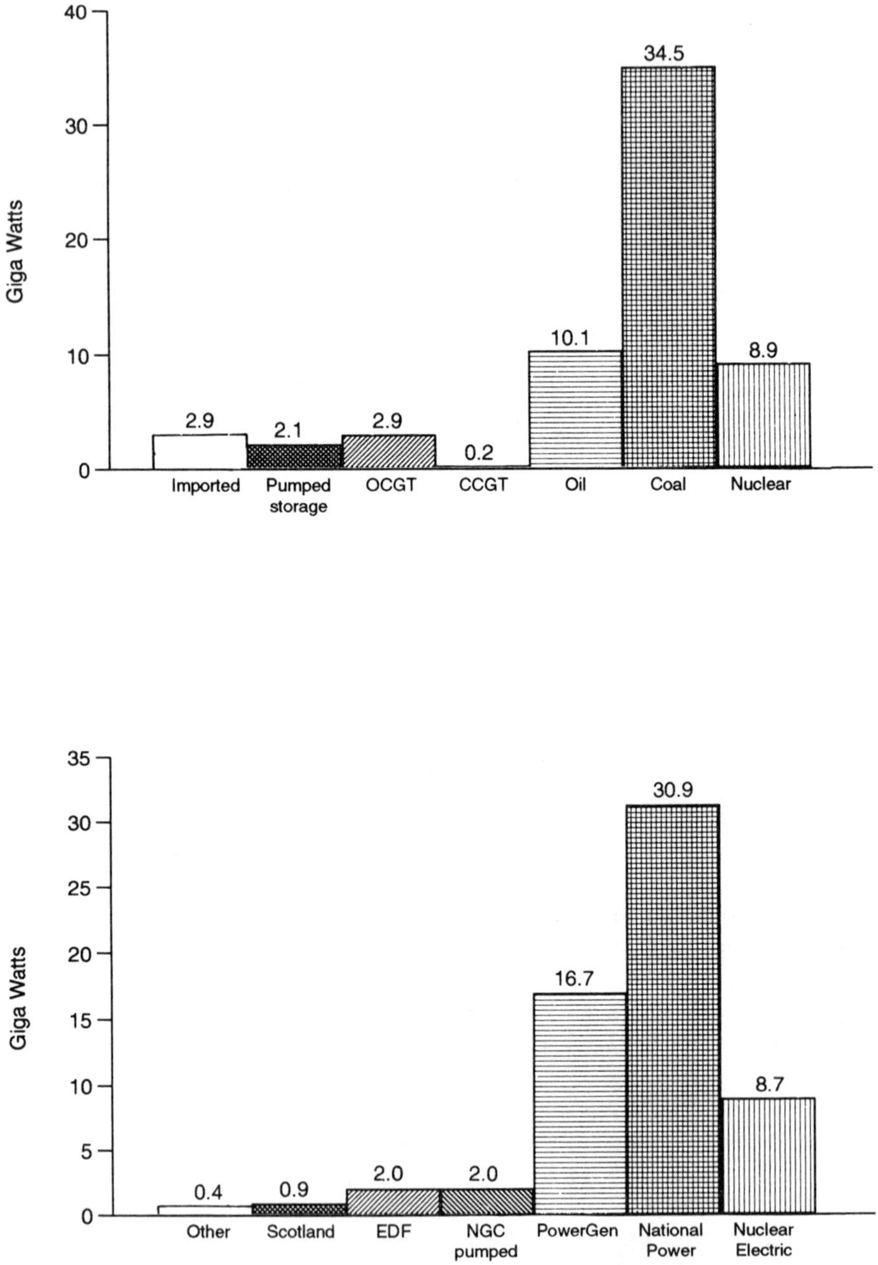

Figure 6.2 Pool Generation Capacity (GW), Broken Down by Type of Generation and by Ownership (1991)

Overall capacity looks set to grow, with the plant margin climbing to perhaps 35 per cent over the next few years. A further 8.2 GW of capacity is now committed to the NGC system by 1995, mainly in the form of CCGTs. Several of these plants are being built by independent generators, which may increase competition in the generation business. Closures announced before March 1991 amounted to only 1,600 MW, and comprised mainly small coal plant.

Electricity Supply

Following the changes in the industry, there are several approaches open to wholesale consumers for purchasing electricity. An agreement can be negotiated with a supplier: this might be a REC (not necessarily the local REC), or it might be another supply company, or it might be direct with a generator. The agreement may be in the form of a fixed tariff, or it may be a pool-related agreement – that is, the consumer agrees a price which varies with the pool price – or possibly a hybrid, such as a capped pool price. An alternative is for the consumer to join the pool and buy direct from the pool. Of course, the consumer may wish to arrange his own generation for all or part of his consumption, bypassing the electricity industry altogether.

THE POOL

The pool was set up prior to privatisation as the main market for physical electricity in England and Wales. The participants in this market are primarily the generators and the suppliers: the large generating companies, such as National Power and PowerGen sell all of their output into the pool, while electricity suppliers (mainly the RECs) buy from the pool, as do some industrial consumers. The vast majority of electricity in England and Wales is traded through the pool.

There are three characteristics of the electricity market which distinguish it from most other markets. First, because electricity is difficult to store in bulk, most of it has to be generated at the time it is required. Second, the variation in demand together with the variation in generating capacity permits enormous volatility in the price of electricity. It can vary from below £10/MWh to £300/MWh or even higher (see Figure 6.3). (Note that £10/MWh is equivalent to 1 pence/unit.) Third, since generated electricity is disseminated over the National Grid, into which it is fed by suppliers and from which it is drawn by consumers, it is impractical to distinguish between different generators or different consumers. Instead, at any given time, all buyers buy from the pool at a single price, the pool output price (POP), and all sellers sell at a related price, the pool input price (PIP).

Operation of the Pool

Pool prices are set for each half-hour of the day, giving 48 periods per day. Pool input prices are set a day in advance, based on the prices at which the various generators are prepared to operate their different generating sets, combined with the demand profiles forecast by the NGC, which runs the pool. The detailed operation of the pool is governed by the pool rules, which are highly complicated, and only an outline of pool operation is presented here.

The Unconstrained Schedule

The first step in setting the price is the preparation of the unconstrained schedule at 10 am each morning, to cover the 24 hours from 5 am the following morning. Each generator submits offers to the grid operator for each plant which is subject to central despatch; that is, each plant whose operation can be controlled by instructions from the grid operator. All generators exporting more than 10 MW must join the pool, and all generating stations with more than 100 MW of capacity are subject to central despatch; while sets whose capacity exceeds 1 MW can elect to be subject to central despatch. The generators' offers detail the availability of each set, its capacity, its operating characteristics and the prices to be charged for its electricity production. A peculiarity of the electricity industry is that this process of offering plant production to the pool is often referred to as 'bidding in'.

System Marginal Price

Given the offers from the generators, together with a forecast for the demand and reserve requirements for each half-hour, the unconstrained schedule is calculated using a computer-based algorithm. In simple terms, this calculates the lowest price which meets sufficient offers to satisfy the projected requirements – that is, the optimum marginal price, known as the System Marginal Price (SMP). In reality, the problem is fairly complicated, and the algorithm has to take into account the characteristics of each generating set to calculate the best arrangement. For example, some sets may offer cheap electricity but start-up and shutdown costs may be high; the algorithm must then ensure that these sets are scheduled for uninterrupted operation as far as possible.

Pool Input Price

At any time, generators are paid at essentially the same rate for generated electricity. The price paid is the pool input price, PIP, which is equal to the SMP plus an extra margin known as the Capacity element. At times of low demand, the Capacity element is zero, but it increases as demand rises towards the point where the possibility arises that generating capacity may be insufficient. The Capacity element is calculated as:

$$\text{LOLP} \times (\text{VLL} - \text{SMP})$$

where LOLP is the loss of load probability, calculated by the NGC for each half-hour and varying between zero and one; and VLL is a figure for the value of lost load, currently set at £2,187/MWh and subject to indexation. PIP is also referred to as Pool Purchase Price (PPP).

Pool Output Price

The price paid by suppliers for electricity consumed is the pool output price, POP. It is equal to PIP plus an Uplift element, covering for example:

- the cost of ancillary services;
- the cost of providing reserve generating capacity; and
- differences between the scheduled and the actual operation.

The Uplift is set so that cash payments by the pool are exactly matched by receipts, so that the pool's net cashflow for each half-hour is zero. The Uplift is typically small or zero.

POP is also referred to as Pool Selling Price (PSP).

Settlement

There is a provisional settlement run 12 days after the trading day, a final run after 24 days, and payments are due after 28 days. All payments are made through the pool.

Pool Membership

One of the key aims of privatisation was to introduce competition into areas where natural monopolies do not exclude it. Hence it is important that newcomers also have access to the pool, either to sell electricity into it or to buy from it. Consumers with their own generation capacity may at different times be both buyers and sellers, depending on whether their own generation exceeds their requirements or falls short of it.

In practice, although some independent generators have joined the pool, as have some industrial consumers, pool membership remains dominated by the original generators and the RECs. On the other hand, there are a large number of wholesale consumers who are exposed to pool prices, even though they are not members of the pool. This is because many RECs have offered their customers tariffs linked to pool prices, with an added administrative charge. This is an attractive strategy for the RECs: since they buy the electricity in the pool, selling it at a pool price tariff eliminates any exposure they might otherwise have to pool price fluctuations.

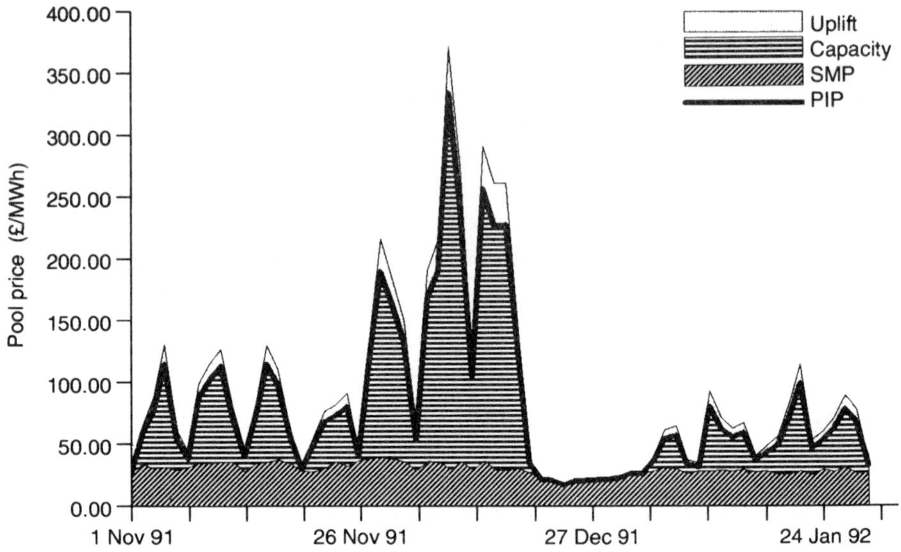

Figure 6.3 Weekday Peak Pool Prices (5.00–5.30 pm) for Winter 1991 (£/MWh)

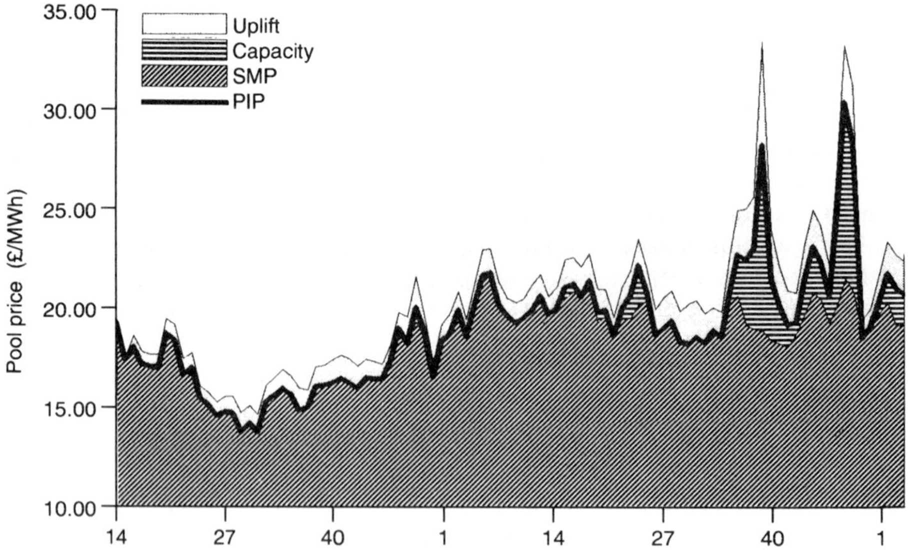

Figure 6.4 Baseload Pool Prices Weekly from Week 14/90 to 5/92 (£/MWh)

Pool Prices

Figures 6.3 and 6.4 provide an indication of the behaviour of pool prices. As Figure 6.3 reveals, peak weekday winter prices (5.00–5.30 pm) are highly volatile, with prices for 1991/92 varying from below £30/MWh to above £300/MWh. It is evident that much of the volatility comes from the Capacity element. However, volatility over longer time periods is far lower. Figure 6.4 shows the weekly average price for constant continuous electricity consumption, known as *baseload* consumption. Weekly baseload prices have typically averaged around £20/MWh, falling towards £15/MWh in the summer of 1990, and occasionally spiking to over £30/MWh in the autumn and winter of 1991.

POOL PRICE DERIVATIVES

Derivative instruments play a substantial role in the electricity market. The volatility of pool prices leaves both buyers and sellers exposed – since the vast bulk of electricity consumed in England and Wales is traded through the pool, the risks would be enormous without some form of hedging instrument.

The derivatives positions of pool members may entirely alter their exposure to the pool. For example, a generator might construct a derivative exposure, so that instead of being at risk from low pool prices, it is entirely neutral to the pool (low pool prices being compensated by the performance of the derivative contracts); or indeed, it might actually reverse its exposure, so that it benefits from low pool prices, being 'short' instead of 'long'. The importance of derivatives is emphasised by the fact that, in 1989–90, 80 per cent of the annual electricity consumption in England and Wales (230 TWh) was covered by OTC derivative instruments.

Partly for this reason, the signals from pool prices may often be less significant than those from prices for trades in the OTC market. For example, for a company contemplating building a power station, the price of a fifteen year electricity derivative instrument is of much more significance than the pool price for the next day. This is analogous to interest rate exposure: for a company wishing to finance a new venture, the medium- or long-term interest rate swap prices are far more relevant than the overnight rate.

Cash Settled OTC Derivatives

The instruments which have developed are cash settled OTC agreements, similar to those in other markets. For example, two parties might agree on a forward pool price for a certain amount of electricity. If the actual price outcome in the pool is greater than the agreed forward price, one party –

the seller – compensates the other – the buyer; if pool prices are lower, the buyer compensates the seller. In the case where the seller expects to sell electricity into the pool, and the buyer expects to buy from it, this form of agreement would act as a hedge for both parties, effectively locking in a fixed price for the electricity in advance.

Cash settled instruments are the natural trading tool in the electricity market. They allow electricity price risk to be traded and hedged independently of arrangements for the physical supply of electricity, and they simplify trading. Moreover, since pool prices are determined for the market as a whole by NGC, suitable cash settled instruments based on pool prices can be used for hedging with little or no basis risk involved.

In principle, cash settled instruments can be used to trade any of the pool price variables: SMP, PIP, POP, Capacity and Uplift. In practice, although contracts on other variables do trade, most of the liquidity in the derivatives market attaches to PIP trading.

Types of Electricity Derivative

There are two broad types of electricity derivative traded.

First, industry participants have been trading individually negotiated contracts with one another from the time of privatisation. Within the industry, these contracts are referred to as contracts for differences, or CFDs. This term is slightly confusing, because it is widely used to refer to any instrument which is settled by means of a difference payment; but, more confusingly, derivative instruments are often called 'options' in the electricity industry, whether or not they involve premium payments or asymmetric risk profiles. CFDs are individually negotiated between the two parties, with little standardisation either of structure or of documentation. Maturities tend to be long, often more than a year and sometimes as much as fifteen years. At the moment, these form the vast bulk of electricity derivatives traded.

Second, since November 1991, another form of contract, known as an Electricity Forward Agreement (EFA), has been traded. EFAs have a standard framework for their structure, and standardised documentation. Trading is normally through a broker; at the time of writing, the specialist derivatives broker GNI Limited is the only firm offering a broking service. The instruments have a straightforward structure, and are aimed at a maturity range of one week to one year. They are particularly flexible in producing a tailored risk profile.

Both CFDs and EFAs are OTC instruments: trades take the form of contractual agreements between two parties, who rely on one another to honour the contract and to make any payments due.

CFDs and EFAs are compared in Table 6.1, and each is described in more detail below.

	CFD	EFA
Reference variable	Mainly PIP; also SMP, POP, Capacity & Uplift	
Structure	Individually negotiated; 'one-way' or 'two-way'	Normally 'two-way' WE1-6/WD1-6 (see below)
Period covered	Normally 6 months+	Normally 1 week–1 year
Documentation	Individually negotiated	EFA Standard Terms
Settlement	Normally daily, after 28 days	Weekly, after 28 days
Trading	Bilateral negotiation; normally written agreement	Telephone market; oral agreement; normally through broker
Market size	Large: covers ~ 80% of pool trading	Small: new market

Table 6.1 Comparison of CFDs and EFAs

Contracts for Differences

CFDs have been the main tool for trading forward pool prices since privatisation. Trading is predominantly between members of the electricity industry. Prices in the CFD market are probably far more significant than those in the pool: while most physical electricity is traded through the pool, the effective price for many participants is determined not by pool prices, but by pre-existing long-term CFDs. However, CFDs are bilateral deals, and prices are not generally published and are therefore not transparent. Moreover, complex variations in structure and in documentation can make prices very difficult to compare.

Structure
There are two broad classes of CFDs, known as 'one-way' and 'two-way' contracts.

In a one-way contract, one party, known as the buyer, pays a premium to the other, the seller. Subsequently, if the pool price exceeds an agreed level, the strike price, the seller compensates the buyer for the difference, based on a certain agreed amount of power. Typically, a generator might sell a one-way CFD to a REC. Thus, with a strike of £30/MWh, if the pool price was £40/MWh for a particular half-hour period, the seller would make a difference payment to the buyer of £10/MWh for half an hour on the agreed amount of power; if the power was, say, 100 MW, the difference payment for that half-hour would be £500.

As described so far, one-way CFDs are similar to cap agreements in the interest rate or commodity markets. However, the structure of a CFD is not standardised, and it may be complicated. For example, it may have elements which vary depending on the time of day or the season. Some one-way contracts have 'MinTake' elements. Suppose, for instance, the contract has a MinTake of 1000 hours and a strike of £30/MWh. This means that the contract is required to cover 1000 hours; if there were 1000 hours or more during the contract lifetime in which the pool price exceeded £30, then the MinTake clause would have no effect, and the buyer would receive difference payments as usual. However, if there were only 900 hours during which the pool price was £30 or higher, the buyer would receive the usual difference payments for those 900 hours, but would be required to make payments to the seller as a retrospective adjustment on a further 100 hours; these would be the periods with the next highest pool price during the contract lifetime after the top 900 hours. For example, if the next highest pool price was £29.50, and there were 100 hours during which the pool price was £29.50, then the buyer would pay £0.50/MWh on 100 hours to the seller as an adjustment at the end of the appropriate period. In effect, the buyer is required to exercise the contract for at least 1000 hours, even if exercise is unfavourable for some of those hours. However, the buyer has the benefit of hindsight to choose the least unfavourable periods.

Structures similar to floors, in which the buyer pays a premium in order to be protected against prices falling below the strike, have not yet appeared in the CFD market.

Two-way CFDs involve symmetrical payments. If the pool price is greater than the strike price, then the seller pays the buyer, while if it is less, the buyer pays the seller. (Note that the industry uses the term 'strike price' in this context as well as when referring to one-way agreements.) Sometimes, the buyer may pay a fee, known as an 'option fee', to the seller. Typically, a generator might sell a two-way CFD to a REC as a hedge for both parties. A two-way CFD resembles a series of cash-settled forward agreements, covering each half-hour of the contract period. Alternatively it may be regarded analogously to a swap in the interest-rate and commodity markets. Of course, contracts may have specific structures, introducing complexities similar to those in one-way contracts. It is usual for both one-way and two-way contracts to include indexation clauses, linking strike prices to extraneous movements in, for instance, the retail price index and certain hydrocarbon prices. Some features of CFDs were introduced at the time of privatisation as methods for passing onto the RECs the costs of the generators' take-or-pay agreements with British Coal.

While CFDs can be used to trade any type of electricity pool price – SMP, PIP, POP, or indeed Capacity or Uplift – in practice most trading is in PIP. As a result, RECs (who, of course, pay POP for their electricity) are typically left exposed to high levels of Uplift.

An interesting development is Nuclear Electric's public offers of CFDs. Nuclear Electric has offered two-way baseload PIP CFDs for various maturities from one to six years. The term 'baseload' refers to a CFD which covers the same amount of electricity for all times of the day, every day. These offers were open to companies of good financial standing outside the electricity industry, as well as to the industry itself. In the event, the contracts were undersubscribed, perhaps because of the offer price. Nevertheless, the move could point to a broadening of the CFD market, as well as to greater standardisation, and hence price transparency.

Maturity

Because negotiation times for CFDs are fairly long, the market tends to concentrate on medium- to long-term transactions – from say, six months up to fifteen years. Numerous PIP CFDs, both one-way and two-way, were agreed between the generators and the RECs immediately prior to vesting, and these had original maturities of one, two or three years.

Documentation

Just as the structure of CFDs is individually negotiated, so is the documentation, and individual contracts may have their idiosyncrasies. For example, a generator may request a *force majeure* element, suspending the agreement in certain circumstances in which the generator is unable to generate. This is not strictly a *force majeure* clause, since the inability of a generator to generate does not of itself prevent compliance with a CFD agreement, as this does not involve physical supply of electricity, but only the making of difference payments.

These clauses can introduce difficulties, not least in terms of pricing. Given two otherwise identical CFDs, one with a *force majeure* element and one without, it would be natural to expect the former to be slightly cheaper, to reflect the fact that the buyer is taking on extra risk; but to estimate a fair price difference is difficult – it is essentially a problem in insurance pricing.

It is also important for traders to be aware of any hidden risks of this kind in their portfolios. For example, in the normal course of events, a trader who buys a CFD with a particular structure from one party, and then sells a CFD of identical structure to another party, will be immune to the actual level of pool prices. While the individual payments to the parties are unknown, the net payment to or from the trader will be the difference between the price for which one CFD was bought and the price at which the other was sold. However, if the CFDs have different *force majeure* provisions, there may be circumstances in which one CFD is suspended but not the other, leaving the trader unexpectedly exposed to pool price risks.

Settlement

Normally, settlement of CFDs follows the timing of the pool, with payments relating to each day being settled 28 days later. In certain circumstances, it is possible for pool prices to be revised after 28 days, and possibly long after; in this event an adjustment payment is usually made to cover the revision. Note that there is no central settlement for CFD payments: payments are made directly between the appropriate counterparties.

Trading
CFDs are negotiated directly between the parties involved, possibly over a relatively protracted period – days or even weeks. Agreements are not normally considered binding until they are signed. Obviously, this practice is not compatible with real-time price movements, and whether the CFD market will speed up as it develops remains to be seen. In principle, significant volatility in the market might be expected, given the range of uncertainty about future pool prices.

Electricity Forward Agreements

Although the CFD market is the most important electricity derivatives market, it is cumbersome to use to fine tune portfolios. Trades tend to be slow to negotiate, and are normally of a relatively long maturity. Moreover, the lack of standardisation introduces problems into both pricing and portfolio management. As a result, there was an impetus within the industry to develop a simple, standard trading tool, backed by, amongst others, all the RECs and the major generators. EFAs, which are a simple, standardised form of CFD, are the results of this industry-wide movement. Following discussions with the industry, GNI Limited, the London derivatives broker, has been offering a broking service in EFAs since November 1991. The service is available to any company wishing to use EFAs to hedge or trade pool prices.

Structure
EFAs are simple two-way contracts, with no upfront fee. A forward pool price is agreed between the two parties: if the actual pool price turns out to be greater, then the seller compensates the buyer for the difference; if less, then the buyer compensates the seller. Although it is possible to trade any of the pool price components, in practice interest has focused on PIP.

A standardised trading structure provides a framework for EFAs. Each day is divided into six four-hour periods, numbered 1–6: 23.00–3.00, 3.00–7.00, 7.00–11.00, 11.00–15.00, 15.00–19.00 and 19.00–23.00. Trades cover one of these contract periods for either both days of a weekend (contract periods WE1, WE2, WE3, WE4, WE5 and WE6), or all five weekdays of a week (WD1–WD6). Table 6.2 summarises this framework. WE1–6 and WD1–6 can be traded for a single week, or a strip of weeks as long as is required; a four- or five-week strip might be traded to cover a month, or a thirteen-week strip to cover a quarter, or even a 52 week strip to cover a year.

Maturity
Although EFAs were planned as a short-term trading tool (from one week to one year), there is nothing in their design to prevent them from being used

Time Period	Mon. Tue. Wed. Thu. Fri.	Sat. Sun.
23:00– 3:00	WD1	WE1
3:00– 7:00	WD2	WE2
7:00–11:00	WD3	WE3
11:00–15:00	WD4	WE4
15:00–19:00	WD5	WE5
19:00–23:00	WD6	WE6

Table 6.2 Framework for EFA Trading

for longer-term agreements if the market develops in that direction. One-year baseload EFAs in particular have attracted a great deal of trading interest.

Documentation

The electricity companies have agreed to trade EFAs on standard documentation, known as EFA Standard Terms, which sets out the characteristics of the trade in general, the settlement arrangements, the events of default, and so on.

Settlement

Under EFA Standard Terms, EFAs are settled weekly with a difference payment between the parties to cover the difference between the agreed traded price and the week's average pool price for the appropriate period. The timing of the payment follows the pool, normally 28 days after the last day of the week.

Trading

Trading EFAs is very different from trading CFDs. Trades are generally arranged via a broker, who matches buyers and sellers by telephone. Once a trade is agreed, it is a contract between the two parties involved. Oral agreement is binding.

The EFA market is essentially anonymous. Although a broker will, of course, know the two principals between whom he is arranging a trade, he will not reveal their names until all other details have been agreed. At this point, either party has the option not to proceed if he is not willing to take the credit risk of the other. Ideally, to avoid embarrassment principals will keep the broker informed of any counterparties which might pose difficulties. If the parties' names are mutually acceptable, the agreement constitutes a binding contract. Responsibility for making payments rests with the parties themselves; and the broker has no further role to play in the trade. Naturally, the parties to trades remain confidential to the rest of the market after the trade is complete.

Since EFAs are much more standardised than CFDs, the EFA market is potentially much more transparent. This transparency is enhanced by the broadcasting of current market prices to participants. For example, GNI enters current prices on certain EFA structures into the S&P ComStock system run by the quote vendor ICV. This allows prices to be transmitted nationally and internationally.

At the time of writing, GNI is the only firm offering a broking service in EFAs. Volumes amounted to 1,000,000 MWh in the first ten months of trading. The market is in its infancy, but has the potential to become an extremely important arena for electricity trading. The transparency of the EFA market should bring benefits to the electricity market as a whole as usage grows.

Regulatory and Tax Issues

Several regulatory and tax issues impact on electricity derivatives, sometimes leading to dissimilar treatment of otherwise similar CFDs and EFAs. In all cases, it is important that traders seek professional advice.

First, the Financial Services Act restricts trading and arranging trades in financial instruments: EFAs, and possibly CFDs may be regarded as financial instruments, and there may be concomitant restrictions, particularly on unauthorised persons. For example, it may be illegal for such persons to market electricity derivative contracts.

Second, the electricity industry is regulated by OFFER, and natural monopolies are subject to fairly strict control. In particular, price increases in the retail supply sector have to be justified against the rate of inflation and the actual purchase cost of electricity supplied. It is understood that the regulator will allow losses on CFDs and EFAs to count as bona fide purchase costs provided that contracts are entered into as hedges, rather than as speculative trades.

Third, the tax treatment of CFDs and EFAs may differ, particularly in relation to VAT. Traders should consult their tax advisers.

HEDGING AND TRADING

Both CFDs and EFAs were devised as hedging instruments, and they are very simple to use. For example, consider an electricity consumer purchasing from the pool who expects demand of 100 MW between 7 am and 11 am on weekdays for the next four weeks. The consumer is exposed to high pool prices: the greater the pool price, the more he pays. Likewise, a generator which expects demand of 100 MW at the same time is exposed to low pool prices; the lower the pool price, the lower his revenue.

The generator and the consumer could both eliminate their risk if the generator sold an EFA covering WD3 for the next four weeks on 100 MW at, say £30/MWh. If the actual pool price turned out to be more than £30/MWh in any of the weeks, the consumer would still pay pool price for his electricity as usual, but would be compensated for the excess over £30 by the generator. Thus, if the actual pool price between 7 am and 11 am averaged £35 for one of the weeks, the consumer would pay £70,000 for 100 MW for the week (5 days × 4 hours/day × 100 MW × £35/MWh); however, the difference payment of £10,000 from the generator (5 days × 4 hours/day × 100 MW × (£35−£30)/MWh) brings the net cost down to £60,000, equivalent to £30/MWh. Likewise, the generator receives £70,000 from the pool, but pays out a £10,000 difference payment, giving a net revenue of £60,000 at £30/MWh. If the actual pool price had averaged £25/MWh, the difference payment would have been from the consumer to the generator. Whatever the actual pool price, both the generator and consumer would have locked in a net price of £30/MWh.

PIP versus POP

The analysis so far has been simplified in that it has assumed that there is only a single pool price. In fact, while the generator would receive PIP from the pool for his output, the consumer would pay PIP plus Uplift, i.e. POP, on his usage. EFAs (and CFDs) are normally based on PIP, so that in the example above the generator would be well-hedged, having locked in a price for PIP, but the consumer would have some residual risk: while the PIP element of the cost would have been locked in at £30/MWh, the consumer would have been required additionally to pay Uplift. If Uplift was £2/MWh, the effective POP would be £32/MWh. Of course, the consumer would have budgeted for this by adding on the expected level of Uplift to the EFA PIP price to arrive at the expected electricity cost. This figure would not be known with absolute certainty: if Uplift were less than expected, the electricity would be correspondingly cheaper, while if it was higher, then the net cost would also be higher. Because Uplift is substantially less volatile than PIP, the uncertainty over Uplift does not render PIP trading entirely useless for suppliers and consumers. By trading PIP, consumers are able to hedge the most volatile element of pool prices, leaving the smaller uncertainty over Uplift as a residual basis risk.

Speculation and Hedging

In the example above, both the supplier and the generator were using an electricity derivative to hedge their positions. Of course, a derivative only provides a hedge against a corresponding exposure. Someone who buys a contract will be hedged if he anticipates a need to buy physical electricity, but if he has no such expectation, the contract will not reduce risk, but rather will increase it. The trader will be exposed to the pool price, benefiting to the extent that the actual price exceeds the agreed price, but losing to the extent that it falls short.

Likewise, the price risk is only eliminated if the amount of electricity which the contract covers matches the expected demand. If the consumer in the earlier example had bought an EFA covering only 50 MW, he would have hedged the purchase price of only half his demand, and would have been exposed to high pool prices on the remaining half. Conversely, if the EFA had covered 150 MW, then the physical demand would have been overcovered, and the consumer would have faced the risk of low pool prices on the excess 50 MW.

Portfolios of Electricity Derivatives

Electricity traders normally build up portfolios of derivatives. The overall exposure to pool prices is then the difference between the net position in derivatives and the demand.

If a derivative is bought, and then an identical structure subsequently sold (or, alternatively, first sold then bought), the trades have no net effect on pool price exposure; the only effect is to lock in a net cashflow corresponding to the difference between the prices of the two trades. Thus if a trader sells an EFA to A for £30, and subsequently buys an identical EFA from B for £25, there is no residual pool price exposure and the trader has simply locked in a net receipt of £5/MWh. Of course, the individual cash flows with A and B are not known until expiry of the trade, but the net cashflow is fixed.

PRICING

Contract Prices

In many non-perishable commodities markets, the pricing of forward agreements is strongly influenced by arbitrage relationships involving the spot market. Even though backwardations are not arbitrageable, forward prices still tend to trade at relatively involatile spreads relative to the spot price. For a commodity such as electricity, which cannot easily be stored in bulk, there are no such arbitrage relationships, and forward prices may move quite independently of spot prices. This gives a great deal of complexity to the market: a trader who wishes to trade a particular time period will only be fully satisfied with a contract covering exactly that period; even small differences in specified time can leave a large residual basis risk. Hence, trading interest in the electricity markets tends to be spread out over a range of instruments.

The obvious approach to pricing is to take the market price (of two-way contracts) as an indication of the expected level of pool price during the appropriate contract period. This is certainly a useful way of viewing contract prices, but some caution should be exercised. In particular, at the time of writing, some traders (both buyers and sellers) appear to expect contracts to trade at prices greater than the general expectation of pool prices to take account of an asymmetry of risk: at moderately low pool price levels, a large price movement upwards is more likely than a downwards movement of the same magnitude. For example, for a contract traded at £20, it is conceivable that the actual settlement price could end up perhaps £30 above this, but the downwards price movement is obviously limited to £20. From this point of view, sellers of contracts take a greater risk than buyers – hence the risk premium.

The take-or-pay agreements between British Coal and the generators introduce a further distortion, as CFDs have been used to pass the costs through from the generators to the RECs. This inflates CFD prices while depressing pool prices (see below).

Naturally, as in any other market, the market price for EFAs and CFDs will settle at the level which equates supply and demand, and market fluctuations may reflect changes in supply or demand which do not relate directly to changes in the expected levels of future prices. One-way CFDs present pricing problems of their own. In other markets, option-like instruments (such as caps) are generally priced using the Black, or a similar option pricing model. The idiosyncrasies of one-way CFDs may make these models inapplicable, and necessitate more subjective techniques.

Pool Prices

Fundamentals

A view of the appropriate level of pool prices is obviously central to trading electricity derivatives. It is commonsense that the time of day and the season of the year are of great significance, and there are other major fundamental influences: the weather, fuel costs, the general level of economic activity, the amount of generating plant which is available, and so on. Because of the importance for scheduling plant, there is a great deal of experience within the electricity industry of forecasting demand from these fundamental factors. When demand is high, pool prices are likely to be high, first because it may be necessary to schedule expensive plant to satisfy the demand, and second, because the Capacity element starts to become significant as anticipated demand approaches the total amount of plant available. However, the variations in pool price are not always easy to relate to fundamental factors, and there are certain elements of the market which introduce distortions and, more importantly, volatility, into the pool price.

Take-or-pay Agreements for Coal

One of these distortions comes from the take-or-pay agreements between the generators and British Coal. Under this sort of agreement, the generator is obliged to pay for a certain amount of coal whether or not it is needed. This increases the generators' overheads, but can decrease their marginal costs, since the coal effectively becomes a fixed overhead. This can depress pool prices, which are based on marginal prices.

Pre-existing Contracts for Differences

In addition, the pool does not operate in a vacuum. Pool participants operate with substantial bilateral contracts for differences already in place, which influence their exposure to pool prices. A generator may decide to alter its 'bidding in' strategy, perhaps to second guess other generators' strategies, or perhaps to maximise the benefits from its derivatives positions. A generator which expects to generate more electricity than it has covered is indifferent to pool price, and one which has overcovered with contracts benefits from a low pool price. In this latter event, it may be beneficial for the generator to offer plant to the pool at 'bidding in' time at prices below the marginal cost of operation: if the pool price is depressed as a result, then the extra payments under contracts would more than compensate for any reduced revenue direct from the pool.

These considerations may contribute to the high volatility of pool prices. Even low demand night-time prices, normally around £15, have swung, sometimes rising almost to £20, and, on one occasion, falling to zero. At peak time, fluctuations can be enormous: weekday prices for the period 5.00–5.30 pm are normally around £30, but sometimes fall to below £20 and occasionally peak spectacularly at over £300.

Historical Price Charts

Historical price charts may be valuable in drawing trading conclusions. Obviously, this approach is dependent on some repetition of history, and the possibility that this might not happen should always be borne in mind. Figures 6.3 and 6.4 illustrate some of the features of pool prices, while Figure 6.5 gives the corresponding weekday PIP prices for the standard EFA periods. The price patterns in the autumn and winter of 1991 demonstrate the danger of imprudent reliance on historical charts. Nothing in previous price history would have given any warning of the price spikes in this period.

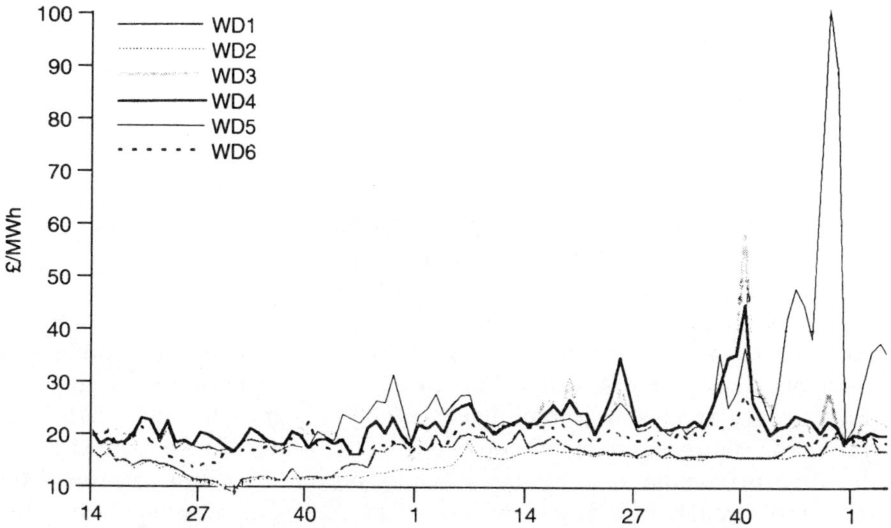

Figure 6.5 Weekly Settlement Prices for Weekday EFAs

SPREADS

A spread trade is simply a trade which involves buying one instrument at the same time as selling another, related instrument. By doing this, the trader assumes an exposure to the difference between the two prices, while remaining indifferent to the overall level of prices.

Types of Spread

There are many different types of spread in the electricity market which might be of interest. For example, Uplift, which is the spread between PIP and POP, and Capacity, which is the spread between SMP and PIP, may be of considerable concern to some companies. These spreads can be traded both through contracts with Capacity or Uplift as reference variables, or through conventional spread positions, by, for example, buying a POP contract and selling a PIP contract.

Other spreads include: the difference between corresponding weekday and weekend prices, such as between EFA periods WE1 and WD1; the spread between different contract time periods, such as between WD1 and WD2; and the difference between consecutive weeks, such as between WD1 for week 40 and for week 41.

Importance of Spread Training

Spread trading is an important activity in many markets. There are two reasons to expect it to be of growing importance in the electricity market.

Natural Exposure
Many companies are exposed to spreads through their normal operations – in some cases, more exposed to spreads than to the outright level of pool prices. A good example of this arises when companies enter into CFDs that might match overall demand, but which are not tailored to the demand profile. For example, a REC which hedges its electricity purchase cost with a baseload agreement might perhaps find that it is overhedged during the night, and underhedged at peak afternoon times; equally it might find itself overhedged during the summer and underhedged during the winter. The net effect is that the REC is immune to the general level of pool price, but is exposed if the spread between night-time and peak day-time prices, or between summer and winter prices, widens.

'Soft' Spread Trading
Traders may from time to time find that the exact instrument required is not available in the market at a reasonable price. They might then find that they are forced to compromise, by buying or selling a contract which is similar but not identical, leaving a residual spread risk. In the event that this residual risk is less than the outright exposure, it may be sensible to do this.

As an example, Figure 6.6 illustrates the WD3–WD4 spread, which is significantly less volatile than its components. While the spread typically lies in the range −£3 to +£3, both WD3 and WD4 can easily vary between £18 and £30. Even in the exceptional circumstance of the price spike in autumn 1991, when WD3 rose to nearly £60, some £35 above its normal level, the WD3–WD4 spread only moved to £12.50.

A trader who is short WD3 and faces the choice of buying either WD3, or WD4 for £3 less, might well prefer the latter option, in spite of the implicit spread risk.

SUMMARY

Since the introduction of the pool as the central market for physical electricity in England and Wales, two distinct derivatives markets have developed. First, CFDs are traded, primarily within the electricity industry, as medium- to long-term hedging instruments. Although these contracts are not standardised, and trading is not transparent, the market is large. Second, EFAs are traded primarily as short-term instruments for tailoring hedge portfolios. The EFA market offers a standardised framework, and greater price transparency because of the involvement of a broker and a network of price screens.

Since movements in pool prices will always be both uncertain and volatile, OTC derivatives should become a permanent feature of the electricity market.

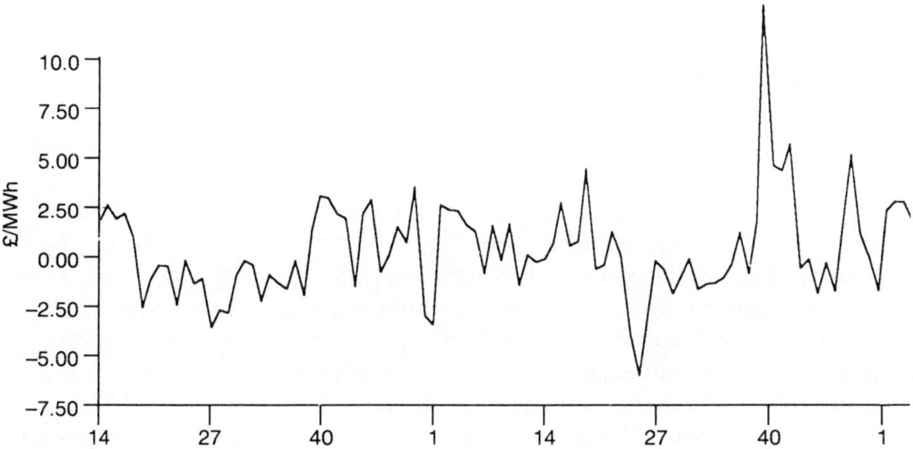

Figure 6.6 The WD3–WD4 Spread (Weekly)

7: The Relationship with Exchange Traded Derivatives

Victoria Ward, NatWest Futures

INTRODUCTION

This chapter considers the relationship between the exchange traded and OTC derivatives markets. It begins by summarising the characteristics of both markets, before exploring the implications of differences in product design, trading environment, liquidity, administration and cost, and regulation and credit risk. An attempt is made to answer the question of whether the relationship is one of symbiotic reinforcement or destructive competition. The chapter concludes with some speculations of the author regarding future developments.

Inevitably, the test contains a number of acronyms. For convenience, these are listed below.

Exchanges and Clearing Houses

AMEX	American Stock Exchange
CBOE	Chicago Board Options Exchange
CBOT	Charges Board of Trade
CBOTCC	Chicago Board of Trade Clearing Corporation
CME	Chicago Mercantile Exchange
DTB	Deutsche Terminborse
FOX	(London) Futures and Options Exchange
LCH	London Clearing House
LIFFE	London International Financial Futures Exchange
LTOM	London Traded Options Market (now merged with LIFFE)
MATIF	Marché à Terme d'Instruments Financiers
NYMEX	New York Mercantile Exchange
OCC	Options Clearing Corporation
OM	(Stockholm) Options Market
OSE	Osaka Stock Exchange
PHLX	Philadelphia Stock Exchange

SIMEX	Singapore International Monetary Exchange
TSE	Tokyo Stock Exchange

Laws and Regulatory Bodies

BIS	Bank of International Settlements
CFTC	Commodity Futures Trading Commission
ERISA	Employment, Retirement and Income Security Act
IMRO	Investment Management Regulatory Organisation
ISDA	International Swap Dealers Association
SEC	Securities and Exchange Commission
SFA	Securities and Futures Authority
SIB	Securities and Investments Board

Products

APT	Automated Pit Trading
CTD	'Cheapest to Deliver' (Bond)
EFP	Exchange for Physical
FRA	Forward Rate Agreement
THS	Transactions Heures Seances

DEFINING CHARACTERISTICS OF EXCHANGE TRADED AND OTC DERIVATIVES

The principal characteristics of the two market-places are described below in order that the relationship may be analysed later in the chapter.

Exchange Traded Products

Product Range
Exchange traded derivatives are normally taken to be futures and options contracts based on currency, interest rate, fixed income, equity, energy, metal, soft commodity and certain other asset classes, which are traded under the rules and regulations of a centralised market-place (the exchange) with a defined membership structure.

Characteristics
Listed exchange products are traded in a publicly accessible, regulated and visible market-place. The range of potential market participants is extensive, including local 'own account' traders, private investors and major institutional users. The variety of uses of the market, from simple hedging to highly leveraged speculation, reflects this diverse list of users.

Most futures exchanges have common characteristics: absolute transparency of trading information (bids, offers, trades executed, number of open positions, and so on); standardisation of products in all respects except the price and number of contracts traded (which are by negotiation in the market-place), leading to ease of offset; and the presence of a central guarantor (or clearing house) rather than individual bilateral relationships.

Beyond this, the nature of exchanges, trading mechanisms and clearing houses varies considerably between countries and regulatory regimes. There are no truly international exchanges, and very few truly international products: with only one exception, mutual offset of contracts between different exchanges has never been successful (the exception is the Eurodollar contract traded on SIMEX, which was deliberately created at the outset to offset with the identical contract traded on the CME).

Trading Mechanisms
Trading takes place either by 'open outcry' in pits or crowds on an exchange floor, or on a screen. Certain screen-based trading systems, such as APT on LIFFE, are specifically designed to show the depth of orders either side of the current bid and offer, while the only current price in a futures trading pit will be the best bid and the best offer. In the latter, traditional circumstance, the assessment of market depth is based purely on the individual knowledge of the traders and brokers on the floor. Some exchanges (e.g. OM) run a hybrid automated central market-place and order matching facility which is managed by exchange employees; others, such as the TSE, run an automated, purely order-driven market.

Futures contracts very rarely have formal market making arrangements, unless these are part of an initial scheme to promote liquidity in a contract as it becomes established. Options, on the other hand, comprise a multiplicity of sub-products within one product because of the number of different strike prices, and these nearly always need some kind of formal support, either by competitive market making (CBOE, MATIF, LIFFE/LTOM) or by the appointment of specialists (AMEX, PHLX). In most exchanges, a complex set of rules governs order priority and market maker obligations. Limit order boards, or order-matching facilities, are maintained in some markets. Some exchanges also permit transactions effectively to take place off exchange through EFP arrangements. These are either a mechanism to allow the futures part of a cash-futures transaction to be traded outside the normal trading environment and then transferred onto the exchange (CBOT), or an opaque out-of-hours trading system (e.g. the THS system on the MATIF). EFP deals are struck bilaterally and then passed onto the exchange for clearing the next day.

Clearing Houses
The clearing house can take one of a number of different forms: it may be integrated into the exchange (CBOTCC, DTB) or independent (OCC, LCH); and it can be mutually guaranteed by all members (CME) or independently guaranteed (LCH, whose financial backing of £200m is partly financed by insurance). The clearing house may have as its counterparty either the clearing member (viz. principal guarantee) or the ultimate holder of the open position (viz. agency guarantee). All clearing houses require initial margin deposits to be lodged in respect of open positions, and all settle or mark losses to market on open futures positions and short options positions. However, on long options positions profits are not always marked or settled to market; nor, in certain markets, are futures positions (for instance, the TSE does not release positive variation margin until the position is closed).

Margining
Initial margin deposit levels are generally set according to market volatility, and can range between 0.5 and 10 per cent of the face value of the contract. The precise method of calculating margins and the offsets available vary between exchanges. A portfolio margin approach (rather than individual identification of offsets) is now common on the major exchanges. There are also wide variations in whether the clearing house pays interest on margins lodged with it and in the range of collateral which the clearing house is prepared to accept. Procedures are governed not only by the chosen rules of the clearing house/exchange (which can be extremely profitable for those clearing houses which pay no interest on cash lodged as initial margin deposits), but also by financial and trust law. The latter may determine who has first right of possession over collateral in the event of a default.

Contract Design
This is one aspect of the exchange traded markets for which there is a common worldwide approach. All futures contracts stipulate either physical delivery or cash settlement; all options are exercised either for cash, physical delivery or for a futures position, and are either European-style (exercised on expiry only) or American-style (able to be exercised at any point up until expiry). Physical delivery is at the seller's option, and is of a defined grade, quality or range of the underlying instrument; cash settlement is by reference to a single price, or an average of a range of prices in the underlying instrument. The method of quotation, minimum price movement (tick size) and the value

	Bund Futures	Brent Crude Oil Futures	Raw Sugar Futures	FT-SE 100 Index Futures
Exchange	LIFFE	FOX	FOX	LIFFE
Unit of Trading	DM 250,000 nominal value German Government bond with 6% notional coupon	1000 net barrels Brent blend crude oil (42,000 US gallons)	50 tonnes of raw cane sugar of a quality as defined under the contract rules	FT-SE 100 index
Standard	Physically settled	Cash settled	Physically settled by FOB delivery	Cash settled
Delivery Months	Mar., June, Sept., Dec.	Nine consecutive months, following current month	Mar., May, Aug., Oct., Dec.	Mar., June, Sept., Dec,
Quotation	Per DM 100 nominal value	US dollars and cents per barrel	US dollars per tonne	Per index point
Tick Size	DM 0.01	One US cent per barrel	US $0.20	0.5 index points
Tick Value	DM 25	US$10	US$10	£12.50

Table 7.1 Illustrative Specifications of Futures Contracts

of the price movement are all defined. The cycle and number of contracts available for trading, and, in the case of options, the number of strikes and method of introducing new strikes, are all predefined. In some markets, there are maximum price limits in respect of daily movement, either across all contract months, or for all except the nearby contract month.

Exchange and Clearing House Membership

Access to the market is obtainable only through exchange members. There are certain minimum requirements in terms of capital adequacy depending on the form of membership offered by the exchange: the DTB permits general and direct clearing, and non-clearing, memberships; while LIFFE, MATIF and the US exchanges offer a wider range including memberships for locals, who trade only for their own accounts and do not handle customer orders. Initial and annual charges for membership vary significantly, as does control over its transfer.

All exchanges charge fees (levied per contract) to cover processing and clearing costs, and there are additional charges for delivery. In addition, exchange members charge commissions, which are usually negotiable (except in Japan, where there is a fixed commission scale). Commissions are usually extremely low in relation to the face value of the contract.

OTC Products

General Definition
'Over-the-counter' is a generic term applied to financial instruments whose main characteristics are that: (i) they are traded, and normally settled, by bilateral agreement on an individually negotiated basis, and (ii) they represent either a contract for differences (e.g. FRAs), or an exchange of payments under different bases (e.g. swaps), or a package of component parts. In the last case, the components are likely to be a hybrid of the cash and derivatives markets, constructed so that the risk characteristics of the tailored package are different from those traditionally available in the cash markets.

Characteristics
A characteristic of OTC products is that they are tailored to the specific needs of an individual institution, which may be a bank, government agency, pension fund or company (amongst others). The product may alter the cashflows (e.g. swaps) or risk profile (e.g. options) of that institution to suit its requirements, or be designed as a more tax efficient way to achieve an asset or liability exposure (for instance, equity index swaps).

The risk that the component parts will provide a different return from the packaged product is borne by the provider. Hence the buyer eliminates basis risk, but becomes exposed to the credit risk of the provider. This risk is an increasing function of the maturity of the OTC instrument.

The distinction with securities markets can be grey. For instance, warrants are traded in a secondary market. Likewise, it may be tax efficient for a UK pension fund, when creating an index swap, to list it in Luxembourg as a security, even though in this case there will be no secondary market.

It might be argued that any 'commoditised' strategy which involves more than one component instrument is an OTC product. For instance, portfolio insurance, which is in effect the creation of a synthetic option whose delta is managed through positions in exchange traded futures (and/or options), or has been perceived as an OTC strategy. Dynamic currency hedging (which employs similar techniques) is certainly identified as such in a recent *Financial Times'* survey on financial futures and options (19 March 1992).

Trading Mechanisms
Innovative products in the OTC markets are usually direct bilateral agreements between two parties. In the early stages of a product's life there is no intermediation, because instruments and approaches are proprietary and are mar-

keted directly by their creators through their own lines of distribution. For some products the market eventually becomes large enough for intermediaries to take an interest. These intermediaries will operate in the style of money or inter-dealer brokers, and should provide market anonymity and enhanced liquidity. Greater price transparency is another consequence. Two recent examples are the extension of swap broking by Tullett and Tokyo to include index forwards and index swaps; and the broking of OTC currency options and bond options by GNI. The role of James Capel in providing price information in the warrants market is another illustration.

A liquid secondary market may not be essential for a product to be attractive, since in many instances an OTC instrument is tailor-made for a specific purpose. However, the product's success may hinge on an accurate assessment of the future liquidity of the derivatives or cash markets which will be used for hedging.

Settlement

The settlement of most OTC products is managed bilaterally, although Cedel and Euroclear settle many of the covered warrant products which have been developed. Typically, option premiums are paid up front. Other products which are forms of contracts for differences (e.g. FRAs) are not normally margined or marked-to-market for daily settlement, except as an internal risk management control. Swap payments are made on a regular basis (e.g. quarterly); in the case of a long-term swap, such as a five-year equity index swap, this periodic settlement plays an important part in the assessment and control of credit risk. Unlike the exchange traded markets, netting does not take place between OTC products, although swap netting is a product currently being developed by the MATIF (using OM technology).

Market Participants

The financial institutions which offer OTC products are, in the main, also key members of the major exchanges. OTC derivatives are nearly always bought by institutional investors, corporate treasurers and other market professionals, and the market is (currently) exclusively wholesale. Market participants include the 'providers' of products (usually banks and securities houses), the end-users and, occasionally, intermediaries who act analogously to inter-dealer brokers. There are probably around thirty significant product providers worldwide, nearly all of whom are characterised by being:

- international and well-capitalised;
- highly rated by credit agencies;
- able to manage their own distribution;
- active in the markets in other capacities, e.g. as banks, primary bond dealers, equity market markers, arbitrageurs, corporate finance houses or brokers of exchange traded instruments;
- aggressive.

Trade magazines such as the *International Financing Review* provide regular information about products and participants/issuers, and 'league tables' where appropriate. In order to be considered a very strong name, some institutions, such as Merrill Lynch Derivative Products, have been established with a heavy capital backing.

The emergence of new entrants tends to push down margins in a relatively short period of time (two or three years), so that there is a constant search for the higher margin, more profitable product areas. Standard interest rate and currency products now attract fairly low margins, and are traded within near transparent markets: the profit margin on a cap or collar probably stands at 5 per cent of what it was seven or eight years ago. Providers of equity-related products have increased from an estimated ten (significant) players in the late 1980s to around twenty today. Commodity-related products are widely cited as the next growth market, although insurance and reinsurance are areas arousing interest.

Following the privatisation of the UK electricity industry, there is now a market in electricity forward agreements involving the generating companies, distribution companies and some larger industrial concerns (see Chapter 6). A broker (GNI) has assumed the role of matching transactions.

Design

A proliferation of products, and the application of design and technology which have been proven in one market-place to virgin territory, are two hallmarks of the OTC market. Most of the more complex options in use or being developed are based on two or more factors, e.g. a currency and an equity market, or the difference in performance between two assets. A thorough knowledge of different tax and regulatory regimes is often necessary for a provider to design a derivative product which suits the buyer better than direct investment.

Developments in the Exchange Traded Markets

Between 1982 and 1990, the volume of futures and options contracts traded on US exchanges grew from around 177 million to 420 million. Most of this expansion was attributable to financial products, although latterly there has been appreciable growth also in energy-related contracts.

Despite this progress, US exchanges have lost their hegemony: in 1982 the US share of worldwide futures trading was close to 100 per cent; by 1991, following the establishment and success of Far Eastern and European exchanges, this had fallen to 53 per cent (excluding individual equity options). Of the ten most highly traded contracts in 1991, nine were financial products (the single exception being the NYMEX contract on West Texas Intermediate

Exchange Traded	Over the Counter
Central market-place, traded under defined rules and regulations; open outcry or screen trading; access only through exchange members	Bilateral negotiation, no rules and regulations in the method of trading; in effect a telephone market with screen-based information available; occasionally broked
Liquidity created by standardisation and range of market participants, either members or users; ease of offset	Not much liquidity; products normally designed to achieve specific goals; not many types of market participant; no offset
Product standardisation; normally high profile, long build-up to launch; can miss the best launch time because of this	Tailor-made; created in secret for quick reactive launch to make the best of prevailing market conditions and keep ahead of the competition
Small number of products	Proliferation
Clearing house as counterparty, i.e. minimal risk at the centre of the market	Product manager or individual counterparty, i.e. risk inherent in the product creation
Initial margin deposits and daily settlement to market	Payment in full at outset, or settlement at maturity; normally not marked-to-market, although there can be regular revaluation
Transparent; equal access of market members	Opaque; individual negotiation
Broker market with commissions and charges	Principal market with bid–offer spread

Table 7.2 Summary of Key Characteristics of Exchange Traded and OTC Derivatives

crude oil). Almost invariably, the liquidity of these contracts exceeds that in the underlying 'cash' or asset markets, sometimes by as much as 200 per cent. But there are now contracts available on almost every key international interest rate, bond, currency and equity market, and in aggregate the exchange traded markets must be considered to be nearly mature. There has been increased international interest in (equity) index contracts, and there may be scope for the introduction of further products relating to the South American and Far Eastern markets.

Size of the OTC Markets

The relative opaqueness of the OTC derivatives markets and the absence of official information ensure that both the volume and the outstanding size of transactions can only be estimated. There can be no doubt, however, that these markets are now very substantial. ISDA estimates that, globally, swaps with a notional value of US$3,000 billion are open. An article in the *Wall Street Journal* (25 March 1992) suggests a figure of $10,000 billion for the total underlying value of all derivatives positions (interest rate, bond, equity and currency). It is plausible to suggest that more than $2,000 billion of OTC interest rate derivatives are now transacted annually.

Equity and commodities markets are obviously smaller, but have also grown substantially. Single transactions in OTC equity derivatives of $100 million are now not unusual. An estimated $3 billion of commodity swaps were open in 1988; before Iraq's invasion of Kuwait in 1990 this figure had grown to $10 billion, and by the end of 1991 to (perhaps) $40 billion. Of this amount, 80 per cent is estimated to be oil related.

IMPLICATIONS OF DIFFERENCES IN PRODUCT DESIGN

The worldwide development of futures contracts has for the most part followed the set of liquid asset classes. A 'funnelling' effect usually occurs, in that a single or limited number of contracts may become established as the hedge medium for an underlying class of assets which is not homogeneous. Inevitably, a successful contract must offer the user an attractive compromise between the (conflicting) requirements of market liquidity and avoidance of exposure to basis or rollover risk.

The standardisation in design of exchange traded contracts can create anomalies in price behaviour, which, being exploited by certain participants, enhance the liquidity of both cash and futures markets. Common approaches include 'pure' arbitrage (cash/futures), basis trading, spread trading and techniques involving the assessed value of embedded delivery options (e.g. monitoring the relative price of the CTD bond and its associated bond futures contract).

In order to reduce risk and speed the process of price convergence, both speculators and arbitrageurs prefer trades with short ('guaranteed') time horizons. As a result, liquidity is greatest in the nearby trading month of almost all futures contracts. For many contracts the market has no depth beyond the second month. Short-term interest rate futures are an exception to this norm, in particular the Eurodollar future traded on the CME which now has listed contract months going out to four years (although open interest in the back two years is only a small percentage of that in the front two).

The process of standardisation has also led to a relatively small number of highly successful exchange products, which have provided opportunities for a wide range of market participants and have fed on their own success. Table 7.3 provides evidence of this concentration in volume.

Top Contracts

Position	Contract	Exchange	1991	1990
1 (1)	f US T-bond	CBOT	67 887 497	75 499 257
2 (2)	o S&P 100	CBOE	63 935 546	68 846 535
3 (3)	f Eurodollar	CME	37 244 223	34 695 625
4 (4)	o US T-bond	CBOT	21 925 578	27 315 411
5 (9)	f Nikkei 225	Osaka	21 643 085	13 589 049
6 (7)	f French notional	Matif	21 087 899	15 996 096
7 (5)	f Crude oil	Nymex	21 005 867	23 686 897
8 (8)	f Euroyen	Tiffe	14 665 521	14 413 693
9 (6)	f Jap gov. bond	TSE	12 822 430	16 306 571
10 (10)	f S&P 500	CME	12 340 380	12 139 209
11 (11)	o S&P 500	CBOE	11 924 719	12 089 035
12 (16)	o Nikkei 225	Osaka	11 835 611	9 186 136
13 (17)	f D-mark	CME	10 928 693	9 169 230
14 (12)	f Corn	CBOT	10 852 909	11 423 027
15 (15)	f German bund	Liffe	10 112 305	9 581 516
16 (13)	f Soybeans	CBOT	9 013 739	10 301 905
17 (20)	o French notional	Matif	8 411 903	7 410 305
18 (18)	f Short sterling	Liffe	8 064 449	8 354 922
19 (22)	o Eurodollar	CME	7 874 551	6 859 625
20 (–)	o Bovespa	BM&F	7 836 256	n/a
21 (–)	o D-mark	PHLX	7 254 687	4 891 902
22 (–)	o Gold	BM&F	7 452 730	n/a
23 (14)	f Gold	Comex	6 799 917	6 730 041
24 (27)	f Copper	LME	6 794 255	5 668 847
25 (24)	f Heating oil	Nymex	6 680 171	6 376 871
26 (26)	f US T-note (10 yr)	CBOT	6 341 432	6 054 222
27 (–)	f Red beans	TGE	6 338 319	2 739 687
28 (19)	f Yen	CME	6 017 012	7 437 235
29 (23)	f Swiss Franc	CME	5 835 480	6 524 893
30 (–)	o D-mark	CME	5 643 031	3 430 374

Fastest growers

Position	Contract	Exchange	Increase
1	o US dollar index	Finex	+1 323%
2	f Natural gas	Nymex	+215%
3	o Highgrade zinc	LME	+200%
4	f Red beans	TGE	+131%
5	o Copper A	LME	+81%
6	o Nickel	LME	+73%
7	f Platinum	Tocom	+65%
8	f Nikkei 225	Osaka	+59%
9	o CAC 40	Monep	+50%
10	o D-mark	PHLX	+48%

Top Futures Exchanges

Position	**Exchange**	**1991**	**1990**
1 (1)	CBOT	139 437 298	154 231 583
2 (2)	CME	108 128 616	102 994 612
3 (3)	Nymex	40 786 714	42 458 727
4 (4)	Liffe	38 583 877	34 169 983
5 (5)	Matif	37 129 032	28 587 734
6 (6)	Osaka	33 478 949	22 775 455
7 (–)	BM&F	19 007 390	9 889 834
8 (–)	LME	16 937 909	13 331 225
9 (7)	TSE	16 476 466	22 679 352
10 (10)	Tiffe	15 152 964	20 889 628

Table 7.3 *League Table of Exchange Traded Futures and Options Contracts* (Source: *Futures and Options World.*)

These figures also illustrate that the most liquid options are either based on the most successful futures contracts (French Notional bond, US T-Bond) or are cash-exercised index options (S&P 100; S&P 500). The liquidity of options on individual equities is far more variable.

There is a long leadtime in the design and launch of futures contracts and therefore a need for a durable design. The US T-Bond contract has been in existence since the mid-1970s, the Eurodollar since 1981 and the S&P 500 future since 1982; all are traded in substantially the same form as that in which they were launched. In contrast, there are cases where a fundamental change in market structure has necessitated the redesign of a product to maintain its relevance and robustness. An example is LIFFE's long gilt future, which has now had at least three changes in contract design, including a lowering of the notional coupon and a change in the definition of deliverable gilts. In principle, however, the overriding need is for consistency of design, continuing applicability, and persistence of market depth and trading interest.

The largest OTC products, such as swaps, currency options and FRAs, share with exchange traded products a simplicity and consistency of design. Yet in other respects the OTC market thrives on variety (however superficial), and products tend to be created and launched quickly to meet perceived interest. There is less concern to create liquidity or a durable product design: option-based instruments can be offered without the need to introduce multiple strikes, or to guarantee a secondary market, since they will often be placed with investors as a long-term untraded 'hedge'. Many OTC products are either listed or designed to have longer maturities (between one and five years) in order to match the demands of investors.

Most important of all, the OTC market tolerates complexity and failure much better than the exchange traded market. For example, one of the most popular (exchange) trades of 1991 was the 'BOAT' spread, the price difference between the LIFFE Bund contract and the MATIF Notional bond contract. The spread was bought or sold on the basis of a view about the future relationship between French and German long-term interest rates. A number of OTC products were created as spin-offs, including warrants and instruments resembling FRAs. It might be imagined that a 'BOAT' product traded on an exchange would have had considerable attractions, in that it would involve only a single trade and one margin requirement.

In fact, the notion of such an exchange traded instrument raises complex questions of design and practicality. Should the spread be measured as an index of the difference in (CTD) prices or yields? In which currency should the future be denominated? The product would be a considerably more intricate analogue of the DIFF contracts (based on short-term interest rate differentials), which failed on the CME. Its introduction might reduce liquidity in the existing core bond futures, if traded alongside them; and since there would be an arbitrage against these contracts, it would not be more attractively priced. Users would gain at best only a limited advantage from trading the product on-exchange, in preference to combining trades in the component futures, or entering into a contract for differences off-exchange.

In addition to these concerns, the expense of development must be recognised. This would include not only the design period, but also the marketing activity to create interest and awareness, and subsequent support to build liquidity.

There have been some interesting examples of failures in exchange products introduced to overlap with an existing OTC or longer-term cash market. On LIFFE the short and medium gilt contracts never gained momentum and were subsequently suspended, and the ('green') third year of contract months in short sterling failed to develop liquidity despite an existing FRA market. The swap products listed on the CBOT in 1991 were similarly ill-starred. In the US, long-term equity options have an uneasy footing on exchanges despite an established and growing OTC market. All of these products were identified as desirable by investment managers, companies and financial institutions. Many of these potential users were already trading similar OTC instruments, and apparently wanted a liquid exchange vehicle to enable investing, hedging or maturity matching decisions in their assets and liabilities. Therefore, it is instructive to examine some of the possible causes of failure.

The first potential problem is an uncertainty in relative price behaviour. If it is difficult to establish current, or predict future, fair value in an exchange instrument and there is a liquid cash or OTC alternative, then the instrument is likely to be avoided. Medium and short gilts were not as homogeneous as long gilts were, and the LIFFE contract designs permitted too much potential basis or yield curve shift – in response to a change in the CTD bond – for these contracts to establish themselves as surrogates for their areas of the gilt market. (In addition, the lower volatility of the short and medium ranges of the market did not appeal to speculators as much as the long end.)

In respect of the money market yield curve, the bid–offer spread implicit in the fair value calculation of a forward-forward rate becomes wider as the maturity of the rate is extended. Users of the third year of the LIFFE short sterling future were therefore not only at risk from the short-term impact of order flows in an illiquid market, but also from the considerable variability in the fair value estimate. Moreover, they would be required to tie up margin in positions (e.g. spreads) which could be held for a long time.

If hedge management becomes uncertain, arbitrageurs and basis traders will also be disinclined to enter the market, since other trades will exist with more certain risk/return profiles. The greatest potential danger is that the exchange contract comes to represent transparency without liquidity. Perversely, this can act to reduce off exchange liquidity, since a transparent exchange traded reference price is available as a benchmark, but the contract has insufficient depth for OTC players to use it to hedge. Some market players believe that the introduction of the third year in short sterling futures had this effect, by apparently crystallising prices in a market in which FRA and swap products provided a good margin business to OTC dealers.

On occasions, OTC products are simply easier to justify in a portfolio. For a pension fund trustee, a two-year index swap, tidily securitised, may be far more acceptable than an asset allocation trade in long gilt and FT-SE 100 futures, given the continuing basis and rollover risks and daily margin administration associated with the management of the latter for the longer term. Sometimes the target audience for an exchange instrument is constrained for regulatory reasons from using the contract. Many building societies, for instance, were unable to make use of the short and medium gilt futures at the time of their introduction. Usually there is only one opportunity available to make a new exchange contract succeed.

TRADING ENVIRONMENTS AND COMPARATIVE LIQUIDITY

While it is difficult to define objectively the term 'liquidity' (used in its market sense), there are some obvious characteristics of a 'liquid' market. Among these are the value of turnover, the tightness of the bid–offer spread and the depth of potential orders on either side of the market.

On at least the first two of these measures, the most highly traded futures contracts are almost invariably more liquid than the underlying groups of assets. For example, taken together, FT-SE 100 futures and options have a turnover approximately equal to the value of the underlying shares traded daily in the UK stock market. These derivative products are by far the most liquid individual UK equity instruments available. The US comparatives, the S&P 100 & 500 futures and options, are still more liquid, in that the combined daily value of contracts traded is well in excess of the cash market turnover. For all of the major international bond futures contracts – the German Bund, US T-Bond, long gilt, French Notional – the value of contracts traded daily is between one and five times the combined turnover of the specified deliverable bonds. For all these futures contracts, the bid–offer spread is as tight as, or tighter than, that available in the underlying market.

A comparision of liquidity in money market instruments is much harder to establish. It is perhaps too simple to assume that the FRA market is the 'underlying' market for LIFFE short sterling futures; could the futures contract underlie the OTC market? FRAs tend to be priced by OTC players using futures quotations, yield curve interpolation, fair value estimates and individual judgement. In addition, since both FRAs and short sterling futures are contracts for differences, the relevance of the value of turnover as a measure of liquidity is less than for other futures contracts: the focus is on market movement between two periods of time, rather than on an overall underlying value. It is common to identify the liquidity advantage that FRAs have over the exchange traded market as the ability to execute a sizeable order at one price and in one transaction. By contrast, there will be times when the futures market is quiet and the market impact of, say, a 1,000 lot order, would need to be managed carefully. In the more distant maturity months, the ease of negotiation by telephone to arrive at a contracted price is often regarded as preferable to the high visibility – and therefore vulnerability – of trading in the futures pit. For many players, the advantage of potential price improvement by moving on-exchange is often regarded as insufficient compensation for the certainty off-exchange.

There is a general presumption that the creation and availability of OTC products whose component parts are hedged using exchange traded derivatives, serve to deepen the liquidity in both the exchange and OTC markets. This presumption should be questioned carefully, particularly given the mechanism of cash settlement (which, it could be argued, encourages an 'inverted pyramid' of exposure overlaying a small base of 'natural' assets or liabilities). As an example, the strategy of portfolio insurance – which, as mentioned earlier, might be considered to be an OTC product – was premised before the crash of 1987 on consistent liquidity in, and relatively consistent pricing of, S&P 500 futures and the underlying stock market. Both of these assumptions were suddenly falsified by the events of October 1987.

ADMINISTRATION AND COST

Some of the differences in the mechanics of the exchange and OTC markets can lead to unexpected results. An example is the effect of the financing bias in short deposit futures, explored in a paper by Josh Danziger published in the March 1991 edition of the GNI *International Futures and Options Briefing*. Danziger identifies that, as a result of variation margin, the fair LIFFE short sterling futures price should be higher that the fair forward-forward or FRA rate (since FRAs are not margined), and that this effect can be significant for the longer maturity dates:

> Consider a trader who is short futures: as interest rates rise, he receives variation margin, and can invest this at high overnight rates; as interest rates fall, he has to pay variation margin, but he can fund this at low rates. This benefits the short position holder and conversely works to the detriment of the long position holder. The effect will be cumulative as rates repeatedly rise and fall over the lifetime of a futures contract; even if the future finally settles at the trade price, the short position holder will have benefited from price oscillation. . . . By contrast, the trader who takes on an FRA position does not normally margin, and does not experience the financing bias effect.

Danziger estimates that there is a 10–25 basis point bias for a three year future.

Variation margin and the additional administrative requirements are two of the most commonly cited reasons for using OTC instruments instead of exchange traded derivatives. Lodging initial margin can also pose difficulties for certain types of institution, particularly in the case of trust assets over which there are restrictions on who can take a charge. Location can also be problematic. For instance, ERISA regulations require that US private pension plan assets are located in the US. Highly cumbersome custodial and banking procedures are normally put in place to comply with these requirements, but these can be offputting to new market entrants.

Because the market is standardised, exchange traded instruments are transparent not only in price, but in their commission cost and day-to-day charges (such as for delivery and exercise). It it hard for brokers to differentiate their services: most market players can see the bid and offer on the screen, and information on market depth is almost equally available to all market participants. It is also very difficult to charge for added value in the overall service (e.g. for provision of written research, client education and support) because commissions are so universally competitive. Much of the broker's remuneration is implicit in collateral and interest management, and most of the added value to clients also takes place in the clearing services provided (e.g. using a single deposit to finance margin requirements on exchanges worldwide).

OTC products are quite different in these respects. First, they tend to be underwritten and distributed rather than broked; where there are brokers, these participants tend to act as intermediaries between market professionals to create anonymity in the market-place, and would not consider their role to be to service clients. Second, the returns on OTC products arise partly from the structure (e.g. a higher implied volatility in an OTC option than the implied volatility of the component exchange traded parts) and partly from a wider bid–offer spread and selective liquidity.

REGULATION, COMPETITIVE ATTITUDES AND CREDIT RISK

Regulation

Regulatory pressures constrain both the exchange traded and OTC derivatives markets. It is often felt – within the industry – that regulators have only a limited understanding of the real risks represented by derivative instruments and the appropriate framework for risk control, particularly in the area of credit and counterparty exposure. However, the obvious demand for these instruments has forced regulators to consider and accommodate them more carefully within the regulatory structure.

There has recently been a discernible increase in regulatory interest: the SIB, BIS and the Group of 30 have all announced their intention to review the risks to financial markets posed by the rising use of derivatives. There is growing concern about the complexity of the instruments, and the risk management systems needed to monitor them, and about the potential for financial instability given the contingent claims hidden in banks' off-balance sheet activities:

> We simply do not know the size of the indirect risks for the individual institution generated by this interdependence. (Mr Alexandre Lamfalussy, general manager of the BIS, quoted in the *Financial Times* of 19 March 1992.)

The BIS and the International Organisation of Securities Commissions intend to issue draft international capital regulations, with the aim of setting guidelines for financial market exposure. In March 1992, the US Financial Accounting Standards Board issued new rules which require banks and securities firms to identify OTC activities on their balance sheets. In its 1991 annual report, Bankers Trust estimated that assets and liabilities would jump by 25 per cent ($16 billion) under these reporting requirements (source: *Wall Street Journal*, 25 March 1992).

However, in terms of the requirement to seek regulatory approval, it is generally agreed that the exchange markets fare worse. In the US, exchanges must apply to the CFTC, or to the SEC, for permission to list a new product. The approval process requires the product to pass an 'economic need' test;

overseas exchanges seeking to market their products to US investors have a still more onerous job along the same lines. In other countries, the approval procedure is normally much more informal, but can still be lengthy.

There are also many overlapping circles of regulatory influence. Consider, for instance, the case of a UK limited company subsidiary of a US broker dealer who buys a FT-SE 100 future on LIFFE on behalf of a UK-based investment management firm managing US private pension plan money. The chain of commercial links involved in this transaction will be: LCH; LIFFE; general clearing member; investment management firm; US pension plan. The laws and regulatory bodies which could, in theory, have a bearing on this transaction include the following:

UK	**US**
Exchange and LCH rules	ERISA
SIB	CFTC
SFA	SEC
IMRO	US solvency law
UK solvency law	
UK company law	

To all intents and purposes, the exact status of the interrelationships between the above, and which set of law or regulation would prevail if tested, are not as yet established.

While an approval process is not necessary before launching an OTC instrument, there can be considerable restrictions over to whom such an instrument may be marketed. Moreover, contradictory and unhelpful case law has made OTC providers wary of maintaining certain counterparty relationships. The most familiar, and damaging, example is the ruling by the House of Lords that the interest rate swaps and swaptions undertaken by UK local authorities in the late 1980s were *ultra vires*, and hence that the transactions were null and void.

Historically, regulators and tax authorities have not been adept in distinguishing hedging from speculation. Often, regulations have precluded institutions from using the very strategies which would prove most effective in the management of their risks, exposures, and costs. This is mostly caused by out-of-date regulation and an understandable caution on the part of the authorities. Moreover, the characterisation of investment strategies is not easy: the duration management of a gilt portfolio may look like the gearing up of a long position, and the adjustment of the beta of an equity portfolio using FT-SE 100 futures, or anticipatory hedging through the purchase of S&P 500 futures ahead of a physical US equity market investment, might also appear to the uninitiated as speculation.

For regulators, the advantage of exchange products is that they are easier to identify, define and label. In addition, their price behaviour and apparent effect on the underlying cash market are more observable than is the case for OTC products. As a result, it has been claimed that the exchange markets have suffered on occasion from an excess of regulatory zeal. Equity index futures and options, in particular, have been linked to undesirable expiry effects (e.g. the 'triple witching' in the US) and sudden 'inexplicable' market movements. The setting by US exchanges of initial margins and 'circuit breakers' has been a politically charged issue since the crash of 1987; in 1991 in Japan, in the face of a falling market, the OSE revised the margin requirements of the Nikkei 225 index future three times and imposed other limits to restrain activity in index arbitrage.

On occasions the demand for competitively priced OTC or exchange traded products can lead to significant structural changes in the underlying markets. An example is the growth in (equity) index arbitrage, which has forced improved efficiency in stock lending and basket trading arrangements. Regulatory developments must keep pace with these changes.

Competitive Attitudes

Many futures and options exchanges have an ambivalent attitude to the growth in OTC products. Some exchanges, in particular those in the US, perceive the OTC markets as direct competition, and have put pressure on domestic regulators to constrain the development of the off-exchange markets. However, this approach is largely impractical, given that the exchanges are grounded in national regulation, and their members, the international players who create OTC products, can easily shift their activities to the most accommodating regulatory environment.

Other exchanges, such as LIFFE, have specifically stated that they have a positive approach to the development of OTC products which are linked to exchange products in some way, but with certain caveats. The LIFFE circular no: 88/100 (issued 6 December 1988) sets out the exchange's views and potential concerns in respect of those OTC products related to LIFFE's listed instruments:

> an OTC product that provided for the creation or transfer of a position in a listed LIFFE contract, either on an ex-pit basis or which involved the later execution of a pre-arranged transaction in an exchange pit, would be in contravention of the Exchange's Trading Procedures.
>
> the Exchange would naturally be concerned if the development of an OTC instrument were to cause the distortion of prices, and so damage the integrity and performance, of a listed contract.

in the case of an OTC development related to a LIFFE contract which is related to a contract which is traded on another exchange (e.g. JGB, US T-Bond), LIFFE would also seek to consult with that other exchange, in the interests of protecting its relationship with the other exchange.

the Exchange requests all Members who are considering the development of such OTC products to contact the Market Secretary's office, at as early a stage in technical development as possible.

The MATIF also takes a pragmatic view, believing that the two markets meet different requirements and that 'it is a question of balance between more or less security and more or less standardisation' (letter from Gilbert Durieux, 3 March 1992).

The CBOE has pointed to two major concerns: first, the effects of the risks created in the overall financial system by OTC products, and second, the potential impact of large scale 'dynamic hedging' and the associated possibility that any resultant mispricing will be blamed on the exchange derivatives markets.

Apart from LIFFE, it appears that few exchanges have to date issued any formal guidance to their members in respect of OTC products.

Credit Risk

There is credit and counterparty risk both on- and off-exchange.

Most exchange traded futures and options are held on a principal-to-principal basis. However, the assessment of credit and counterparty risk can be complex, given the interaction between the role and responsibilities of the clearing house, exchange regulations and the laws governing international investment and trading. The earlier example showed how tortuous this interaction can be. A user of an exchange market should consider also the manner in which the broker holds clients' funds, and the different risks which are represented by clearing and execution-only broking relationships. The default procedures in place, and the powers that these give to the clearing house and the exchange in realising collateral and closing or transferring positions also need to be well understood. Understandably, a broker will have mirror image concerns about collateral, and the creditworthiness of clients.

However, most of the potential risk in the exchange traded market is managed by:

- initial margin deposits held by the clearing house and daily settlement to market. In addition, there can be intra-day margin calls in times of market volatility;
- capital adequacy requirements laid down by the exchange and the clearing house for different levels of clearing and non-clearing membership;

- client monies' regulations established by bodies such as the CFTC and SEC (in the USA), and the SFA (in the UK);
- formalised client agreements setting out the terms of the relationship.

It is extremely important for the integrity of the exchange traded market that the counterparty at the end of all chains of open positions is an adequately capitalised clearing house without direct market price risk: the clearing house should always have a matched position, except when a broker defaults.

Users of OTC instruments are nearly always faced with greater credit risks, even when selecting excellent names as counterparties. Credit quality changes over time, and counterparty exposure can vary significantly with swings in market prices and volatility, particularly where option-type products are involved. The longer the maturity of the product, the more pertinent the need for detailed evaluation of these risks. Some credit concerns can be overcome by frequent settlements and resettlements. However, this is not always possible (or desirable), and it is essential that the user understands the risk characteristics of the instrument being provided, and that the provider has analysed the risk management implications of the product.

Moody's Investors Services issued a helpful Special Comment paper in November 1991 entitled 'Credit Implications for Firms that Use Derivatives', which identified the key risks associated with derivative instruments as: market, management, credit, legal, regulatory, and liquidity. The paper includes particular examples of large-scale derivatives transactions which have gone wrong and provides a useful analytical checklist. It also defines some key considerations for vendors and intermediaries in respect of OTC derivatives, including the following:

- the substantial market risks inherent in many derivatives can lead to large, sudden losses – particularly if management controls are weak;
- credit risks are expanding. This reflects two facts: that more and more derivatives written and traded by these participants are long term in nature – often not maturing for many years – and that counterparties tend to be other corporations, not just clearing units of securities exchanges. Such corporations can have weak and fluctuating credit standings;
- principal activities in derivatives are a use of a firm's credit capacity. This use can affect a firm's ability to place its debt, and potentially result in greater funding risks.

ISDA has produced a standard master agreement to cover bilateral OTC derivatives transactions, and, for most of the main types of product, has also published suggested contract confirmation documentation and a 'dictionary' of definitions. The standardisation of legal documentation is evidence that the OTC markets are moving, in some respects, closer to the exchange traded environment.

FUTURE DEVELOPMENTS

The interrelationship between the two markets is complex and shifting. There is no doubt that OTC products can significantly enhance the liquidity of exchange instruments which are often already highly traded. But equally, the reluctance of active OTC traders to support newer and more marginal exchange traded products (such as the long-dated short sterling futures and swap futures) has stunted the growth in some potentially highly useful products.

A potential user of either market faces key choices, including:

- the rollover and future transaction uncertainties implicit in exchange traded derivatives; and the assumption of counterparty credit risk in OTC positions;
- the basis risk arising from the use of standardised contracts, weighed against the usually greater cost of buying a tailored (OTC) product;
- the ease of reversing an exchange traded position, compared with an OTC position which may have an illiquid or non-existent secondary market.

By way of conclusion, the following are some personal observations and speculations of the author.

- The creation of OTC products is initially tightly controlled by a few players, but rapidly becomes available to a wider range of participants. Instruments become 'commoditised', and increased competition brings down prices and/or profit margins. The inevitable result is a search for ever more arcane products from which to make money. At some stage, distribution becomes a problem, because the market is saturated, or because products become too complex, too multi-dimensional, or too obscure in their payoff;
- The market in equity-related OTC products has considerable remaining potential. Commodity instruments will be the next focus, followed by more exotic classes such as insurance and reinsurance. The embryonic UK forward market in electricity should be followed closely;
- Exchange traded products have to stay simple to be effective. There is room for very few additional products, and none for the long lead times involved in the historical, high profile attempts to create liquid futures and options contracts in new areas;
- The debate concerning the relative merits of on and off exchange instruments will continue. The exchange markets may have a slight advantage overall, because regulators prefer these markets and because the central clearing house structure is appealing from the viewpoint of credit risk. However, settlement netting and other OTC market developments will challenge the exchange structure significantly;

- The growth of managed futures funds (currently estimated to be a $20 billion industry) will eventually collide with the growth of OTC and structured products; these investment classes have very different roots but an overlap will emerge;
- There will be heated intellectual and regulatory debate over the appropriateness of mechanisms such as cash settlement, given the possibility that these enable the creation of artificial liquidity which far exceeds the real assets or underlying 'natural' exposure. The rights and wrongs of this will never be definitively established.

BIBLIOGRAPHY

Periodicals

Equity International (especially October 1991. 'Equity Derivatives: Over the Counter . . . or Over the Top')

Financial Times (and futures and options surveys, e.g. 19 March 1992)

Futures and Options World (and supplements)

GNI International Futures and Options Briefing (especially March 1991. 'Short Sterling Deposit Futures: Financing Bias')

IFR

Institutional Investor (especially September 1991. 'The Risk Collectors')

Risk Magazine

Wall Street Journal

Books

Robertson, Malcolm. *Worldwide Futures and Options Manual* (Thornhill Bridge Publishing)

Articles/Reports

BIS. 'International Banking and Financial Market Developments during Q4 1991', May 1992.

Carlson, Charles A. 'Darwinism and the European Futures Markets'. Unpublished paper available from the Gelber Group, Chicago.

LIFFE. *Circular no. 88/100.* December 1988.

Moody's. 'Credit Implications for Firms that Use Derivatives'. Special comment paper, November 1991.

Stoll, Hans R. 'Derivatives: Exchange Traded versus Off-Exchange'. Vanderbilt University: policy paper 91-72, December 1991.

8: Investment Management Applications

Karen Mason, BZW Investment Management

INTRODUCTION

One of the most widely quoted numbers in the City is the FT-SE 100 share index: the aggregate measure of the value of the UK's 100 largest stocks. The FT-SE 100 represents the most accessible way to measure the performance of UK shares within a trading day or over a period, and, along with other popular indices, has become a base for some of the OTC instruments discussed in this chapter.

The FT-SE 100 index, and the wider-based FT-A All Share index, have become benchmarks for UK investment managers because they represent the returns from investing in the UK equity market, and because they are used to calculate the relative gains or losses arising from specific stock or sector bets. In a world in which competition between fund managers has intensified, the continuous evaluation of a fund's performance against an index provides a timely, objective and quantifiable assessment of the success of a manager's investment strategy.

Funds which track the FT-SE 100 and other indices, known as index funds, have become increasingly popular amongst the investment community in the UK; and much of the developmental work in equity-based OTC derivatives in particular has been stimulated by the passive management techniques of quantitative fund managers, who seek low cost methods to pursue theoretically based, objective investment strategies. Active fund managers are also finding a growing role for OTC derivatives, as improved technology allows analysis of a greater range of opportunities within any given investment approach. In between these two poles, a range of strategies exists which blends passive management with active management, and these too can usefully profit from a greater diversity of derivative investment products, be they OTC or exchange traded.

A BRIEF HISTORY OF QUANTITATIVE FUND MANAGEMENT

Harry Markowitz was one of the first theoreticians to approach the world of investment from a statistical and objective base. In a paper published in 1952, he plotted the historical returns and risks (standard deviations of annual returns) of combinations of US stocks. His analysis showed that there was always one combination of stocks which had the highest return for a given level of risk or, alternatively, had the lowest risk for a given return (both possibilities highly desirable from the fund manager's perspective). A series of 'optimal' portfolios could then be constructed to form an 'efficient frontier' (see Figure 8.1).

The idea of risk minimisation was enhanced by focusing on (a) a stock's market-related systematic risk which could be eliminated by diversification, and (b) the non-diversifiable, specific risk which was unique to that stock. This distinction formed the basis for William Sharpe's capital asset pricing model (CAPM), and led to the concept of a market portfolio (the portfolio of all stocks in the market, weighted by capitalisation).

It was subsequently argued that, for every fund manager who was able to pick successful stocks, there would be one who did not, and in aggregate these managers would hold the market portfolio (equivalent to an index fund).

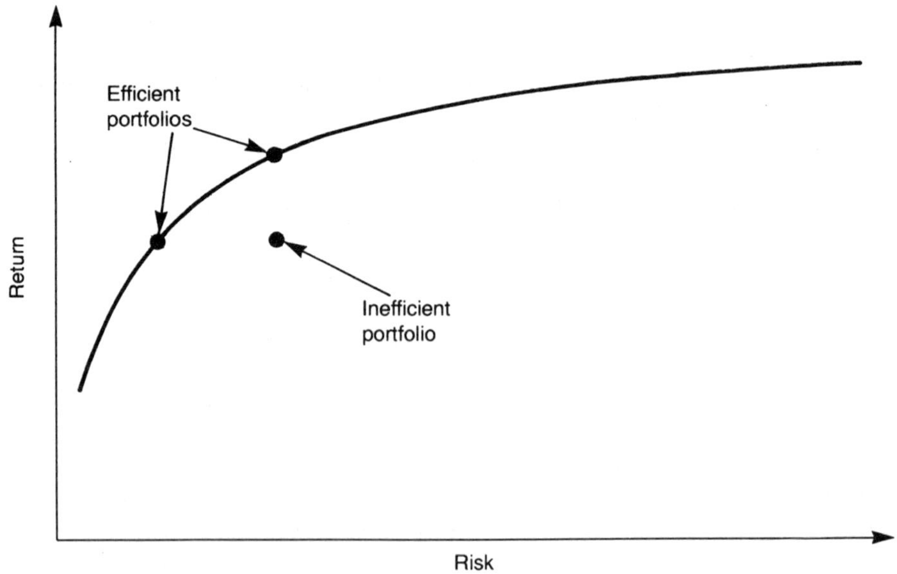

Figure 8.1 The Efficient Frontier

However, the trading costs incurred by the active fund managers would in fact introduce a downward bias to their performance, relative to the index. In other words, the average fund manager could be expected to underperform the broad market index.

It was academic work of this nature which prompted some of the early conversions to index funds in the US in 1971. The conclusions drawn from the theoreticians' work were borne out by subsequent performance statistics, which showed evidence of sustainable superior returns from the index funds compared with those of the average stock picker. As a result, the popularity of passive funds has grown to the point where an estimated 20 per cent of US pension fund assets are indexed.

Developments in the UK have been slower, and indexation did not take hold until the early 1980s; but, according to the National Association of Pension Funds, index funds now amount to approximately 13 per cent of the UK pension fund market.

THE CHANGING SHAPE OF INDEX FUNDS

The early index funds were marketed and differentiated on the premise that they provided the most efficient use of risk, combined with significant cost savings which could be passed on to clients. A variety of techniques were introduced: full replication, which mirrored holdings in all the constituent index stocks; sampling, which took a selection of stocks from each sector to match those of the index; and optimisation, which also matched key index characteristics such as price/earnings ratios, growth, dividends, size, and so on.

All of these techniques were evaluated by comparing their ability to minimise the risk of the portfolio relative to the index (the tracking error) with the cost of running the strategy. It is no surprise that, as traded stock index futures were launched around the world, 'synthetic' futures index funds, which combine a long cash position with a long stock index futures position to give an equivalent index return, began to emerge. Not only were commissions on futures low, but there were cost savings in terms of custody fees, withholding tax on dividends and ease of implementation.

Index fund managers are always searching for cheaper, more cost effective methods of tracking an index, and the more recent growth in OTC instruments is likely to change the shape of index fund management still further over the next few years. The attraction of such instruments and their possible applications are discussed later in this chapter.

FURTHER DEVELOPMENTS IN QUANTITATIVE FUND MANAGEMENT

The development of quantitative investment did not stop at index funds. Over the years a number of other computer-driven, objective and systematic investment strategies have experienced varying degrees of popularity, including:

- *Dedication* A dedicated portfolio is a computer-selected fixed income portfolio whose cashflows match a predetermined liability stream. Dedication can be used, for example, in a pension scheme to ensure coupon receipts match known future pension payments.

- *Immunisation* An immunised portfolio is one designed with a specific duration, to protect an asset/liability position against the broad effects of interest rate movements over a given time period.

- *Portfolio insurance* This strategy, which was highly popular in the United States until the stock market crash of 1987, aims to replicate the payoff of a cash plus call option position by progressively selling equities in a falling market and buying equities in a rising market.

- *Currency dynamic hedging* Based on the same principles as portfolio insurance, currency dynamic hedging varies the percentage of currency exposure which is hedged back to the base currency, to give an option-like payoff.

- *Tilted index funds* An index fund can be biased towards or away from specific stocks, such as those with a low P/E ratio or a high dividend yield, while still controlling the tracking error. Provided the factors are successfully selected, the portfolio will have an inherent bias towards outperformance.

- *Tactical asset allocation* In tactical asset allocation, a computer model determines which asset classes are likely to outperform based on historical relationships, and then constructs an appropriate portfolio to maximise expected return for a given level of risk.

- *Active stock selection models* These models analyse fundamental data on the basis of historical relationships, with the intention of exploiting structural inefficiencies in equity markets.

The increasing depth of traded futures and options markets enabled new methods of implementation which were, in theory at least, ideally suited to the techniques just described. Portfolio insurance, for example, could be implemented by selling stock index futures against an equity portfolio, rather than disturbing the underlying portfolio through physical liquidation and rebuilding of positions, hence avoiding the associated costs of trading.

THE INTEREST IN OTC DERIVATIVES

Unfortunately, exchange traded markets brought with them a new set of problems such as temporary illiquidity, pricing inefficiencies and a lack of longer-dated instruments. As a consequence, the volume of OTC instruments began to grow, enabling fund managers to construct long-term positions in a tailor-made fashion.

As a form of alternative investment, a fund manager must consider the relative advantages and disadvantages of using OTC instruments. Often, the deciding factors will be specific to the strategy and instrument in question, but some of the more general considerations are listed below.

Custody Fees

The majority of equity OTC derivatives are based on quoted indices rather than individual stocks, and consequently the custody fee normally charged on each stock can be avoided. For overseas equities this saving can be substantial.

Stamp Duty and Other Taxes

A significant benefit of an OTC approach is that any duties or taxes payable on the underlying equities can be avoided. In the UK, for example, stamp duty of 0.5 per cent is currently payable on any purchase of physical equities. Many foreign countries levy a withholding tax: often 15 per cent on all dividend payments. In such cases the tax saving from derivatives investment can be substantial (for example, on a dividend yield of 4 per cent, a saving of 60 basis points per annum).

German investors receive 75 per cent of gross dividends on the payment date, and then receive tax credits which, depending on their tax status, entitle them to a combined dividend close to the gross amount. Typically, international investors in German stocks receive only 85 per cent of the gross dividend: 75 per cent on the pay date and 10 per cent in tax refunds. A buyer of, say, an equity index swap is one step removed from the underlying equities; hence, provided the swap counterparty is a German investor, the fully dividend can be reclaimed and passed on, even when the receiver of the equity-linked flows is a non-German investor.

Temporary Illiquidity in Traded Derivatives

Exchange-traded futures and options sometimes experience temporary squeezes, or a decline in traded volumes, which can push the market price away from its theoretical fair value. For an investor running a traded futures or options position this can result in significant costs: where, for example, a futures position needs to be rolled from one maturity to the next at a time when the future is trading disadvantageously away from its fair value.

Because OTC derivatives tend to be longer-dated than their traded counterparts, rollover risk is substantially reduced, and the temporary squeezes in exchange traded markets may not be of concern.

Tailored Products
The possibility of tailoring is one of the main attractions of using OTC instruments in an investment strategy. Each derivative can be customised to meet the client's needs as closely as possible, particularly with respect to time horizon, benchmarks, tax status and size, resulting in a specific desired payoff under different market outcomes.

Ease of Investment
An index fund manager has to buy and sell a large number of securities in order to switch assets between index funds in different markets. In the derivatives markets, the investor can gain exposure to an entire market (i.e. all the stocks in the index on which the derivative is based) in just one transaction.

Unwinding
By their very nature, OTC derivatives are tailored and tend to be longer-dated instruments, struck with one counterparty broker. This means that they can be difficult and often costly to unwind, and should therefore only be used as part of a long-term strategy. Many brokers give a commitment in principle to provide an after market, or will offer a buyback clause as part of the instrument, in order to help overcome this problem. However, investment strategies which involve active trading or repositioning are more likely to be suited to the exchange traded markets, where the implicit transaction costs are lower and price visibility is greater.

No Share Ownership
In an OTC position, the investor does not physically own the underlying securities. In most instances this presents no practical problems, but some investors may wish to maintain the trappings of ownership, such as voting rights.

Large Minimum Investment
This excludes the smaller investor from the OTC markets, except via pooled funds.

Counterparty Risk
Because OTC instruments are, by definition, not traded on a recognised exchange, any profit accruing on a contract will be settled directly between the two counterparties. As a result, the choice of counterparty broker becomes

critical, and the introduction of rigorous credit controls inevitably forms part of the fund manager's brief when using the OTC markets. It is not surprising that some intermediaries are keen to emphasise the strength of their credit rating.

Pricing

Since an OTC instrument is tailored to the client's needs, it is harder to assess how competitive the price is. Obviously, one control is to ask for comparable prices from other brokers, but this is time-consuming and impractical on a regular basis (for example, for monthly valuations). More often than not, fund managers will either use quoted prices on other comparable derivatives or will calculate a theoretical price using their own valuation software.

Performance Measurement

There has been a great deal of discussion about the appropriate treatment of futures and options in fund management, culminating in a report recently published by LIFFE in conjunction with actuarial consultants William M. Mercer Fraser, in January 1992. Performance measurement and attribution is playing an ever-increasing role in the fund management business, yet historically derivatives have usually been measured as a separate asset class. Combined with a sketchy understanding on the part of the ultimate investor, inaccurate performance attribution has made clients wary of using these instruments.

SOME APPLICATIONS OF OTC-BASED PRODUCTS

Among the OTC instruments available in the market-place, options and warrants are the derivatives most commonly used by fund managers. Typical applications are described below.

Guaranteed Funds

An investor who has a desire to participate in the equity market, but who is averse to suffering losses over a given time period (say one or two years), may be attracted to a guaranteed fund. In such funds the majority of the portfolio is invested in either cash or bonds which mature at the time horizon selected by the investor. In this way the fund 'locks in' a minimum rate of return.

The first step is to establish how much money needs to be invested to return the minimum capital required at the end of the period. For example, if interest rates are 10 per cent, an investor only needs to invest 90.9 per cent of capital in cash to return 100 per cent after one year (once the 10 per cent has been received).

The remaining 9.1 per cent is available to invest in risky assets. The gearing of options is such that a large nominal exposure can be obtained for only a modest investment (the cost of the premium). Typically, guaranteed funds buy near- or at-the-money call index options with a maturity matching the time horizon (in this case one year). OTC options are ideally suited for this application (compared, for example, with traded options), since not only can the time horizon, strike price and choice of index be matched perfectly, but little, if any, subsequent turnover is required.

Guaranteed funds are attractive to the less sophisticated, risk averse investor who has perhaps never invested in equities before. It is therefore unsurprising that in the UK a number of money purchase schemes are starting to show an interest in cash/option strategies. Such schemes will typically compare the return they achieve on the fund with the return on cash and/or bonds. The level of equity participation will vary according to the prevailing level of interest rates, the duration over which the scheme is to run and the implied volatility used to price the option. However, an investor who is considering this strategy must take into account the opportunity cost of investing either in cash or in a straight equity position.

Figure 8.2 compares the proforma return of a typical guaranteed fund with the returns on cash and a 100 per cent equity investment.

Table 8.1 and Figure 8.3 display the one-year historical returns from each of these three strategies for the period 1978 to 1991. The success of the guaranteed strategy in participating in market advances is apparent; however the equity market was in a bull phase for much of the period, and, while in eight of the fourteen years the guaranteed strategy outperformed the one-year LIBOR rate, in only two years (1982 and 1990) did it surpass the FT-A total return.

Protection Strategies

Most textbooks on options cite examples in which equity put options are bought to hedge portfolios against the adverse effects of bear markets, without losing the full benefit of any market advance.

OTC Index Put Options

Short-term hedges are often best implemented through the use of traded index and stock options, but longer-term protection (say six months or more) is more suited to OTC derivatives. Fund managers can select carefully the exact time horizon, together with a range of strike prices, in order to maximise returns under their particular scenario of market forecasts.

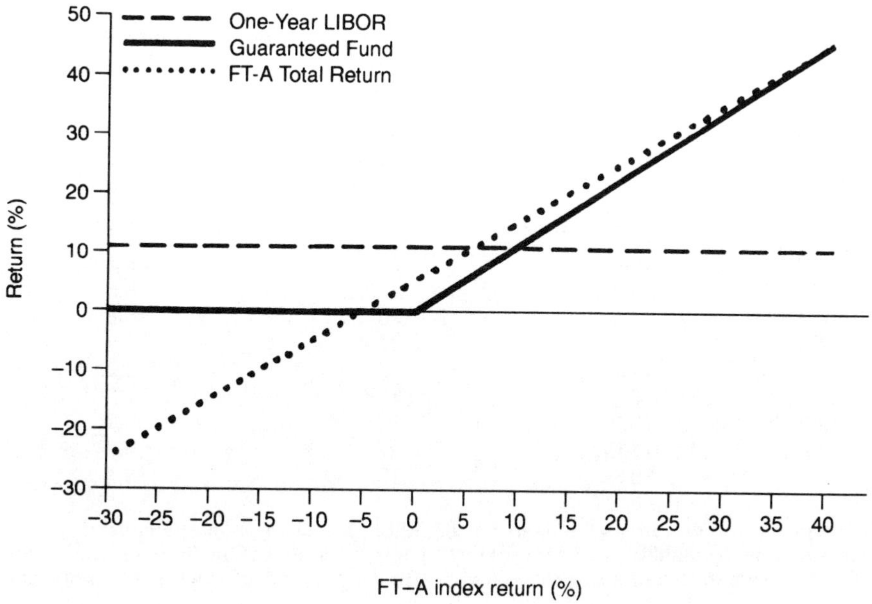

Figure 8.2 Guaranteed Fund Return Profile

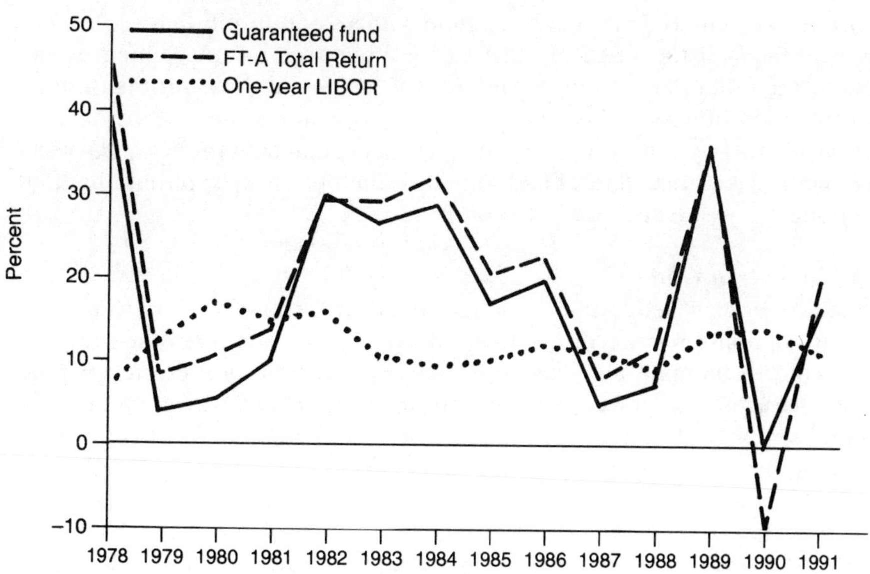

Figure 8.3 Comparison of Strategy Returns

Year	One-Year LIBOR at Start of Year (%)	FT-A All Share Index Total Return (%)	Guaranteed Fund*
1978	6.6	49.2	41.9
1979	12.6	8.5	3.8
1980	17.1	10.5	5.4
1981	14.8	13.7	10.0
1982	15.8	29.1	29.8
1983	10.6	29.1	26.4
1984	9.4	31.9	28.6
1985	10.0	20.4	16.8
1986	11.9	22.4	19.7
1987	11.2	8.0	4.9
1988	8.9	11.5	7.2
1989	13.2	36.1	35.7
1990	14.0	−9.7	0.0
1991	10.9	19.7	16.4

* Guaranteed fund returns have been calculated on the assumption of a constant one-year implied volatility of 16 per cent for the option element of the fund; the purchased option is assumed to be at-the-money (relative to the spot index) at the start of the year.

Table 8.1 UK Interest Rates, Equity and Simulated Guaranteed Fund Returns (Sources: Datastream: BZW Investment Management)

Many pension fund investors, for example, have specific year-ends for reporting and actuarial purposes. If a fund with a small surplus has succeeded, part way through the year, in meeting the minimum return applied by the actuary, then there are strong arguments for locking in those profits through the protection of an OTC put option.

Typically this option would have an expiry date matched to the fund's year-end, and a strike price determined so that, if the option is exercised, the fund would meet the actuarial rate of return.

OTC Basket Put Options

Provided they can hedge their resultant exposure, some brokers will quote prices for options on a specific portfolio of stocks. This is attractive to investors who want to eliminate any chance of negative returns on a given portfolio whose characteristics differ markedly from the index. However, the cost of the put option will increase in line with the difficulty the broker faces in matching the portfolio to traded instruments.

OTC Equity + Currency Options

An investor with overseas equity exposure can protect against falls in his portfolio in two ways. For example, a Japanese equity index fund can be protected by buying an OTC index put option which will protect against any equity market falls. However, if the yen depreciates against sterling the investor will still lose money in base currency terms. To overcome this problem, it is possible to purchase an OTC option which protects against both equity and currency risk.

It should be noted that this form of protection is quite different from buying two separate options to hedge the specific market exposures: one on the sterling/yen exchange rate and the other on the TOPIX index. Table 8.2 presents four different potential returns for both the yen and TOPIX, which are used to compare the return to the investor who purchases an at-the-money OTC TOPIX option offering currency protection with the return on two separate at-the-money currency and index options.

	Case 1	**Case 2**	**Case 3**	**Case 4**
TOPIX Index Return:	−20%	−20%	+30%	+20%
Yen Currency Return:	−20%	+30%	+30%	−30%

Table 8.2 Illustrative Market and Currency Returns

In Case 1, both currency and equity returns are negative, giving a return in sterling of −36 per cent. Both the combined option and the two separate options would be exercised. Ignoring premium costs, the overall return from the former strategy would be 0 per cent, while the latter strategy returns 4 per cent (= 20 + 20 − 36).

In Case 2, the equity market falls while the yen rises, giving a sterling return of +4 per cent. The combined option would expire worthless, producing a return of 4 per cent (less the cost of the option premium). In the separate options strategy, the currency option would expire worthless but the equity option would be exercised. The total return would be 24 per cent (= 20 + 0 + 4), less the option premiums.

In Case 3, the market and the yen both rise sharply, giving a sterling return of +69 per cent. Both the combined and the two separate options would expire worthless, resulting in a return of 69 per cent less option premiums. However, the total premium on the two separate options would be higher than the combined premium, so that the combined option strategy would yield a slightly higher net return.

In Case 4, the market is up but the yen falls, giving a sterling return of −16 per cent. The combined option would be exercised, to leave a net return of 0 per cent, less the premium cost, to the investor. For the separate options, the equity option would expire worthless and the currency option would be exercised, resulting in a combined return (ignoring option premiums) of 14 per cent (= 0 + 30 − 16).

The choice of strategy depends on the investor's views on currency and equity markets: in general, if he believes that there will be a significant divergence in the currency and equity market trends, he should select the separate options strategy; but if returns are correlated, then the combined option approach will usually be cheaper.

Relative Performance Options

Other OTC options offered by brokers will give the investor the relative performance between two indices. The assets on which the option is based do not need to be related, and can be any combination of equity, interest rate, foreign exchange or commodity markets. The relative performance option can therefore be used as a convenient, and relatively inexpensive, tool for asset allocation.

For example, a fund manager whose benchmark is the FT-A All Share index, but who has discretion to invest up to 10 per cent in Japan, might wish to buy a put option on the relative performance between the Japanese market (in sterling) and the UK market return. If Japan underperformed the UK, then the investor would receive the difference in sterling from the broker who had written the option. Like any option, the strike can be set in-, at- or out-of-the-money. For instance, if the strike was 5 per cent out-of-the-money, the option buyer would only receive a payment if the Japanese market underperformed the UK by more than 5 per cent.

Relative performance options can be priced using a modification of Black–Scholes known as the Margrabe model, which uses the covariance between the two asset classes as the measure of volatility – this takes into account both the volatility of each asset and their correlation. The higher the correlation, the less likely it is that large differential price movements will occur, and therefore the lower the option premium.

Portfolio Insurance

In portfolio insurance, the investor effectively cuts out the intermediary by designing a synthetic put option to vary dynamically the amount of exposure to the equity market.

Based on option pricing theory, a portfolio insurer will select a time horizon and level of protection – for example, a minimum return of 0 per cent over one year. A computer model will then estimate the recommended initial equity exposure given these requirements, and the portfolio insurer will need to switch the remainder into cash. This can be achieved either by physically selling the underlying assets or by hedging with stock index futures.

The portfolio must then be monitored on a continuing basis. As equities rise, the model will recommend an increase in the fund's allocation to equities, subject to certain rebalancing parameters. This increase can be implemented either by physically buying equities, or by buying back some of the short futures position. If the market continues to rise, this process will be repeated until the fund is fully exposed to the equity market and participating in all rises.

On the other hand, if equities start to fall, the model will start to recommend a decrease in the fund's exposure to equities, and in a severe bear market this will continue until the fund becomes fully exposed to cash.

The result is a strategy which, in theory at least, delivers an 'insured' minimum return, but participates in any equity rises. Rather than paying an explicit premium, the option premium is 'paid' in the form of an opportunity cost of lost upside in rising equity markets, the reason being that the fund is initially only partly exposed to equities. Equally, in a bear market the fund does not instantly eliminate its equity exposure; and in an erratic market, the premium is paid through the cost of buying the market on each advance only to sell it after a subsequent decline.

It is argued that, because the financial intermediary has been eliminated, the cost of portfolio insurance will be lower than the option premiums quoted by brokers for OTC put options with a similar strike price and maturity. However, this depends in part on the subsequent volatility of the market: higher levels of volatility than expected will cause the strategy to be less efficient.

Portfolio insurance became very popular in the US prior to the stock market crash of 1987. Most schemes were implemented by hedging with S&P 500 stock index futures. Unfortunately, the experience of the crash was not a pleasant one for portfolio insurers, as index futures traded at heavy discounts to fair values and markets moved sharply downwards. Among a number of technical, and perhaps foreseeable, problems, the most significant was that the futures market was falling too quickly for the portfolio insurers to implement their required sales, with the result that many funds fell below their floor returns.

Since the stock market crash, portfolio insurance has been largely discredited in the US, and few investors now implement portfolio protection strategies of this type, preferring to purchase OTC index options if protection is needed. Although the premium must be paid in advance, the minimum return from an OTC-based approach is more certain.

It is worth reiterating the value of a high quality, creditworthy counterparty. In the event of a very sharp market fall, purchasers of OTC index put options would be owed substantial amounts by brokers, and it is exactly in such market conditions that these firms will be at their most vulnerable.

As the volume of OTC index options grows, so the advantages of portfolio insurance will be increasingly outweighed by the disadvantages. Competition has led to more aggressive pricing, and increased volumes have ensured that the flexibility which portfolio insurance offered, in terms of the ability to change time horizons and minimum returns, is increasingly matched by OTC instruments.

Cashflow Management

One of the more common applications of derivatives in fund management is to hedge expected or actual cashflow pending investment in the underlying asset class. For example, an investor who knows a cash injection will be received in nine months' time, but considers that equities will rise sharply during this period, could buy a nine-month at-the-money OTC FT-SE index call option. If the index did subsequently rise, the investor would then be able to invest the new cash at original index levels.

Stock Options

Active fund managers frequently write call options against individual holdings in their portfolios as a means of enhancing income on the portfolio while providing a limited amount of protection in falling markets. Such 'covered call' programmes are usually introduced when the manager believes that the stock is not going to appreciate markedly over a given time period. Writing an option against a stock holding will have the following effect on the portfolio return:

- *Stock price rises* The buyer of the option will exercise at the lower strike price – the positive stock return is offset by the exercise of the option, leaving the investor the return from the option premium and any difference between the option's strike price and the level of the stock at inception of the position.
- *Stock price remains steady* The option is left to expire and the investor receives only the premium earned from writing the option.
- *Stock price falls* The buyer leaves the option to expire and the seller keeps the premium, which either partially or wholly offsets the losses arising from the fall in the stock.

In summary, covered call programmes enhance income, and provide some protection against falling markets, but cap the level of upside potential. The strike price and time horizon of the option can be tailored to match the investor's views regarding future market performance.

Interest Rate Options

The principles of hedging and protection can apply equally to bond portfolio management as to equity management, and interest rate derivatives play an important role in the management of interest rate risk. OTCs are particularly attractive for those areas of the yield curve not covered by exchange traded derivatives, and for longer-term strategies which cannot be implemented using traded instruments.

Covered call strategies are also applied to bond portfolios. However, a more interesting application makes use of relative performance options. For example, if an investor holds bond positions in two markets (say Germany and France), and believes that the relative performance of these two markets will be similar, he might write a call option on the outperformance of, say, France over Germany. At the maturity of the option, the seller will have to pay the amount by which France has in fact outperformed Germany. If his views are correct, and neither market has outperformed, or if Germany has shown stronger performance, he will keep the premium.

OTC Currency Options

In the same way that an investor can protect against a fall in the equity market, so currency depreciation can be avoided through the purchase of currency options. However, because fund managers do not always treat currency as a separate asset class, currency options are often embedded into equity derivatives, or are linked in some way to the underlying equity or bond market.

For example, a fund manager might invest in the Japanese equity market, but if he is worried about the yen depreciating, he could purchase an at-the-money OTC option whose nominal underlying value varied with the equity index return. This would allow him at maturity of the option to sell the equity portfolio at the exchange rate prevailing when the option was purchased.

Example: Quantity Adjusting Currency Option
An investor buys £1 million of a Japanese index fund, at an exchange rate of Y230. He purchases an at-the-money put option which allows him to sell yen for sterling at Y230 in one year's time, with the nominal value linked to the performance of the TOPIX index.

After one year the equity market has risen 10 per cent and the index fund is now worth Y253 million. The currency has depreciated to Y253, so that if the manager converted the portfolio back into sterling at current exchange rates, the investment would still only be worth £1 million. However, by exercising his option he can convert the Y253 million portfolio into sterling at Y230, to give £1.1 million.

Note that if the investor had purchased a conventional put option rather than the 'quantity adjusting' OTC instrument described, he would only have been able to convert Y230 million at Y230; the remaining Y23 million (i.e. the profit on the equity investment) would be converted at the depreciated rate of Y253, to leave the total investment worth only £1.09 million, rather than £1.1 million.

Although in theory quantity adjusting currency options should be no more expensive than conventional comparatives, in practice they tend to trade at a premium. An explanation for this is that the writer must mark-to-market the currency hedge to adjust for equity market movements. Typically, OTC quantity adjusting options tend to cost around 1 to 2 per cent more than the comparable conventional option, although this varies with market conditions.

Currency Dynamic Hedging

Curiously, although the events of October 1987 virtually caused the death of portfolio insurance in the US, more recently US funds have turned to strategic currency management programmes which incorporate dynamic hedging techniques. Currency dynamic hedging, like portfolio insurance, attempts to replicate the payout profile of a 'quantity adjusting' currency option.

Using option replication software, an investor selects a time horizon and a minimum acceptable return below a fully hedged position. The model then determines what initial proportion of the foreign currency should be hedged back into the investor's base currency. If the foreign currency subsequently starts to appreciate, the proportion of exposure hedged is progressively reduced, leaving the fund increasingly exposed to the benefits of currency appreciation. Conversely, if the foreign currency starts to depreciate, progressively more and more of the exposure is hedged back into base currency, until the portfolio is fully hedged.

For a number of reasons, currency dynamic hedging is thought to suffer fewer problems than equity portfolio insurance in its practical application. First, the forward foreign exchange and currency futures markets are highly liquid, and dynamic hedging only forms a very small proportion of daily volume. Second, central bank intervention will often ensure depth of both buyers and sellers of a currency even in a strongly trending market. Finally, the very existence of currency trends can make the implied cost of the option relatively low.

The increasing popularity of currency dynamic hedging is a reflection of the increased concern of US investors about the value of foreign currency assets; and OTC options provide a further tool for currency risk management. Indeed, dynamic hedgers can use OTC options as part of the strategy to minimise the risks of market gaps. This is usually achieved through the purchase of inexpensive, deep out-of-the-money options which provide a low level of 'disaster' protection.

Equity Index-linked Notes

These instruments are fixed income securities issued by corporations, banks or sovereign agencies. The bond's principal repayment will typically be linked to the return on an equity index. Most equity-linked bonds have small or very low coupons, and tend to be issued with a one to five-year maturity. Sometimes the coupon will be linked to the dividend yield payable on the equity index so that the investor receives a total rate of return equivalent to the return on a conventional index fund.

As with both OTC options and conventional corporate bonds, the credit risk of equity index-linked notes lies with the issuer. When the principal is related directly to the equity index, the bond is an unprotected note. Sometimes, however, securities will have an option structure built into them, and so become protected notes. In this instance the minimum value of the final principal repayment is determined by the strike price of the implied option.

Occasionally, the repayment of principal is either in local currency or hedged back to the currency of the investor, with or without currency option protection included.

More complicated features have been applied to equity index-linked notes. The instrument is perceived to be attractive to investors who, for whatever reason, cannot invest in futures, options or equities. Psychologically, purchasing a bond rather than an equity can appear a less risky investment, and those index-linked notes with inherent option structures offer investors limited downside exposure to the equity market without the need to enter into specific, and perhaps tailored, derivative positions.

The packaged nature of the product makes it easy to sell; and its simplicity appeals to the investor who does not want the added complexity of evaluating the precise mechanics of the required option position, or determining the specific stocks and combined proportions necessary to make a good index fund. But they do not offer the investor as much flexibility as an OTC option, and this disadvantage must be weighed up against the apparent advantages.

Equity Index Swaps

In recent years the interest rate swaps market has become increasingly competitive, and there has been a narrowing of spreads in core products. This trend has encouraged participants to look elsewhere for higher margin business, and the equity markets have been the principal beneficiaries of this attention.

The most heavily promoted of the new OTC equity products has been the equity index swap. This instrument is in most respects comparable with the plain vanilla fixed/floating interest rate swap. An investor who manages a portfolio in LIBOR-related cash instruments (e.g. certificates of deposit, commercial paper and Treasury bills) might enter into an equity index swap with a bank counterparty to create a synthetic index exposure without disturbing the underlying portfolio.

The cash flows exchanged are straightforward. Every six months (or at a different frequency agreed in advance between the counterparties), the bank (the 'index payer') pays the investor (the 'index receiver') an amount equal to the capital appreciation of the index over the period and (usually) a sum reflecting the attributable dividend income. In return, the index receiver pays the index payer a floating interest rate (e.g. six-month LIBOR) prevailing at the start of each reset period applied to the notional principal amount of the swap. Typically, these payments will be netted. As with the majority of conventional (interest rate) swaps, no principal payments are exchanged.

The only material complication relates to dividend receipts, which for physical equity investments are receivable on ex-dividend dates unlikely to be coincident with swap reset dates. In practice, a dividend yield may be negotiated in advance and included as a negative spread to the LIBOR-based payments, or the index payer may pay the 'total return' of the index as calculated by various actuarial bodies. (Conveniently, one index underlying much swap activity – the German DAX index – is calculated to reflect total returns.)

Figure 8.4 illustrates the anatomy of an equity index swap based on the FT-SE 100 index. The numerical example which accompanies this illustration is based on an original paper by Guy Austin of BZW Equities Ltd (and is reworked here with the kind permission of the author).

Example

An investor is assumed to enter into a one year FT-SE 100 index swap with an opening notional principal amount (NPA) of £10 million and quarterly

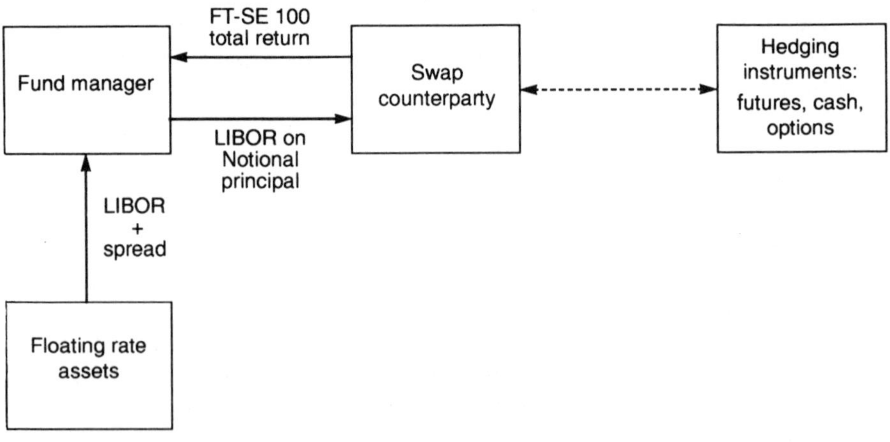

Figure 8.4 Anatomy of an Equity Index Swap

reset dates. On these dates, the following market levels and interest rates are observed:

		FT-SE 100	Three-Month LIBOR
Inception of swap	1 January	2500	10.00%
First reset	31 March	2700	10.25%
Second reset	30 June	2700	9.75%
Third reset	30 September	2600	10.00%
Termination of swap	31 December	2750	

As outlined above, three factors determine the net payments under the swap:

(1) Capital Performance
On each reset date, the movement in the NPA is paid by the index payer. The amount payable is based on the closing value of the index at the end of each quarter as follows:

First reset NPA = Opening NPA × (Index on 31 March)/(Index on 1 January)

= 10,000,000 × 2700/2500

= 10,800,000 ,

leading to a payment of £800,000 (= 10,800,000 − 10,000,000) to the index receiver. The remaining quarterly payments relating to capital performance are calculated similarly.

(2) Dividends
Dividends on UK stocks are paid on an 'account' basis, whereas under a swap contract dividends will be paid on each reset date. As suggested above, the resulting timing differences must be allowed for under the terms of the swap. However, for the purposes of this illustration, the following accumulations of dividends are assumed in each quarter:

	FT-SE 100	Accumulated Dividends (Points)	Accumulated Dividends (£)
1 January	2500		
31 March	2700	35	140,000
30 June	2700	30	120,000
30 September	2600	28	112,000
31 December	2750	32	128,000
		125	500,000

(3) Interest Payments and Receipts
The floating interest payment under the swap is calculated by reference to the new NPA and the interest rate fixed at the start of each reset

period. Hence at inception the interest payable by the index receiver will be calculated as:

Interest = Initial NPA × Initial LIBOR × (days from 1 January to 31 March)/365

= 10,000,000 × 10.00% × 90/365

= 246,575.34

This amount will be payable on 31 March. Interest payable on 30 June will be based on (three-month) LIBOR and the reset NPA on 31 March (£10,800,000) as follows:

Interest = 10,800,000 × 10.25% × 91/365

= 275,991.78

One further interest rate calculation is required: the income from the underlying cash portfolio. This amount should include reinvestment or funding income associated with payments or receipts under the swap for the capital performance of the index. For simplicity, this example assumes that the asset portfolio returns three-month LIBOR, while reinvestment of dividend income is ignored. The calculations for the first two resets are then as follows:

Interest income to 31 March = 10,000,000 × 10% × 90/365

= 246,575.34

Interest income to 30 June = (10,000,000 + 800,000) × 10.25% × 91/365

= 275,991.78

Table 8.3 now summarises all of the investor's payments and receipts.

		Net Swap Payments					
	Date	Difference in NPA	Dividends	Swap Interest Payable	Net Swap Receipt	Income	Total Return
Inception of swap	01-Jan						
First reset	31-Mar	800,000.00	140,000.00	(246,575.34)	693,424.66	246,575.34	940,000.00
Second reset	30-Jun	0.00	120,000.00	(275,991.78)	(155,991.78)	275,991.78	120,000.00
Third reset	30-Sep	(400,000.00)	112,000.00	(265,413.70)	(553,413.70)	265,413.70	(288,000.00)
Termination of swap	31-Dec	600,000.00	128,000.00	(262,136.99)	465,863.01	262,136.99	728,000.00
Totals					449,882.19	1,050,117.81	1,500,000.00

Table 8.3 Total Return to the Investor

It should be apparent that in this simple example the total return from the swap strategy is identical to that from straight physical investment in the FT-SE 100 index. Ignoring transactions costs, under the latter there is capital appreciation of £1,000,000 (= 10,000,000 × (2750 − 2500)/2500) and dividend income of £500,000 (= 10,000,000 × 125/2500).

In some practical applications, however, an equity index swap may return a yield in excess of the benchmark. Usually this opportunity arises because of the presence of withholding taxes or a persistent undervaluation of a related futures contract. As an example of the former, the purchase of S&P 500 index futures to overlay a portfolio of short-term US dollar cash instruments enables a UK investor to avoid the US withholding tax of 15% on equity dividends. Comparable benefits should attach to a swap-based strategy, which is little more than a tailored futures position. Given an S&P 500 yield of around 3%, these techniques could add up to 45 basis points to fund performance.

The swap counterparty will use stock index futures to hedge the residual exposure of his book. To the extent that these trade beneath fair value, an arbitrage gain may be obtainable, and passed on (in part) to the index receiver under the swap. The (German) DAX future, in particular, has become most noted for its semi-permanent cheapness to fair value (a fact remarked upon in Chapter 1). It is natural to question why in such circumstances an institutional investor would prefer an equity index swap to direct purchases in the under-priced futures market. There are two possibilities: either the investor may be precluded from using futures contracts (a common restriction in trust deeds) or he may wish to avoid all basis risk attaching to the quarterly roll of futures positions. If the (future's) discount to fair value later becomes a premium, all arbitrage benefits will be eradicated; but under an equity index swap this implicit rolling risk is passed on to the counterparty broker.

Brokers are keen to emphasise also some administrative advantages inherent in the swap structure. These include the absence of a requirement to respond to rights issues or to reclaim taxes on dividends (e.g. for a UK gross fund), and the possibility of exploiting expertise in managing the underlying cash portfolio to outperform a LIBOR benchmark. Swaps also enable a manager to go short of a market for a longer period than is possible securely by using index futures.

The structure is highly flexible. Payments can be made in the investor's base currency, in local currency or hedged back to a particular currency. Frequency of payment dates can be set largely to suit the investor's needs: a pension fund manager, for example, may be keen to receive payments which tie in with the periodic reporting requirements to trustees. Moreover, equity index swaps are not restricted to cash/equity exchanges: some contracts enable long-term asset allocation switches from one equity market to another.

In fairness it should be added that, while there has been considerable excitement in these products shown by the banking and brokerage community, end-user (i.e. fund manager) demand has been fairly sluggish. To an extent this reflects the existing use of index futures by the more sophisticated investors and a lack of comprehension in the less sophisticated. Restrictive mandates and concerns in the wake of the local authorities swaps fiasco have also limited demand. But management in the numerous banks which have rushed to set up structured equities operations clearly believes that there is a significant future in this area.

STUMBLING BLOCKS FOR THE FUND MANAGER

Traditionally, the fund manager's role has been to analyse securities to identify misvaluation at a stock, and market, level. The translation of the manager's conclusions into portfolio management has focused on the physical purchase and sale of the securities in question.

Traded futures and options and, more recently, OTC instruments have brought an entirely new range of tools to the fund manager; and, perhaps unsurprisingly, these have been met with a certain degree of investor suspicion. Nevertheless, their application as both strategic and tactical tools for overlay management and in risk minimisation techniques means that they cannot be ignored.

Clearly, an important step is the improvement of fund managers' understanding of derivatives. This has been enhanced by external training and the promotional efforts of brokers, but ultimately the best understanding comes from using the instruments. This means that the manager needs to be persuaded of the potential benefits of derivatives, but also aware of the liquidity issues and counterparty credit risks. Many investment management companies have internal credit committees, and the process of education must extend beyond the fund manager into these functional areas.

Once the internal issues have been resolved, a manager must approach his clients. Many pension fund trust deeds do not permit the use of off-exchange derivatives. This may not be a conscious decision – such instruments did not exist when many trust deeds were originally drawn up. For trustees to approve an amendment to their deed, they too must understand the instruments, how they can be used and the risks involved, as well as the benefits to the fund. Unfortunately, bad publicity of any sort will concern trustees, even when not related to the strategy being considered.

Finally, there is the problem of valuation and performance measurement. Many internal valuation systems were developed before the dramatic growth in OTC derivatives and consequently are not able to reflect their value appropriately. Although the recent report published by LIFFE in conjunction with William M. Mercer Fraser dealt competently with the measurement of traded futures and options, other instruments such as equity swaps have yet to be addressed.

CONCLUSION

Since the market in OTC derivatives is relatively new, it is difficult to assess the influence that these instruments will have on investment management over the next few years. Initially it is probable that most managers will limit their use mainly to tailored strategies, rather than in everyday applications. For example, in anticipation of a sharp reduction in a scheme's contributing beneficiaries (e.g. as a result of a planned programme of redundancies), the fund manager may consider the purchase of an OTC equity index put option to protect the fund's value, in preference to an immediate sale of all equity assets. The option approach will permit the scheme to benefit from rises in the market before its liabilities become due.

Two concerns may come to the fore. The first is the issue of counterparty credit risk. Intermediaries with a good credit rating should have a clear competitive edge. The second relates to both the trading volumes and open exposures represented by OTC instruments. For the more traditional managers, the events of October 1987 highlighted the dangers of 'the tail wagging the dog', particularly in the USA where it is arguable that sharp falls in the futures markets were the cause of corresponding movements in the underlying stock market. Systemic risks represented by OTC positions are likely to increase, particularly since equity derivatives are cash settled, inherently concealed and potentially of unlimited size.

9: Corporate Applications

Mike Shilling, Record Treasury Management

INTRODUCTION

In the last five years, there has been dramatic growth in the range of derivative instruments available to the corporate treasurer. It is a matter of contention whether this growth has arisen from the demand of the corporate sector, or whether it has been generated by the suppliers (e.g. investment banks) and a new breed of 'rocket scientists'. But in either event, it is clear that the value and application of derivative instruments cannot be properly assessed without first examining the nature of corporate risk.

Unlike the risks encountered by investors or investment managers, corporate exposures are seldom created intentionally for their own sake. They almost always arise as a result of commercial decisions – although they may well influence those decisions – and are consequently secondary and largely unwanted. It is a truism that businessmen will argue in political and economic arenas for interest rate and currency stability; whereas movement in markets is the *raison d'être* of investment managers.

The identification and quantification of market exposures is therefore of considerable importance to most medium-sized and large corporations. Application of derivative instruments to these corporate exposures can then be classified under four headings:

- The systematic management of strategic exposures, under a well-defined hedging policy, in order to control the continuing risks created by the company's long-term commercial decisions.
- The adjustment of the company's strategic financial positions while avoiding the need to change or renegotiate underlying contracts and associated documentation.
- The management of short-term *ad hoc* exposures, which may be unexpected or uncertain, but will nonetheless arise from normal commercial operations.
- The short-term exploitation of market opportunities or 'views' with the intention of enhancing the day-to-day performance of the treasury department.

The category into which a particular operation falls will determine the type of (derivative) instrument and application which is most suitable, as well as the form of analysis that is required in order to assess the expected costs and benefits. Having evaluated the products on offer in terms of their cost and expected benefit, hedging policies can be developed which are both objective and well-structured. Finally, the practical implications of implementation and performance measurement must be carefully considered. These processes of analysis and application are explained in detail in the remainder of this chapter.

IDENTIFICATION OF EXPOSURES

Corporate exposures to fluctuations in interest rates and foreign currencies range from the obvious to the esoteric. If a company borrows money at a fixed rate for five years, the funds will look expensive if interest rates fall in the interim. Consider, however, the case of a UK chocolate manufacturer with a continuing requirement to import cocoa. The international cocoa price is US dollar-denominated, so that it might be imagined that the manufacturer's principal currency risk is to a fall in sterling against the dollar. Yet, insofar as the demand for cocoa is widespread within the major Western economies, its price is effectively dependent on a 'basket' of currencies. Hence it is conceivable that a strong deutschemark might adversely affect the manufacturer's costs even in the event of a stable sterling/dollar rate.

In most organisations, attention tends to focus on 'strategic' exposures: risks which are perceived to be fundamental to the business. These are generally of a long-term nature, and arise consistently and predictably. Typically they relate to long and medium-term funding decisions, importing and exporting issues, and the translation of the results and assets of overseas subsidiaries. Derivative instruments have considerable application in the management of these risks, and it is now commonplace for such instruments to provide the cornerstone of the hedging process.

The following section deals exclusively with currency exposures; the subject of interest rate management is covered later in the chapter.

CURRENCY EXPOSURES

The foreign exchange market is probably the closest to the 'perfect' market described in economics textbooks. It has innumerable participants none of whom dominates, a near instant flow of information and considerable depth and liquidity of transactions. It is therefore a natural breeding ground for derivative instruments: demand arises from practically every major corporation in the world, and supply from a host of inventive financial intermediaries.

Some corporate currency exposures are straightforward. For instance, a UK distributor of Japanese videos is systematically 'short yen/long sterling' (he would like to see the pound strengthen against the yen). However, other exposures are complex, as in the case of the cocoa importer mentioned earlier. Exposures may have a direct impact on the company's reported profitability (typically where turnover or direct costs are affected), or they may affect only one corner of the balance sheet. It is conventional to classify currency exposures in the following way:

- *Transaction Exposures* Imports, exports and other flows where cash actually changes hands and exposures are crystallised on specific dates.
- *Economic Exposures* These arise from transactions which have yet to be confirmed. For this reason they are often considered to be 'future' transaction exposures, and are of a contingent nature.
- *Translation Exposures* These arise from the periodic translation of the value of profits or assets denominated in a foreign currency into the company's base (accounting) currency for financial reporting purposes.
- *Indirect Exposures* These are not easily quantified, and usually arise from competition in a foreign market as a result of movements in a third currency. For example, a UK motor manufacturer exporting to the US will benefit from a strong dollar/weak pound, but if the deutschemark is weak (against sterling) then German manufacturers will gain a competitive advantage in the US market. The company may therefore consider that it has a deutschemark/sterling exposure even though it does not undertake any trade with Germany. Even a company which supplies only its domestic market may encounter this type of risk if it competes with imports from foreign producers.

  There is an overlap between indirect and economic exposures which can be a source of confusion. This is probably because both exposures tend to affect a future price (in local currency) rather than the value of a known transaction at a fixed price.

Prior to the development of sophisticated hedging instruments and techniques, the typical UK company had a very traditional approach to these exposures.

Transaction exposures were hedged as soon as they became certain. The hedge was effected by buying (or selling) the relevant currency forward for the specific date on which it would be required (or received). Transaction risk can be significant, because it has a direct impact on the profitability of the company. An exchange rate can move by as much as ten, or even twenty, per cent in a matter of months and such a movement may be sufficient to turn a profitable transaction into a loss-making one. Once a contract has been formed, it is prudent to fix exogenous variables, such as the exchange rate on subsequent conversion. Clearly this eliminates the potential for extraordinary gains, but a 'worst case' outcome is avoided.

Traditionally, *economic* exposures have only rarely been hedged. This is principally due to their contingent nature, and the associated problem of quantification.

Translation exposures come in two forms: the translation of the value of foreign assets (balance sheet) and the translation of the earnings which those assets generate (profit and loss). Translation risk is usually not perceived to be as dramatic as transaction exposure, since it is not possible for a profit to be turned into a loss, or an asset into a liability, simply by a change in the exchange rate. In addition it is quite possible that no cash will actually be transferred from one country to another (profits being retained in the foreign country for further investment). Where profits are remitted, it is often in the form of dividends paid from subsidiary to parent and these may be treated by the parent in much the same way as other transaction exposures. Translation exposures are often left unhedged, although it is common to arrange funding in the same foreign currency to finance the acquisition of a foreign asset. The argument against hedging is supported by the observation that translation exposures originate from an accounting requirement to report results in a single currency, and do not reflect actual cash flows.

In the past, *indirect* exposures have been largely ignored and it has been very rare for companies to undertake hedging operations in this area. There are several reasons for this, the most important being the difficulty of quantification and the objection to hedging 'non-cash' exposures.

In addition to the above, companies also face one-off risks, frequently of a contingent nature. Familiar examples include: a bid for a construction project which has to be priced in a foreign currency; a possible future acquisition or disposal in another country; and a major item of capital expenditure. These exposures are very difficult to manage with traditional tools (forward contracts) because of their uncertain nature. For example, if the bid for the foreign construction contract is accepted, it may no longer be profitable if the foreign currency has fallen in value during the period between tender and acceptance. On the other hand, to 'lock-in' the exchange rate with a forward contract when the bid is made could be disastrous if the bid fails and the domestic currency has fallen in value. Attempts to remove or reduce the contingent currency risk through commercial means – such as by pricing in domestic currency or introducing an exchange rate variation clause – may make the bid unattractive by comparison with local competition.

Contingent exposures can be managed more efficiently and profitably through the use of derivative instruments, in particular currency options and their offshoots. However, this requires the development of a hedging policy and a consistent approach to the categorisation of exposures.

Policy Formation

It can be argued that a hedging policy need concern itself only with two broad types of risk: those which are recurrent in nature, and those which are one-off.

Recurring exposures include the transaction risks from trading operations; economic exposures; the translation of the profits of, and dividends received from, foreign subsidiaries; balance sheet translation of foreign assets and debt; and indirect exposures. One-off exposures include single, isolated sales or purchases, and bids and tenders (although these may contain recurring elements).

The management of recurring exposure requires a systematic policy with a minimum of discretionary input. The management of a one-off exposure requires commercial judgement applied on an *ad hoc* basis. This does not mean that the traditional categories identified above – transaction, translation, economic and indirect risks – should be ignored, since they provide the components for the specific policy of the company, formed according to perceptions about their relative importance and the attitude of the Board. The primary issue is to determine the possible impact of currency movements on the business as a whole, measured in terms of implications for the balance sheet, profit and loss account and cash flow.

Ideally the rules which define the hedging policy should be such that they can be agreed by the Board and then implemented without the need for continual revisions or new authorisation. Periodic reviews will identify opportunities for refinements, and as new instruments become available they can be assessed within the policy's stated objectives.

If the policy is to be effective over the longer-term, it should possess the following characteristics:

- *It should be testable over time* It will shortly be seen how empirical analysis can provide a foundation for assessing the expected value of derivative instruments. This analysis is particularly important for dynamic hedging techniques and other strategies which are designed to react progressively to market movements. The relationship between the price of an instrument and market conditions must also be understood and taken into account if these historical simulations are to be realistic.

  It is also important that historical analysis does not lead to 'curve-fitting' – adjusting the policy retrospectively in order to obtain the best empirical result. It should be appreciated that, while probably necessary, it is not sufficient for a policy to have performed well in history.
- *It should produce predictable results under different prospective market assumptions* However long the period covered, no historical analysis can encompass every conceivable outcome. On the other hand, a mathematical analysis (such as may be produced by a Monte Carlo simulation) can do

this, but simplifying assumptions will be necessary for even the most sophisticated modelling techniques to be effective. If the company's exposure is well understood, then possible outcomes which have not been experienced in history, but which would nonetheless have a material impact, can be assessed in relation to the proposed policy.

- *It should incorporate predetermined rules* A policy is defined by the rules which it follows. Without rules, there can be no policy and the looser the rules the less useful the policy. These rules will state which instruments can be used under different circumstances, so that a degree of flexibility is maintained. Dealing limits, minimum hedge cover, hedging horizons, stop-loss and profit taking limits should all be formally identified.
- *It should have specific objectives* It is important to decide what the policy is intended to achieve. For example, is this simply to cover the one-sided risk (of loss)?; or also to minimise the potential opportunity cost, and therefore actually add value over time? The primary concern of the risk manager is to protect against the worst case outcome, but the businessman will always have an eye on the potential gains, which under some strategies he may have to sacrifice. Regarding economic exposures, the policy can also be expected to provide greater flexibility in future pricing decisions, especially if option cover is taken out before contracts are finalised.
- *It should not rely on* ad hoc *judgemental inputs* This is a difficult area, since any policy must have the flexibility to accommodate changing circumstances. However, if success is dependent on the subjective judgements of either individuals or a committee, then it becomes impossible to evaluate the effectiveness of the policy itself. Moreover, it is no longer possible to predict performance on a 'what-if' basis. Judgemental input should therefore be limited to certain parameters which need to be adjusted only if the exposures or commercial considerations change.
- *Its performance should be measurable* A benchmark is required in order to assess the effectiveness of the chosen policy. This should be kept as simple as possible and should clearly show the value added by the policy. The majority of derivative instruments settle for cash – that is, at regular intervals during their life, or at maturity, a calculation is made to determine the net position between the two parties and a cash settlement is made. This means that if a hedge is being implemented for the first time with a particular instrument (for example an average rate option is bought to hedge an accounting exposure not previously hedged), then the net cash received or paid at maturity is itself a measure of success. Alternatively if the exposure was previously hedged with forward contracts or debt then this would provide the benchmark. Either of these will of course depend on market movements and if it is felt desirable to remove this effect then a theoretical 50 per cent hedge would provide the best benchmark. The more systematic the policy, the easier performance measurement will be.

There are no hard and fast rules for quantifying the exposure itself. If the Board prefers not to manage accounting exposures, or the more esoteric indirect exposures, then these may not be included at all. It is, however, worth remembering that one potential benefit of using derivatives is that it is possible to overcome many of the cash problems which previously formed the basis for arguments against active exposure management. For example, using forward contracts to hedge the profits of an overseas subsidiary can have serious cash flow implications if the foreign currency rises in value and the profits are not repatriated. However, by using options, the negative cash flow is limited to the premiums paid rather than the gross currency movements.

For most companies, the prime consideration is the profit and loss account, and therefore all of the categories of exposure listed above will be regarded as recurrent (although the translation of assets, as opposed to profits, will often not be regarded as a key concern). As the hedging policy takes shape and its expected impact is assessed, so cash flow and balance sheet considerations (and possibly tax and accounting issues) will be examined.

The exposure to be hedged is generally expressed in the form 'x dollars per annum' or a changing amount per month if there are seasonal variations. For instance, a UK company with income derived in the US may wish to hedge \$60m per year or \$5m per month. It is probably unnecessary to be far more specific than this since the aim of the policy will be to protect against the company's overall risk rather than match specific cash flows or accounting dates.

Clearly the most important function of a currency hedging policy is to protect the company against adverse currency movements over a specific period (the 'horizon' of the hedge). However, its attraction will lie in the extent to which it does this without absorbing or neutralising the gains that the company makes when rates move favourably. It is with this objective in mind that option-based derivative instruments have been developed. But before examining their application in detail, it is appropriate to consider the horizon of the hedge.

Hedging Horizon

For many companies, the most important aspect of the financial results is the change from one year to the next. A smooth increase from year to year in profits, earnings per share and dividends is usually received favourably by analysts, banks and investors. Therefore, it would not be unnatural for a hedging policy to reflect this horizon and provide protection from currency movements from one year-end to the next.

This does not conflict with the probability that transaction exposures are generated over a shorter (or longer) horizon. If a company takes orders three months in advance of payment, it does not have to limit its hedging strategy to a three-month horizon or to a specific contract-by-contract basis. There is no reason not to hedge the expected revenue a year in advance or to any horizon for which the company has plans and reasonable expectations. In other words, it can be argued that transaction and economic exposures should be treated in the same way. In fairness, this conclusion is not uncontroversial. But in practice a systematic hedging policy based on a one-year horizon can be extremely effective in managing an exposure generated by shorter-dated transactions, provided the expectation is for these transactions to be continued in the future. This approach may often provide the opportunity to price future transactions at exchange rates which would otherwise have been unobtainable, offering greater flexibility and competitive advantage to the operating unit concerned.

Interpreting the exposure on an aggregated, recurring basis, rather than as a set of individual transactions, enables the hedging horizon to be determined by practical, rather than conceptual considerations.

Three such considerations are: the impact on the company's reported results; the chosen horizon for business planning and budgeting; and the efficient use of available hedging instruments. For the first two of these, a one-year hedging horizon is eminently appropriate; regarding the last, the choice is not immediately apparent.

There has been much debate about the appropriateness of applying option-based instruments, offering a skewed risk/return payoff, to many currency exposures. The discussion now turns to this issue.

Currency Options

The currency options market is large, very sophisticated and, in most market conditions, reasonably liquid. These attributes make its use ideal for the corporate treasurer. In particular, the OTC market offers a high degree of flexibility, competitive quotes being available for premiums on options of most durations, strike prices and currency pairing. All of the major banks now offer a currency option facility and there is a wide range of pricing software and specialist advice available. Given this, the corporate treasurer's principal residual concern is how best to apply the instruments to the management of the company's currency exposure.

Mathematical models for valuing currency options can be complex, and may be of less worth than imagined to the corporate user in the light of the various assumptions which they require about the market. There is, however, an abundance of historical data available, and an empirical approach (as used in most insurance-type analysis) has much to recommend it.

As a rough guide, the price of an at-the-money currency option tends to increase with the square-root of the time to its maturity. Figure 9.1 illustrates the premium payable for a currency option struck at-the-money forward

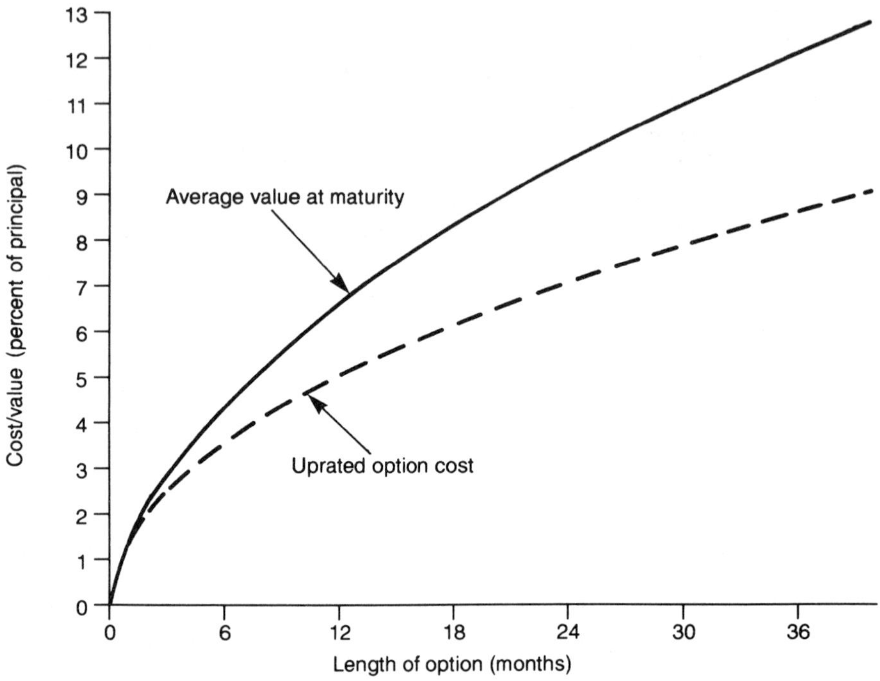

Figure 9.1 Cost and Historical Value of Currency Options

(i.e. the strike price equals the forward rate for the option's maturity). It is based on a one-year premium of 4.5 per cent, which would have been fairly typical for a US dollar/sterling option during the late 1980s and early 1990s; an interest rate is applied to the premium cost – in practice payable in advance – to arrive at the cost at maturity. The shape of this curve is fairly constant although its absolute position will vary with market conditions – high levels of market volatility will move it up (increasing option premiums across the board) and low levels will bring it down. Its position here approximates to the average that has been observed since the currency option market became established in the early 1980s.

An option may be compared loosely to an insurance premium. Pursuing this analogy, it is possible to examine also the 'claims record'. A curve reflecting this record is also contained in Figure 9.1. This curve shows the value at maturity for at-the-money US dollar/sterling options (puts and calls) of various lengths. Figures are derived from data since 1980 and consist simply of gross cash settlement values, disregarding the premium. The most obvious (and interesting) observation to make is that this set of returns is higher than the cost curve: the 'claims record' has exceeded the 'insurance premium' on the basis of all the historical information available over the period. A closer

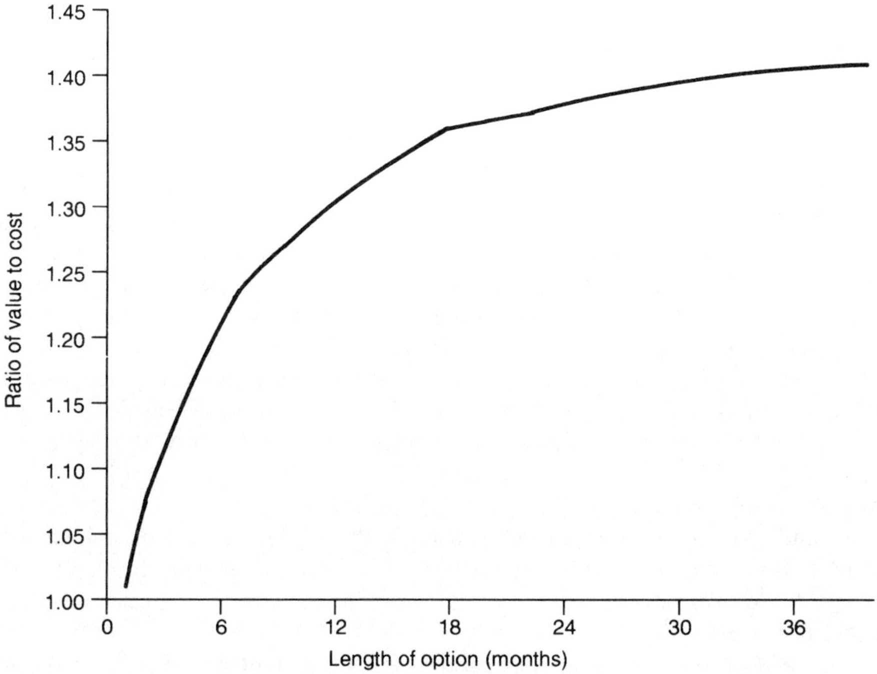

Figure 9.2 Ratio of Historical Value to Cost of Currency Options

examination of the figures reveals that this relationship has actually been fairly consistent throughout time. In particular, during 1985 and 1986 currency options were (historically) very expensive, but as a rule they turned out to have abnormally high value as well.

It is also revealing to examine the ratio between value and cost for different option maturities. Figure 9.2, which is also based purely on empirical data, summarises the ratio between cash settlement value and cost for every US dollar/sterling at-the-money forward option that could have been bought, on a monthly basis, since 1980, and plots the data by the length of maturity. This ratio increases with time but the rate of increase declines.

Consequently there has been very little to be gained, in terms of the balance of value and cost, from buying options whose maturity exceeds eighteen months, and for practical purposes twelve-month options are nearly optimal. One practical consideration is the degree of protection that an option provides once it moves substantially in- or out-of-the-money. Longer-dated options are more likely to move in this way, and there is then a temptation to 'trade' the option in order to move the strike rate closer to the market. Such an adjustment will introduce a new discretionary element to the hedging strategy, and will be executed at the least liquid end of the market, incurring potentially high transaction costs.

In summary, for several reasons a one-year horizon provides the most suitable basis for a systematic hedging policy. This means that for continuing exposures, one-year options can be used regularly, on a rolling basis. An effective approach is simply to buy a one-year, at-the-money forward, option each month for one twelfth of the annual exposure. Figure 9.3 estimates the cash flow that would have occurred each month during the period 1980 to 1991 had this policy been adopted to cover an income exposure of \$5m per month for a sterling-based company. It can be seen clearly that strongly positive cash flows compensate for periods of dollar-weakness, while smaller, negative cash flows are associated with a strengthening dollar (in which periods the company benefits from the exposure itself). These cash flows may be considered in a variety of ways and are often used to calculate an 'average rate achieved' for the year. This leads on to the consideration of an instrument which has been steadily gaining in popularity since the start of the 1990s.

Average Rate Options

The value rate of an average rate option is the average spot rate calculated from a number of exchange rate observations. These observations may be quarterly, monthly, daily or even on an irregular or infrequent basis provided particular dates are defined.

The strike rate is specified separately, and the extent to which the option is in- or out-of-the-money will be discernible by comparing the strike rate

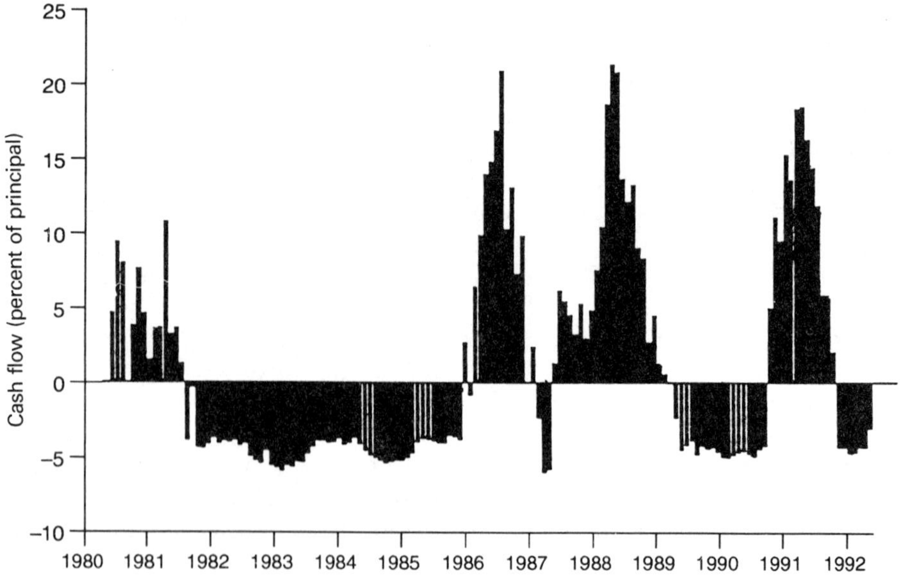

Figure 9.3 Monthly Cash Flow from Systematic Option Hedge

with the average of all the forward rates from the initiation date to the observation date. It is also possible for the strike rate to be the average of several observations, and therefore unknown initially.

Because the value of an average rate option is dependent upon the average performance of an exchange rate over a period, it will usually be a less volatile instrument than a standard currency option. For this reason the premium charged will be considerably lower, a fact which is perceived as a major benefit to the corporate user, especially since most other attempts to reduce option premiums tend to result in increased risk, or loss of upside potential for the buyer. But if the company is genuinely concerned to protect annual average rates, then the average rate option may appear in any event to be the most suitable instrument, and the cost saving merely a bonus.

However, the last observation is not as straightforward as might first appear. The value of an average rate option depends on the average rate for the year, whereas in most circumstances the company's exposure is between average rates from one year to the next. The exposure is therefore only matched precisely if the previous year's average rate is taken as the strike rate. This will result in the purchase of an option which may be substantially in- or out-of-the-money according to the actual spot rate at the start of the year. In-the-money options can command very high premiums and for this reason most users prefer options whose strikes are at or fairly near to the current rate.

The systematic rolling option strategy described earlier also hedges the average rate for the year, but each component of the average rate is hedged from one year to the next with a separate option. This may even be done on a daily basis but it is generally equally effective to use weekly or monthly observations since the correlation between these and daily average rates is in practice very high.

In comparison with the use of average rate options, this method of hedging translation exposure has three major advantages:

- Currency movements within the year can have a direct impact on the value of the strategy, beyond their contribution to the average rate.
- Cash-flows are distributed throughout the year.
- The rate hedged is always at least as 'good' as the previous year's average rate, even though the options are always set at-the-money.

Figure 9.4 compares the two approaches in terms of profits achieved. The graph shows the sterling value of $60m of earnings per annum on an unhedged basis, hedged with a single at-the-money average rate option purchased at the start of each year, and hedged with a rolling portfolio of one-year-at-the-money forward US dollar put options as described above. Historic option premiums have been estimated where necessary using current pricing techniques.

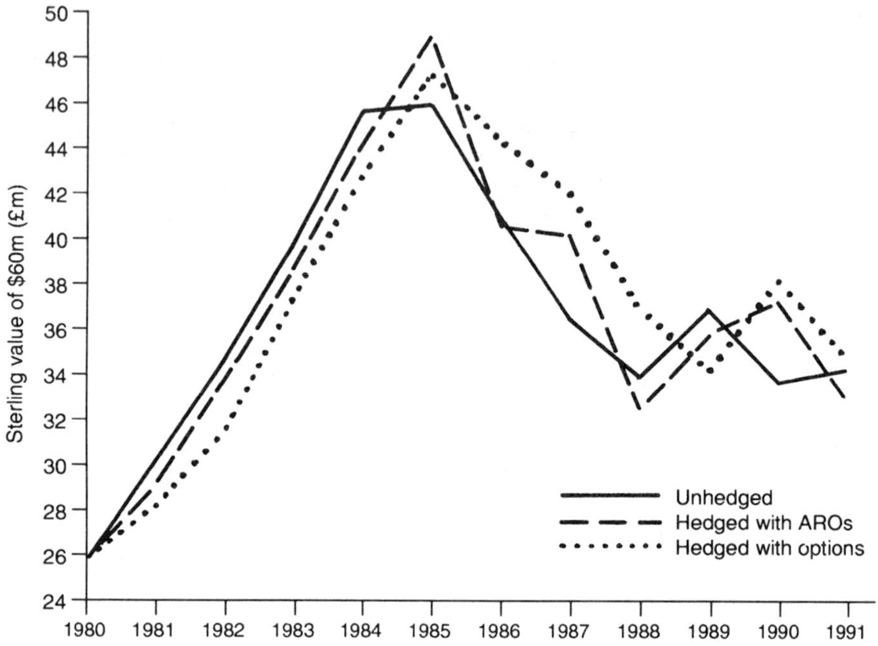

Figure 9.4 Hedging Performance from Straight and Average Rate Options

It is clear that the results of the hedge using average rate options are both inferior and more highly variable than those of the hedge which uses a portfolio of conventional one-year currency options, despite the lower premiums of the average-rate options (on average about 25 per cent less).

In other words, the ratio of historical value to cost has been lower for average rate options (in fact it is very close to parity). Hedge performance is also more variable, because the hedge is based on the year-end rate for the previous year, whereas the profits are calculated on each year's average rate.

These empirical results show that the systematic use of simple currency options would, for the period analysed, have been both more efficient and more profitable – adding 1.25 per cent per annum on average above the use of average rate options.

Other Options

It has been shown that a straightforward systematic hedge of a recurring exposure using one-year at-the-money-forward options is both effective (it provides protection against the downside risk) and profitable (it has added value of about 1.25 per cent of the amount hedged per year) when measured against an unhedged strategy. It can also be shown that the approach has been successful to a similar extent when measured against a strategy of constantly covering the exposure with forward contracts.

Most of the recent developments in 'currency option technology' have attempted to provide the active manager with instruments which might enable him to improve upon these results.

An active manager is one who will trade in and out of positions in an attempt to add value, eschewing the rather disciplined procedure described above. However, risk must also be controlled, implying that 'straight' instruments such as forward and spot foreign exchange contracts can be unsuitable – while efficient for taking positions, use of these instruments means that the actual exposure either remains or is reversed. Ordinary currency options are rather expensive to buy and sell frequently (although, as shown above, not expensive to buy and hold), particularly when they are significantly in- or out-of-the-money. These considerations have led to the design of more complex option-based derivatives intended to reduce the up-front premium payable.

In general an instrument which has a lower premium than a standard option either has a lower return or involves extra risk for the buyer. As a consequence, it is very important to recognise and quantify these effects before using an 'exotic' instrument. For example, an average rate option has a lower expected return to compensate for its lower premium. A complete list of the various hybrid products in this rapidly evolving market would include barrier, basket, compound, look-back and participating options. These have been described elsewhere in this book (see, for instance, Chapter 4), and no further details are given in this chapter.

Summary

In summary, currency options provide an effective means of managing recurrent exposures if used systematically, and are also useful for 'one-off' and contingent exposures. Systematic use of currency options can be replicated with dynamic hedging techniques which offer the possibility of substantial cost savings. However, costs are more variable and somewhat unpredictable.

For corporate users, an empirical approach to the valuation of derivative instruments is extremely useful and can be most enlightening. It imposes the discipline of realism, while the analysis itself generates an intuitive understanding of the way in which markets behave in practice.

INTEREST RATE MANAGEMENT

Turning now to interest rate exposures, it is apparent that there is a third dimension to consider. This is the element of *time*, which becomes a complicating factor because an interest rate instrument usually does not have a cash impact on only one occasion (as with a forward contract to buy or sell a currency on a particular day, for instance). An interest rate transaction takes the form of a commitment to borrow or to lend at a given rate from a certain date, for a certain period of time.

Despite this complication, many of the principles of currency risk management can also be applied to interest rate exposures.

Funding Decisions

Apart from the relatively straightforward consideration of price (relative to the market), the key issues which affect a funding decision are: flexibility; counterparty risk; re-financing risk; timing; and the application of funds.

Different companies will ascribe varying degrees of importance to these issues:

- *Flexibility* will be a major issue for those companies whose future funding requirements are uncertain.
- *Counterparty risk* is important for those whose sheer size dictates that they must deal with a wide range of counterparties (or have a dangerously disproportionate exposure to just a few).
- *Re-financing possibilities* are particularly important when there is a mismatch between the maturity of a source of funds and the term of its application.
- *Timing* refers to the possible delay between the raising of funds and their use (for example raising debt in anticipation of an acquisition).
- *Application* of funds involves matching the type of funding to the returns which are expected from it. Typically a long-term fixed asset would be financed with long-term fixed rate debt, whereas requirements for short-term liquidity may be more suited to a floating-rate facility, or the use of bills and commercial paper.

Once a particular funding strategy has been put in place, an exposure to future changes in interest rates is generated. For instance, a decision to borrow at a fixed rate may not have disastrous consequences if this rate is commercially viable, but there is an opportunity cost if rates then fall. Conversely, borrowing at floating rates would be costly if rates subsequently rise, but profitable if they fall.

The instruments available to manage interest rate risk usually offer one of three outcomes:

- The funding will vary with market rates;
- The present market structure of interest rates will be 'locked-in' for a period; or

- A choice between the above extremes will be made at some future date with the benefit of hindsight.

The use of derivatives enables changes to be made to the type of funding originally chosen. The initial funding strategy need not reflect a view of future rates since a company can borrow in a structure and market which is most efficient, and then change the profile of the debt by an overlay derivative position. Derivative instruments therefore perform two tasks: they enable a company to tap its cheapest or most secure source of funds regardless of the view of future rate movements; and they permit an alteration to an interest rate view to be made without the necessity of expensive and time-consuming re-structuring and documentation.

In general, a company will have a mixture of fixed and floating rate debt, and a variety of short-term timing mismatches to manage. The proportion of fixed to floating debt should be a matter for strategic policy, having regard to a number of issues:

- *The effect of interest rates on the business itself* For instance, if rising interest rates reduce demand for the company's products, then it may be desirable to keep the proportion of floating rate debt low (to avoid a 'double hit').
- *The level of underlying debt in the business* If this is fairly constant it often makes sense to borrow long-term, since long-dated swaps are not particularly liquid instruments. Anticipated levels of future debt clearly need to be considered carefully.
- *Specific views on future interest rate levels and/or the future shape of the yield curve* Predicting the future is always a hazardous affair and it must always be remembered that adopting a particular stance on the basis of a forecast does not reduce risk, however confident the forecaster may be. But it would be unnatural for the manager to disregard his views when making a decision about the mixture of fixed and floating debt.

The ideal management of the debt portfolio would enable the company to follow interest rates down (with a high proportion of floating rate exposure) whilst maintaining protection against sudden or unexpected rises. As rates 'bottom out', the portfolio would shift in favour of fixed rates, locking in the cheaper money as rates rose again. If the underlying debt portfolio remains unchanged, such hedging activities require the extensive use of derivatives.

Hedging Instruments

The most straightforward instruments are probably forward rate agreements (FRAs) and interest rate swaps. These trade in liquid markets, so that transactions can be executed at a reasonably low cost and positions can be unwound as circumstances change. Under an FRA, a borrowing or lending rate is agreed with an intermediary in advance for a future period; a (simple) interest rate swap is an exchange of fixed payments for floating payments (or vice versa). Both instruments involve a clear contractual obligation. This is satisfactory if it is known that a change in interest rate profile is required for business considerations, or if certain financial targets become guaranteed, or perhaps even if there is considerable confidence in the view of the future that is being taken. But in the absence of these certitudes, it may be necessary to look elsewhere for instruments which limit the opportunity cost of a wrong decision. These are the option-based instruments: caps and floors and their associated spin-offs, the most common being collars and swaptions.

These latter instruments are often complex and difficult for the corporate user to analyse accurately. Particular importance should be ascribed to assessment of a 'fair' price.

Figure 9.5 illustrates the advantage that a cap may have over a swap, although it excludes the premium that has to be paid for the cap. The graph shows the final values of three-year caps on three-month LIBOR and three-year swaps (fixed/floating) maturing on each quarter; these having been taken out on a quarterly basis from 1980. The values are expressed as percentages, enhanced for the impact of interest over the period. Therefore each bar represents the percentage gain or loss compared with the floating rate cost over the previous three years. As might be expected, the swap return is broadly

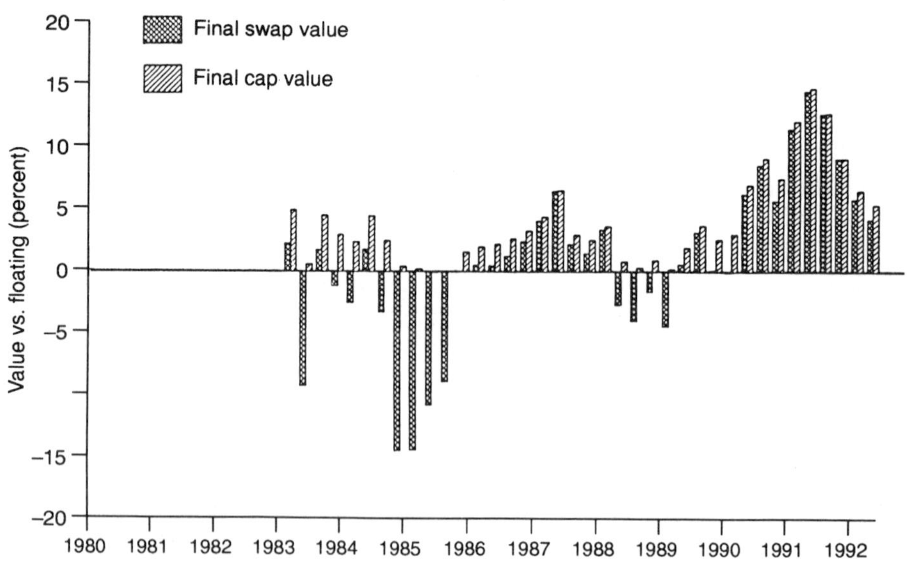

Figure 9.5 Comparison of Value between Three-year Swaps and Caps

neutral: an average gain of 0.9 per cent, reflecting the predominantly negative-sloping yield curve, which has not been a good predictor of future rates; the range of values is −14.4 per cent to +14.7 per cent. The cap return is obviously positive (a cap cannot have a negative value by this measure) and had an average of over 4 per cent in the period (with a range of 0 per cent to 14.9 per cent). A swap has no expected value, but a cap does, and a premium for the latter will therefore be required. There are two ways to perceive this premium:

(i) From the seller's point of view, it needs to be at least as great as the expected cost of covering the resultant exposure by hedging directly in the underlying market. This leads to complicated mathematical pricing models which make various assumptions about the market, the details of which lie outside the scope of this chapter. Valuation models can be bought off the peg from various software houses and provide a useful check for the corporate customer of the reasonableness of the market price.
(ii) From the buyer's point of view, it must not be so high as to exceed his perception of unacceptable downside risk. This in turn depends both on his aversion to risk and his expectation of volatility within the market.

Aversion to risk is a subjective judgement which will vary considerably from person to person and company to company, and will be affected by the nature of the underlying business. Volatility, on the other hand, can be looked at rather more objectively. However, because this chapter is concerned with the practical considerations for corporate users, a rigorous mathematical approach to the subject of volatility is probably inappropriate.

Figure 9.6 shows three-month sterling LIBOR for the period 1980 to 1991 and provides a good overview of the potential movements in interest rates to which a company can be exposed. It is also easy to see how different policies would have performed over the period. In particular a policy of maintaining 100 per cent of borrowings at this floating rate would have produced an average cost of funds of 12.25 per cent over the period. For many companies this may even represent a valid benchmark against which to measure the funding and hedging strategies.

By contrast, borrowing at fixed rates for five years, on a rolling basis over this period, would have locked in an average rate of 11.5 per cent. However, timing is critical when making this type of comparison since the results are dependent on one observation from the yield curve at the time of initiation. The figure of 11.5 per cent takes an average of each available five-year period, starting at three-month intervals, from 1980 to the beginning of 1987.

The 'ideal' line in Figure 9.6 shows the effect of swapping optimally from fixed to floating rates and back, each decision being taken every three months. The average rate falls to just above 10 per cent.

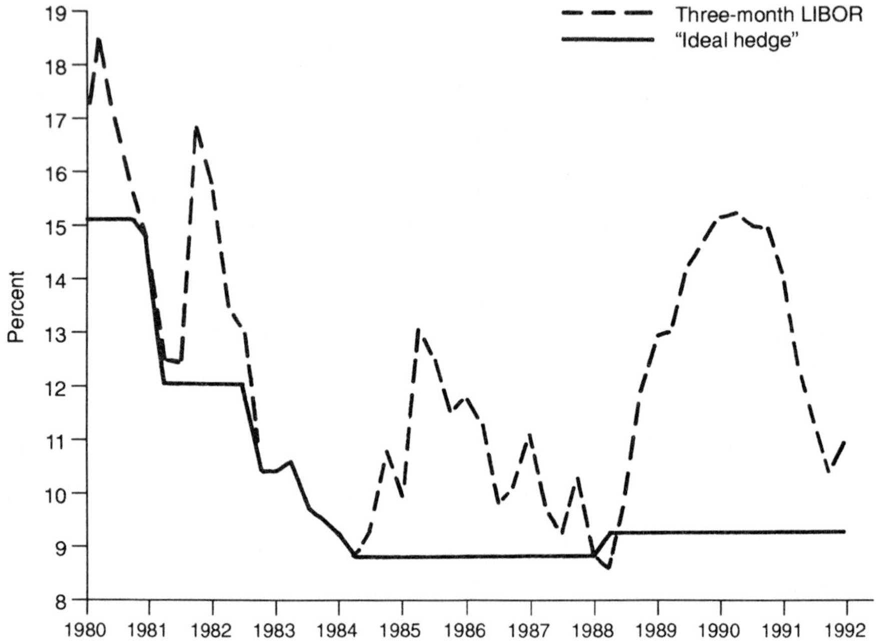

Figure 9.6 Three-month Sterling LIBOR and the 'Ideal Hedge'

Clearly this would have been an extraordinary performance, since it requires that every decision was taken with perfect foresight. However, the improvement in overall rates shows the margin that is available for spending on option-based derivatives to enable similar decisions to be made, but with the benefit of hindsight rather than through forecasting the future.

For example, caps on three-month LIBOR could be purchased on a systematic basis. The period of the cap would then become a key variable. The longer the cap, the more advantage is gained from low interest rates when they occur; but fewer 'readings' are taken from the market and brief periods of low rates are more likely to be missed.

Swaps, FRAs and the funding decisions themselves reflect the current structure of rates (the yield curve) and therefore do not require pricing in the way that an option-based instrument does. A financial option has been compared to an insurance policy, but a distinguishing feature is the two-way nature of the risk: if the insurance is not required the exposure itself will probably be profitable. It was seen earlier how empirical analysis can be applied to the currency options markets, enabling a systematic approach to be taken to the application of derivative instruments. With interest rate exposures the element of time makes the analysis rather more complex. In addition, the exposure itself tends to be less predictable and more vulnerable to change in the future.

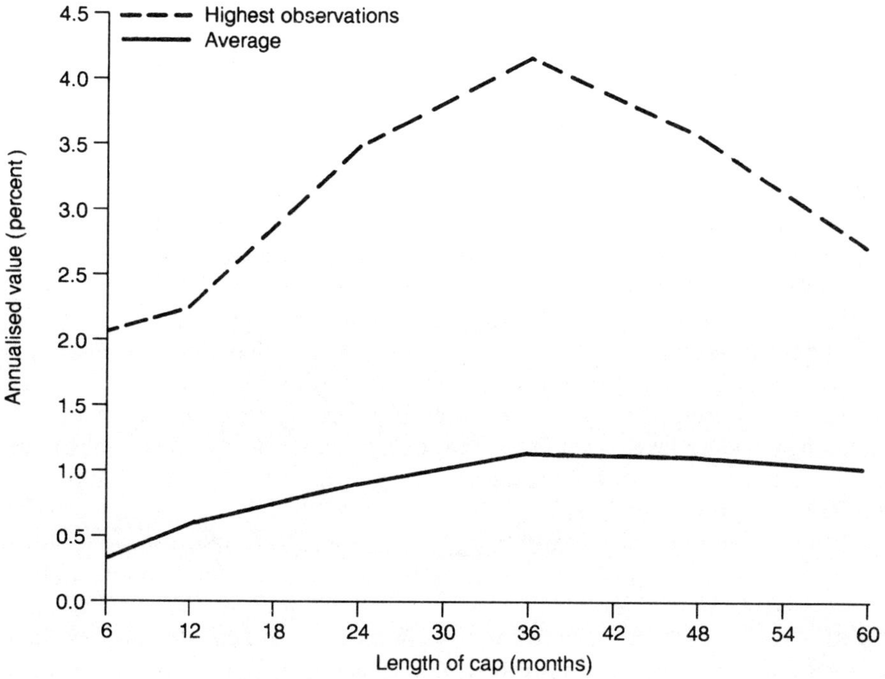

Figure 9.7 Historical Value of Caps on Three-month LIBOR

However, as a starting point it is useful to look at the annualised values of caps of various durations. Figure 9.7 shows the average and maximum values (the minimum is always zero) for 6, 12, 24, 36, 48 and 60 month caps on three-month LIBOR. For these caps to be at-the-money, the strike rate is taken to be the same as the initial fixed rate for the term of the cap (since a cap is in effect a strip of options on FRAs).

Although somewhat crude, this analysis suggests that the most valuable caps have a maturity of three to four years, and that historically a premium of under 1 per cent per year would have represented good value. The degree of risk protection is highlighted by the range of outcomes (given by the maximum observations), the most extreme of which is a three-year cap which produced a saving of over 4 per cent per year against floating rates (third quarter 1988 to second quarter 1991).

If four-year caps had been used on a rolling basis over the period shown in Figure 9.6, the results would be quite similar to the 'ideal' hedge – an average rate of about 10.5 per cent (excluding premiums). Therefore, if the premiums had averaged under 1.75 per cent per annum (12.25–10.5), the cap strategy would have represented good value (compared with an unhedged benchmark floating rate exposure). However, the timing of the start of such a hedge is critical if the cap is only rolled every four years. To start one year later, for instance, would have produced an average rate of 10.8 per cent, compared with an average floating rate of 11.8 per cent, leaving only 1 per cent per year for the premium.

In order to identify what can be expected from a systematic approach, a rolling portfolio of caps needs to be constructed comparable to the currency option approach discussed earlier. If a three-year cap is taken out each quarter for one twelfth of the underlying debt, the path-dependency of the results will be reduced, and the average rate becomes 11.3 per cent over the period, again leaving about 1 per cent per year for the premium in order to break even.

In contrast to currency options, it seems unlikely that the systematic use of caps can be expected to add value over time, although premiums vary considerably and are often much lower than historical average values. But, as a hedge against the large fluctuations that can occur, such a policy does have the advantages, on a continuing basis, of both 'smoothing' overall results and minimising opportunity cost.

In summary, an empirical approach to the valuation of interest rate derivatives provides not merely a rigorous analysis, but an enhanced understanding of the nature of the products.

Indeed, it could be argued that an emphasis on practicality rather than theory tends to produce a more disciplined and systematic attitude towards hedging risk, since the need for subjective decisions is minimized.

Under a systematic hedging policy, derivative instruments can produce 'smooth' results, giving protection against both unacceptable downside risk and the opportunity costs that are introduced by traditional hedging techniques. For exposures with a contingent element, option-based derivatives may have particular attractions. The use of derivatives, as an alternative to subjective hedging, has other benefits in terms of policy formation, performance measurement and control procedures, each of which is examined briefly below.

MANAGEMENT AND CONTROLS

For a hedging policy to work in practice, it is necessary to ensure that its operation can be integrated within the corporate treasury structure.

A number of questions need to be addressed at the outset:

- What resources will be required?
- How will progress be monitored?
- How will performance be measured?
- Over what time-scale will judgements be made?

The resources available to the treasury function vary enormously from company to company, and if a policy is implemented which over-stretches these resources, then the chance that an expensive mistake will be made is increased. It is essential that the company is able to implement the policy, monitor its progress and measure its performance, as well as to administer and check individual transactions.

Beyond financial considerations, derivative products may have unforeseen risks which involve management. For example, a policy may preclude the writing of uncovered options but permit the purchase of a cylinder or participating forward. These instruments incorporate an option-writing element which for most applications will be covered by the underlying exposure (the buyer 'gives back' some of the upside potential in order to reduce the premium). However, if the exposure subsequently changes so that the upside is in any event reduced, this transaction can create an uncovered liability which may not be immediately obvious.

Over the years there have been a number of well-publicised examples of disastrous events within treasury departments. Poor control procedures, when compounded with the gearing implicit in derivative positions, can quicky cause escalating losses.

It is important, therefore, to review authorisation, reporting and checking procedures regularly, as well as the policy goals and strategy underpinning the trading and hedging activities. In addition, treasury staff must fully understand their role and the scope of the treasury department's objectives and strategies. This will involve continuing training programmes to maintain awareness of the latest developments in instruments and techniques. When implementing the company's policy, the individuals concerned should have a strong intuitive understanding both of the instruments being used and the objectives which are sought.

Even with sophisticated systems in place, mistakes can occur, and a thorough system of reports and checks should be in place to catch both the simple error, and something more deliberate. In all checking routines the concept of independence is critical: all checks need to be undertaken by someone who is not involved in the dealing process but who understands the underlying strategy.

If an error is made, then the quicker it is discovered and rectified the less it will cost. For derivative instruments, a small market movement can have a dramatic financial impact. An efficient checking and control system will minimise this risk and reduce both the opportunity and the desire for an individual to attempt to conceal information.

MONITORING AND PERFORMANCE MEASUREMENT

If a company is to have a well-defined hedging policy for its key exposures, then it is important that these exposures are reported within a specially designed system. It must be possible to monitor, and mark-to-market, all the company's outstanding positions and transactions to date, segregated within the individual hedging schemes. This will enable the company to separate areas of responsibility and check that the policy is being implemented according to plan.

This system should also enable performance to be measured, a requirement which must relate to the specific objectives that have been set. As has been seen, for a systematic policy this can be straightforward, since comparison with an unhedged position is measured simply by the net cash generated. Measurement against other benchmarks requires the additional simulation, or monitoring in the case of an index, of the benchmark itself.

Performance can be monitored on a continuous basis and should comprise two elements:

- *The implementation of the policy* This relates to the performance of the individuals responsible for running the hedging policy. Are transactions being executed as planned? Are prices, costs, and spreads evolving as anticipated?
- *The success of the policy* Given the market movements that have taken place, has the policy performed as expected? Does it match up to the historical simulations and projections analysed in its development? This type of performance analysis requires an agreed timescale over which measurement is made. This timescale must be realistic with reference to the hedging objectives, since measuring performance over too short a period runs the risk of reactive changes being made prematurely, undermining the principle of a systematic approach and potentially frustrating the longer-term benefits which are being sought.

CONCLUSION

Derivative instruments are powerful, yet flexible, tools to manage the exposures which naturally arise within a substantial business. However, their price characteristics and applications can be complicated, and when used irresponsibly, or in ignorance, they may increase risk in unexpected ways. An intuitive understanding of their properties and a clear statement of intended objectives are of great importance. This chapter has suggested that this understanding, as well as a realistic assessment of policy, is most easily gained through a practical and empirical approach, exploiting the great amount of historical data and past experience that is now available.

10: Risk Management

Chris Currington, Arthur Andersen & Co.

INTRODUCTION

In the last ten years there has been substantial volatility in the foreign exchange and interest rate markets. Not surprisingly, a need has arisen for methods to manage the commercial risks arising from this volatility, and financial institutions have met this demand in part by developing and promoting new financial instruments.

These instruments – often called derivatives – may have been designed to cater for corporate exposures, but financial institutions have used them extensively in the management of their own risks. The 'off-balance sheet' nature of derivatives appealed to financial institutions because they permitted efficient capital utilisation. Hitherto, traditional risk management techniques required increasing credit risk (i.e. 'grossing up' the balance sheet) to manage price risk, and worsened capital adequacy constraints. In addition, as capital utilisation was often measured in terms of a proportion of 'notional' principal, income from these instruments was attractive in that it could be earned without substantially increasing required capital.

The growth in the traded volumes of derivative instruments has been such that their application has gone beyond that of tailoring (corporate) customer requirements and enabling financial risk management. In particular, financial institutions now actively trade these instruments with a view to profit, in the process building and maintaining market liquidity. Market and instrument innovations have enabled the needs of investors and borrowers in different spheres to be linked or arbitraged, and have contributed to the growth of particular markets (an obvious example being the Eurobond and swap markets). Financial institutions, in their familiar role as intermediaries, have encouraged this trend.

As the number and type of instruments available to investors and borrowers have increased significantly, there has been substantial competition amongst intermediaries to serve the needs of these investors and borrowers. As in all markets, increased competition has reduced returns, and has made the risk-return balance more dangerous for the unwary institution.

Yet risk has not only been influenced by competition, but also by the nature of the financial instruments themselves. The new instruments are to some degree an extension of traditional risk management tools; for example, the interest rate swap is analogous to the earlier parallel loan and the cross-currency swap comparable with a set of forward foreign exchange contracts. However, some attributes differ fundamentally. Instruments such as futures, forward rate agreements, options, caps and swaps, which have the ability to transform asset, liability and income streams, are complex for legal, commercial and control reasons. As a result, the risk characteristics of OTC derivatives can be significantly greater than those typical of the more traditional markets.

An example is the asymmetrical risk and return of option-based derivatives. In option-based applications, there is limited risk to the purchaser, but, in theory, unlimited exposure to the writer. For instance, in exchange for a fixed premium payable in advance, the writer of an interest rate cap agrees to compensate the buyer if interest rates exceed a set level (i.e. the cap rate). Once interest rates exceed the cap rate, the writer may possibly have to keep compensating the buyer over the term of the interest rate cap agreement. A prudent approach might be to hedge this exposure as interest rates approached the cap rate. This might be achieved by increasing a short position in an interest rate vehicle (for example, a bond position). However, this 'hedge' can quickly turn into an exposure if interest rates suddenly fall. If the short bond position has not been removed in advance of a drop in rates, then the 'hedge' will become a loss-making position with little offset, as there is less exposure under the cap which then requires protection. After its opening sale there is no additional income to be earned from the cap to offset any hedge losses.

The complexity of derivatives requires that a different approach must be adopted to identifying and managing risks. This chapter discusses these risks and then sets out a risk control framework for their management.

RISKS

The key risks relating to OTC derivatives can be summarised as follows:

- Market price;
- Credit;
- Market liquidity;
- Settlement; and
- Transaction and technology.

This section of the chapter explains the nature of the above risks and their relevance for derivatives.

Market Price Risk

Market price risk reflects the probability that the value of a financial instrument will decline as a result of changes in exchange or interest rates. The concept of price risk is well understood by financial institutions. In addition to market volatility, price risk may arise from factors such as (interest rate) term structure, market liquidity and portfolio concentration.

An additional consideration is basis risk: the possibility that the bases on which the prices of two different instruments change do not conform. For example, the impact of a 1 per cent change in LIBOR on the two 'legs' of a futures – FRA hedge may not be identical: futures are exchange-traded and subject to (initial and variation) margin payments, while FRAs are OTC instruments which pay off at expiry; and the FRA may have underlying dates not coincident with those of the futures contract. For these reasons the initial interest rate differential or margin on a futures–FRA hedge will not remain constant over time, and accordingly must be reviewed periodically.

Understanding and evaluating price risk is fundamental to the control of derivative positions. Almost invariably this requires 'marking-to-market' every instrument within a portfolio. Again, the 'mark-to-market' concept is relatively well understood, but the valuation techniques can be complex, especially for OTC options and other 'exotic' instruments.

The valuation of exchange-traded options is usually straightforward in that there is a readily available market quotation. However, for OTC options there is no single objective valuation, and alternative procedures must be adopted. There are essentially two possibilities:

- The use of an option-pricing formula. Perhaps the earliest, and certainly the most well-known, formula is attributable to Black and Scholes (1973), and is derived from the concept that opportunity for risk-free arbitrage between the option and the underlying commodity should not exist. Analytic extensions to the Black–Scholes model have been developed in the course of the last two decades but many of the core principles have remained unchanged. Providing that the holder or writer of an option is acquainted with the model used, and the assumptions made, it is possible to recalculate the value of an option at any time. However, in most circumstances the choice of market volatility (when not observable) will be more contentious than the choice of pricing model.
- The request of a current valuation from the counterparty. This would be an appropriate course for a trader who is holding an option, but is unaware of the pricing formula used by the writer.

In addition to the above, issues of credit and liquidity (discussed in detail below) will also influence the pricing of OTC derivatives. For example, a prudent valuation of a cross-currency swap will depend, *inter alia*, on the:

- Credit-worthiness of the counterparty;
- Liquidity of the currency;
- Term of the swap; and
- Structure and complexity of the swap (i.e. termination clauses, form of settlement, option arrangements, etc).

Of particular importance for the evaluation and control of price risk is the performance of a sensitivity or 'what-if' analysis. This technique evaluates how an exposure changes under certain assumptions regarding changes in market prices; it uses information about the volatility of the market and is a fundamental tool in controlling option-based derivatives such as caps, floors and swaptions. Employing a sensitivity analysis in combination with 'stop-loss' limits is a powerful control technique, and also provides management with a quantitative assessment of potential risk.

The application of sensitivity analysis is not limited to financial institutions, and it is now commonly seen in the corporate sector. It can be argued that it is a primary tool to be used by those large companies whose treasury functions take sizeable trading and hedging decisions. In recent years, examples in the corporate sector of substantial option trading losses would support this view.

Credit Risk

Credit risk is the risk that a counterparty to a financial transaction will fail to perform according to the terms and conditions of the contract, thus causing the other party to suffer a financial loss.

When considering this risk as it applies to derivative instruments, some participants have taken the view that the exposure is intrinsically in the nature of a market-price risk. In particular, the exposure in a derivative position is not for the full (notional) amount of the contract, but for the cost to replace the contract if the counterparty fails. This is often referred to as replacement risk. However, an undue emphasis on a portfolio's instantaneous replacement cost is not an adequate approach to the identification of risk. The first step should be the assessment of the creditworthiness of the counterparty, an evaluation which should include the impact of market-price risk on the counterparty's ability to honour the contract.

Moreover, the wider use of derivative instruments has resulted in a broader range of participants whose creditworthiness is less well known. This necessitates a strict application of the 'know your customer' concept.

Credit risk is often perceived in terms of bankruptcy or insolvency, but it may also arise from:

- Failure to understand custody and ownership issues;

- Concentration in particular instruments and positions, and to particular counterparties;
- Technical and legal issues which delay or render enforcement of contracts.

Failure to understand particular custody and ownership issues is often associated with an unfamiliarity with new instruments. This is a particular form of transaction risk which is discussed below.

An international financial services company must deal with exposures created by the different divisions within it, and the wide variety of internationally traded derivative products. Concentrations of exposure can be difficult to monitor because of the the problems in establishing compatible systems to measure aggregate exposures. In addition, measurement usually needs to occur on a 'real-time' basis. Concentration risk is as, if not more, important as the institution's exposure to a particular instrument, and both will need to be monitored closely. Unfortunately, most financial institutions currently do not have the systems to adequately measure, monitor and control world-wide exposures to any particular counterparty.

Assessing credit risk for derivatives can be difficult. Options, for example, are generally felt to carry minimal credit risk. However, in some cases, premium payment dates are flexible, so that some risk may remain. Moreover, credit risk will attach to purchased options (i.e. where the customer is the writer) and to instruments subject to margin payments.

Credit risk on swaps is more complex. Most institutions will ascribe some long-term exposure to each swap that they write: often a simple percentage is applied, while occasionally sophisticated computer analyses are performed. In any event, the exposure will always be substantially smaller than the notional principal amount involved, indicative figures being 10 per cent for an interest rate swap, and 25 per cent or more for a cross-currency swap.

It is a matter for debate whether credit risk increases or decreases over the life of the swap. Some institutions maintain that, while the term risk is greater at the beginning of a swap since it stretches out into the future, both credit and interest risk are less at that point, because of the greater certainty that the counterparty will not default (assuming an adequate initial credit investigation) and the small chance that rates will yet have moved substantially.

A contrary view is that the period of least risk occurs as the swap approaches its termination date, since replacement cost is related to a swap's remaining duration even if rates have moved dramatically or the creditworthiness of the counterparty declined. However, the delivery risk in a cross-currency swap serves as a counterpoint to this view.

A key feature of derivative instruments is that they enable participants to hedge, transfer or transform market-price risk while assuming a credit risk which is substantially smaller than the 'notional principal' underlying the transaction. In addition, most settlements of derivatives contracts are for 'differences' (i.e. the net gain or loss is paid or received), thus enabling the transfer of market-price risk to occur in a credit, capital and transaction cost efficient manner.

Yet, as a consequence the credit risk associated with derivative instruments must be interpreted very differently from that underlying the more traditional instruments. As suggested earlier, a critical factor is the relationship with market-price movements. An interesting illustration is provided by the débâcle of the interest rate swaps undertaken by UK local authorities in the latter part of the 1980s.

Typically, the local authorities entered into interest rate swaps and other derivative contracts (swaptions) under which they received fixed rate and made floating rate payments. The volumes contracted were significant, and followed from the local authorities' assumption of stable or falling UK interest rates. Local authorities were perceived by financial intermediaries as representing a very fine credit risk, but this analysis was limited to a judgement of the risk of default and did not extend to the wider legal considerations. The majority of the banks who acted as counterparties in these transactions offset their positions with other banks.

UK interest rates then rose significantly, so that the local authorities began to pay out substantially under the swap transactions. In 1990, the UK courts ruled that the actions of the local authorities constituted 'trading', and accordingly exceeded their legal powers. As such, the contracts were ruled to be *ultra vires* (i.e. null and void). The counterparty banks subsequently incurred significant losses in closing out their 'hedges' with other parties. These events had an effect on other local authority markets, as financial institutions became wary of the legal ramifications. There was also an impact on the liquidity in the swaps market, as banks 'retreated' to counterparties for whom the assessment of credit risk was more straightforward.

It is noteworthy that the legal judgement would probably not have taken place had interest rates moved in the local authorities' favour.

This example is powerful evidence of the relationship between credit and market-price risk. The latter must in aggregate sum to zero, while credit risk is related to the volume of contracts outstanding. In essence, derivative financial instruments are two-sided with respect to market-price risk (i.e. the gain on a long position should be equal to the loss on the equivalent short position) but are one-sided in terms of credit risk. Admittedly the market-price risk on certain (option-based) derivative instruments is skewed (i.e. the risk to the buyer of an option is limited, but to the writer, in theory, unlimited). However, there is still risk to both parties; and this is not the case with credit risk as, once the premium is paid, the writer has no credit exposure to the buyer, but the buyer has an exposure to the writer.

Clearly, market expansion should not increase market-price risk as it will remain a 'zero-sum game', but this expansion does increase overall credit risk in the market as the price risk is spread among a wider number of participants. In summary, while price risk and individual counterparty creditworthiness does not change, overall credit risk in the market increases.

This conclusion, in conjunction with the impact of increased competition on margins, reinforces the need for strong credit assessment.

Market Liquidity

Market liquidity risk measures the possibility that a financial instrument cannot be sold quickly at a price which equates to its fair market value.

Liquidity will change over time and rapid changes will occur in highly volatile conditions. Often, liquidity will initially increase with volatility, as participants enter the market to hedge or to attempt to make short-term profits. However, if volatility continues for a sustained period, liquidity is likely to decrease. Some participants will have established neutral positions, and, in a climate of general uncertainty, other participants may take the view that the risks posed by higher volatility outweigh the potential returns.

Derivative products are still relatively new and it is arguable that the liquidity of certain markets has yet to be fully tested. Some exchange-based markets (typically in interest rate products) are undoubtedly very deep, and it is a familiar claim that these markets can occasionally dominate the straight 'cash' markets (the 'tail wagging the dog'). The liquidity in the more tailored form of OTC transaction can disappear quickly.

Liquidity risk does not arise solely when opening or closing a position: perceptions about liquidity can also influence market prices. For instance, a major deterioration in the credit-worthiness of a significant participant may affect market liquidity as the participant becomes a 'forced seller' of a particular instrument or position.

There are numerous illustrations of markets whose liquidity suddenly evaporates, and relatively few pertain uniquely to the derivatives markets. Examples include the stock market crash of 1987; the downturn in the UK property market at the end of the 1980s; the US 'junk bond' market following the collapse of the US investment bank Drexel Burnham Lambert; and the disappearance of the perpetual FRN market in the late 1980s.

Settlement Risk

Settlement or delivery risk is the risk that on a particular settlement or contract maturity date, a financial institution pays out funds before it is certain that it will receive the appropriate payment from its counterparty.

Examples specific to derivative instruments include the payment of variation margin to an exchange and the corresponding margin from the customer not being received on time; and a counterparty not making swap differential payments on time. Settlement risk can also involve failure to deliver 'stock' (e.g. a commodity-based OTC option where physical delivery is expected) to the correct location on the correct day.

In general, settlement risk is temporary and is of an operational nature. Likewise, while settlement risk can give rise to market-price risk (adverse price movements occurring before closing out a position arising from the settlement errors), losses may be recoverable from the counterparty. However, this will not be the case for 'own account' settlement errors, or where the settlement problem results from the counterparty defaulting on the transaction. In the latter case, settlement risk becomes credit risk.

The large number of corporate failures in the recent recession has highlighted the relationship between settlement and credit risk. One of the first signs of difficulty has frequently been a failure in the settlement of transactions. It is important to remember that settlement risk may be the first indication of default, rather than a simple issue of 'timing'.

Errors can arise from backlogs in transaction volume, poor settlement controls and inadequate knowledge of contract terms and settlement procedures. As mentioned previously, the majority of derivative products are settled for 'differences'. The transactions can be complex (i.e. based on net present values), involving different currencies and countries, and, in the case of futures and traded options, daily cash settlements.

The rapid increase in derivatives market volumes has occasioned many players to make significant investments in communications, payment and transaction processing systems. These have been largely technology-led with the objective of improving control and reducing transaction costs. This trend is likely to continue, especially given greater competition and the impact that settlement inefficiencies and errors can have on margins.

Transaction and Technology Risk

Transaction risk is the risk that a financial loss is incurred because a transaction is not executed properly. Some types of settlement errors are a subset of transaction risk. However, the nature of the risks relating to each type of transaction will depend on the quality of controls, systems and personnel (front and back office); transaction volumes; and the complexity of the particular instrument.

The majority of transaction errors will result from inexperienced personnel dealing with a high volume of complex instruments in the absence of proper systems and controls. Errors are more likely to occur in a growth stage, and managing transaction risk is really a question of proper management planning and supervision, and ensuring existing personnel and systems can cope with present and anticipated volumes.

In addition to the above, managing transaction risk requires risk management and processing systems which monitor transactions and exposures from transaction to value to settlement date.

Clearly, a substantial level of technological support is required to achieve this in a cost effective manner. Technology is also required to analyse market risk on a day-to-day basis and to perform the required sensitivity analysis. For certain instruments, such as options, existing risk management techniques cannot be effective without substantial technological support.

The fundamental role of technology in successful derivative operations cannot be over-emphasised. Technology is required to trade and to manage risk successfully, and to enable a player to be a low-cost transactor. At a more basic level, the failure of a computer system could lead to significant losses being incurred following a change in market prices.

In addition to market price, credit, liquidity, settlement and transaction and technology risks, there are a number of other factors to consider. These include the risks of inadequate capitalisation; regulatory considerations; lack of appropriate senior management review and supervision; and 'over-stretching' for profitability and market share. The last two points are often the fundamental cause of loss. In addition to managing the individual risks, senior management must have a clear understanding of the overall objectives and risk profiles acceptable to the firm and its shareholders and regulators. This is especially true in a highly competitive market-place characterised by 'tight' margins which can be quickly erased through poor risk management.

Having described the main categories of risk, this chapter now turns to a discussion of the ideal framework for risk control.

RISK CONTROL FRAMEWORK

The current market environment requires a greater awareness by management of the restrictions on activity, the requirements of the regulators and the need to balance profitability and risk exposure. It is the management of risk that determines profitability.

The pursuit of profit through increased risk taking in difficult and volatile markets has inevitably led to significant losses being taken by major participants. These losses have not only weakened financial positions but, just as importantly, have damaged reputations. Recognising that unforeseen losses of this magnitude are unacceptable, many participants are now questioning whether their risk control is adequate. The following sections describe how financial and other organisations can structure themselves to optimise control over trading risks and set out some of the steps to success.

What is Risk Control?

Risk control is the process of:

- Identification, approval and communication of the risks appropriate to a firm's objectives, capital base and abilities;
- Operating a control and reporting system which ensures that actual and potential risk correspond to those approved by senior management; and
- Assessing and communicating actual and potential risks quickly and accurately to the appropriate people in the organisation.

Risk control is in essence an exercise in communication. Its overall objective is to ensure that trading activities are planned, conducted, evaluated and reported in accordance with criteria set down by senior management, who are in turn accountable to the shareholders.

Risk cannot be controlled effectively if trading or operational personnel are insufficiently aware of senior management's risk tolerance or if lines of communication are blurred or too lengthy. No risk control system, however rigorous, can give absolute assurance that all operating risks and control weaknesses will be identified quickly enough. Indeed, an over-zealous approach to risk control will inhibit the ability to capitalise on opportunities which present themselves in volatile and changing markets.

Effective risk control requires an environment in which risks are managed within approved levels, allowing sufficient flexibility for traders to make the decisions with a view to profit. The most important features of such an environment are:

- The existence and communication of clear *corporate objectives* and strategies, for both the firm as a whole and for individual business units;
- An appropriate level of *management control*, achieved by promoting an acceptable attitude to risk taking and relevant constraints within which each trading or operating unit can work;
- The existence of *dealing controls* such that day-to-day strategies and short-term positions are assumed, controlled and reported in accordance with agreed limits;
- A system of *operational controls* which ensures that trades are processed efficiently and that trading results are communicated promptly and effectively to both management and traders;
- Planned and integrated *technology* which ensures that individual trades and operating performance are captured, analysed and reported accurately and promptly to all levels;

- The establishment of an *organisational structure* which ensures that lines of communication can respond quickly to the 'real-time' demands of a trading environment.

Each of these features is now considered in turn.

Corporate Objectives

Many financial entities lack a clear statement of corporate objectives and, as a result, lack a focus for their activities. A clear summary of objectives provides a cohesive force for an organisation which operates in a diverse range of products, activities and locations.

In order to develop such a statement, most firms will need to undertake a strategic review of their activities. This review should include:

- A critical assessment of the strengths and weaknesses of each area of operation, including the quality of management;
- A detailed assessment of the existing and potential profitability of each activity, identifying the reasons, commercial or otherwise, for participation;
- A detailed analysis of the existing or potential synergy between the organisation's different divisions and lines of business;
- An analysis of the desirable mix of activities in, and between, the firm's core and peripheral activities.

This process should not place undue empahsis on how the markets will behave in the future, but focus instead on operational plans to achieve objectives. One result should be an agreement concerning the acceptable degree of risk. The review should also incorporate practical guidelines to assist trading and operational management in evaluating business opportunities and developing operational plans. These guidelines will indicate the safeguards required before any risk is accepted and should identify the manner in which risks are to be evaluated, as well as the nature and extent of controls to be maintained over underlying exposures.

A coherent set of corporate objectives and strategies, focusing on operational considerations, should provide clear and concise risk parameters and a structure which enables trading and risk consideration to be communicated and acted on quickly and decisively.

Management Control

Management control consists primarily of the establishment of formal plans and strategies for each major business area. This process incorporates the risk guidelines identified in the determination of corporate objectives, and should be the responsibility of each business or operational manager. The plans and strategies should be compiled using a 'bottom-up' approach, but requires senior management coordination, review and approval. This will ensure consistency with overall group objectives and strategies, and will reduce conflicts and inconsistencies between operating units.

Trading and operational management should establish detailed risk limits which reflect the agreed plan. These limits should cover all material exposures and risks inherent in the operation's business activities, and the basis on which the authorised limits are delegated to various management levels must be identified. Management should then define the nature and periodicity of reports they will require in order to manage the performance. Trading is a dynamic activity, and it will therefore be necessary to change and update plans and limits; this should be acceptable with appropriate management approval.

It is essential that the individuals responsible for operational control are involved in the planning process as failure to include them may result in:

- Poorly designed and implemented procedures, and systems and technology which do not adequately process and control transactions; and
- Failure to accumulate, analyse and report meaningful information promptly for management and traders.

In many respects, management control is the most important feature of risk control since, if effective, it should identify and highlight potential losses before they arise, even when dealing and operational controls are failing to operate adequately.

Dealing and Operational Control

Dealing controls ensure that the transactions that are executed are consistent with business objectives and fall within predefined risk limits. Examples of these controls include authorisation of transactions, approving counterparties and recording transactions; in addition to reporting short-term strategies and risk positions. Operational controls include accurate and timely processing, settlement and recording of transactions; and the assessment and reporting of performance and actual and potential risks.

The content and timing of management and dealing reports is of the utmost significance. Risk information must be both accurate and timely, and must be sufficiently tailored so that management and traders can take appropriate decisions and, if necessary, remedial action. Reports to dealers must either correspond to their perceptions of risk and performance, or must be reconciled by explaining significant differences.

Preferably, management reports should be limited to the main areas of existing or potential risk, positions and performance, and include details of all positions which are in excess of approved limits. Excessive reporting is not an effective management tool and may result in the underlying information being ignored or analysed incorrectly.

The basic exposure and limit structure should include:

- Counterparty limits;
- Position verification and profitability;
- Position limits;
- Liquidity, interest and maturity analysis;
- Stop loss and sensitivity analysis.

COUNTERPARTY LIMITS Counterparty limits cover credit and concentration risks and should be analysed by overall exposure, broken down by sector and product. Limits should be 'weighted' for 'off-balance sheet' products and should incorporate related party relationships.

Global exposures must be monitored, and if possible the comparison of exposures with limits should be made on a real-time basis. Failing this, the analysis should be performed daily.

POSITION VERIFICATION AND PROFITABILITY Positions should be recorded on a 'trade-date' basis and must be agreed on a daily basis between the 'front' and 'back' offices. Agreement of positions is fundamental to risk management as unreconciled positions cause an institution not to know what risks are being managed.

Likewise, profitability should be measured and agreed on a daily basis and complex position structures should be reviewed critically to ensure hedge criteria and basis risk are being properly assessed. Ideally a 'mark-to-market' valuation approach – as amended to reflect liquidity and credit risk – should be used.

All aspects of the above should be subject to review by a control function independent of the trading operation.

POSITION LIMITS Position limits are designed to control market price and liquidity risks. Limits should exist for each product, currency and maturity profile and for the overall risk.

Overnight and daylight limits should be in place, and followed real-time at the dealing level and daily at the management level.

LIQUIDITY, INTEREST AND MATURITY ANALYSIS This type of analysis is an additional control on market-price and liquidity risk. It should cover source and concentration of deposits and funding; and 'gap' and duration risks.

Analysis should cover product, currency and maturity profiles and the overall risk. As in the case of position limits, the level and frequency of reporting will vary.

STOP LOSS AND SENSITIVITY ANALYSIS This form of analysis covers all financial risks and is especially critical for 'asymmetrical' products such as options. The sensitivity analysis should be performed by product and currency, and on an overall basis; the level and frequency of reporting will vary by user.

In addition to the above, it is critically important that the calibre of operational personnel is sufficient to assess the risks associated with derivative products. The risk characteristics of today's products are complex and exposure can often change radically and in an unforeseen manner. Failure to detect and assess these complexities, particularly in new product areas, can obviously lead to loss. As an overall control, it is also essential that the individuals responsible for controlling dealing activities should have no responsibility for operational controls and the reporting process.

Technology

Most sophisticated trading environments are wholly dependent on computer technology and systems for transaction processing and reporting. The complexity of new instruments results in substantial technical support being required in order to assess, evaluate and control risk. Unfortunately, many organisations fail to plan their technology needs properly and hence fail to achieve the right degree of integration of their systems. This leads to systems which are decentralised, badly coordinated and often ineffective.

The importance of technology, especially in difficult market conditions, cannot be over-emphasised. Systems which are poorly planned, or which fail to function as required, pose significant business and control risks. In addition to the peril of systems failure, poorly planned and integrated systems can inhibit the risk control process in the following ways:

- The lack of a well defined systems strategy will result in piecemeal developments or short-term solutions without regard for long-term business plans or information requirements;
- Risk control information will be lacking in quality and frequency and will not meet the needs of all users. Accordingly, the information will fail to communicate the appropriate messages;
- Appropriate technology and systems will not be available or sufficiently flexible to meet the demands of changing markets and products. Operational personnel will therefore be unable to assess and report changes in risk quickly enough;
- Incompatible systems will emerge and the lack of integration will hinder the ability to accumulate, assess and report risk consistently between the trading desks, operational units and locations. Senior management will therefore be unable to take a consolidated or global view of risk;
- Operational personnel will waste substantial amounts of time attempting to extract meaningful information from the data provided by the systems. The completeness and quality of information will suffer as a result.

A well considered systems plan which is focused on operational considerations, in combination with an appropriate level of integration, will provide technology which is responsive to traders' and management's information needs.

Organisational Structure

An essential element in effective risk control is an appropriate organisational structure. Many such structures reflect historical development as well as the traditional independence of operating units, and, as a result, do not necessarily reflect a firm's growth, nor the change in its mix of activities. If so, management information and control systems intended to support decision making and the monitoring of risk will not have kept pace with the change in environment.

As risk control hinges on communication, a disjointed organisational structure can severely reduce the effectiveness of any risk control process. In particular, too much emphasis on the individual units or profit centres within a structure can pose the following problems:

- Objectives and risk issues pertaining to the entire group may not be communicated or understood, or may simply be ignored;
- Problems may be identified, but communication to senior management outside the relevant unit may either not occur or be too slow;
- Operational and financial control functions may lose their independence if they are tied too closely to particular trading operations;
- The effectiveness of the central financial control function may be reduced. This can result in lack of uniform standards over accounting policies, the quality of processing, internal control and management information;
- The deterioration of financial and operational controls may go unnoticed until too late.

Any organisational structure which restricts communication between levels of management will impair the effectiveness of risk control.

11: Accounting and Regulation

Robert Rountree, J.P. Morgan

INTRODUCTION AND SCOPE

The growth in the derivative markets and increasing variety of financial instruments available has led to much discussion and research by professional accountancy bodies worldwide. Several projects are underway, all of which are aiming to set consistent standards for the accounting treatment and disclosure of the various instruments. The magnitude of the task cannot, however, be underestimated and the pace of development in the financial markets is continually widening the brief of the accountancy bodies and regulators.

As will be seen, the user of derivative products now has a number of authoritative sources for accounting guidance. These range from discussion papers to draft accounting standards, but there is still no definite framework in place. As has been the case since the derivative markets started, users of financial statements must still recognise that the accounting treatment and disclosure of both new and not so new financial instruments can vary enormously from company to company. The guidance currently available is open to differing interpretations, and those charged with the task of accounting for the products may still find it necessary to resort to the four fundamental accounting concepts of going concern, accruals, consistency and prudence when formulating a specific method of accounting treatment.

These fundamental accounting concepts, on which there is at least general worldwide consensus, are summarised below:

Going concern:	The profit and loss account and balance sheet are prepared on the assumption that the enterprise will continue in existence for the foreseeable future;
Accruals:	Revenue and costs are matched so far as the relationship can be established, and dealt with in the profit and loss account of the period to which they relate;
Consistency:	There is consistency of accounting treatment of like items within each accounting period and from one period to the next;
Prudence:	Revenue and profits are not anticipated. Provision is made for all known liabilities whether the amount is known as a certainty or is a best estimate given available information.

The problem for users is that these concepts are necessarily very general and can be accommodated relatively easily into many different proposed accounting policies for derivative products. In the final analysis it is the purpose of the transaction that must be ascertained, and based on this the accounting treatment should aim to follow the economic substance while adhering to the fundamental accounting concepts detailed above.

It is generally agreed that there are two broad purposes for any derivative transaction, either 'trading' or 'hedging'.

'Trading' involves taking an open risk position with a view to profiting from perceived future market movements or earning bid/offer spread. It covers both market making, traditionally the domain of financial institutions, and speculation, open to financial institutions, corporates or indeed individuals.

'Hedging' involves taking a position to cover or reduce risk on an open or anticipated risk position. Any profit on such a transaction would normally be offset by an equivalent loss on the transaction being hedged. Hedging transactions provide liquidity to the market and are entered into both by corporates and by financial institutions.

In following economic substance and fundamental accounting concepts, intuitively one would expect some form of mark-to-market accounting to be appropriate for a trading transaction, and an accounting treatment consistent with that adopted for the hedged item (either accrual accounting or mark-to-market) to be appropriate for a hedging transaction.

Accrual accounting involves spreading income recognition over the period to which the transaction relates. For example, income on a swap transaction would be recorded in the same way as if it were a loan and matching deposit, by accruing interest on each leg on a straight line basis over the relevant accounting period at the rates in force on the swap during that period.

Mark-to-market accounting involves recognising changes in market value, both positive and negative, as and when they occur. Hence for the same swap, recognition would be made in the income statement of movements in market interest rates during the relevant accounting period. If the swap was for five years receiving fixed and paying LIBOR, and five-year rates declined significantly, the swap's value, or cost to unwind, would increase accordingly and under mark-to-market accounting that increase would be recorded currently in income.

Clearly, the practicalities of mark-to-market and accrual accounting are different for the various derivative products available. The majority of instruments discussed in this book will be covered in this chapter, both from an accounting and a regulatory perspective. After a section on current accounting standards and developments, there is a detailed accounting policy section, dividing the products into two broad categories as follows:

Swap Products:	Interest rate and currency swaps, commodity and equity swaps;
Option Products:	Bond, commodity, equity and swap options, interest rate caps and floors.

A final section on the regulatory environment provides background information on how supervisory bodies and regulators exercise control over the use of these instruments.

CURRENT ACCOUNTING STANDARDS AND DEVELOPMENTS

United Kingdom

Background

In November 1987 a Review Committee, under the chairmanship of Sir Ron Dearing, was established to review and make recommendations on the setting of accounting standards in the United Kingdom. The Committee presented its report in September 1988 and on 26 February 1990 the UK Government announced the setting up of a new independent Financial Reporting Council to guide a newly established standard-setting body, the Accounting Standards Board (ASB).

Under the Companies Acts 1985 and 1989, companies are required by law to adhere to certain 'accounting standards' when preparing their accounts. The ASB adopted all standards already set by the previous standard-setting body, the Accounting Standards Committee (ASC), and by doing so effectively ratified the accounting standards to be followed in accordance with the Companies Acts. There are currently 27 such accounting standards, being 25 Statements of Standard Accounting Practice (SSAPs) issued by the ASC and 2 Financial Reporting Standards (FRS) issued by the ASB. All future statements issued will be known as FRSs.

To allow sufficient time for consultation prior to issuance, an FRS will generally be preceded by a Discussion Paper on the relevant topic, and then a Financial Reporting Exposure Draft (FRED), both of which are widely circulated for comment. This follows the ASC's previous policy of issuing an Exposure Draft (ED) prior to issuance of a full SSAP.

In addition to FRSs and FREDs issued by the ASB, certain bodies recognised by the ASB are empowered, under an agreed code of practice, to produce their own Statements of Recommended Practice (SORPs). These are aimed to provide guidance on the application of accounting standards, which are by nature general, to specific industries, for example the financial services sector. The ASB's involvement in the issuance is restricted to a 'negative assurance statement' required to be appended to each SORP. This statement indicates that the ASB sees nothing fundamentally at odds between the SORP and existing or contemplated accounting standards.

Existing Authoritative Guidance
The standards listed below are those currently available which have relevance to the accounting and disclosure requirements for derivative products:

SSAP 18	(ASC: August 1980): Accounting for Contingencies
SSAP 20	(ASC: April 1983): Foreign Currency Translation
SORP	(British Bankers' Association (BBA) and Irish Bankers' Federation: November 1991): Off-Balance Sheet Instruments and other Commitments and Contingent Liabilities

In addition to the above, the Institute of Chartered Accountants in England and Wales (ICAEW) issues Technical Releases (TRs) on topical accounting issues, of which the following are of interest in relation to derivative products:

TR 677	(ICAEW: November 1987): Accounting for Complex Capital Issues
TR 773	(ICAEW: December 1989): The Use of Discounting in Financial Statements

It should be noted that, with the exception of the SORP issued by the BBA, none of the statements or papers above specifically addresses the practical accounting treatment of individual derivative products. Taken together, however, they do provide a background from which users can develop appropriate accounting policies. A summary of the relevant guidance in each is provided below:

SSAP 18: ACCOUNTING FOR CONTINGENCIES This very general accounting standard addresses all types of contingency, this being defined as 'a condition which exists at the balance sheet date where the outcome will be confirmed only on the occurrence or non-occurrence of one or more uncertain future events'. The standard requires contingent losses (i.e. losses dependent on a contingency) that are considered probable to be accrued in the financial statements. Conversely, contingent gains which are probable should not be accrued, but merely disclosed as a note to the financial statements. Various disclosure requirements are also set out in the standard. The tenor of the standard is towards prudence in accounting for issues with an uncertain future outcome.

SSAP 20: FOREIGN CURRENCY TRANSLATION This standard covers all aspects of foreign currency translation to the extent that they are relevant in the preparation of financial statements. Its relevance for derivative instruments is clearly restricted to those products which generate foreign exchange exposure (e.g. foreign exchange forwards and options, and currency exchanges). The standard lays down requirements for individual companies and for consolidated financial statements. It requires monetary assets and liabilities denominated in foreign currency to be translated at the closing rate, or, where appropriate, rates fixed under terms of the transactions. Exchange gains and losses arising are to be reported currently in the profit and loss account. Distinction in accounting treatment is made dependent on the objective of the transaction. Its interest for derivative products is that it allows for current recognition of unrealised gains, not distinguishing between the treatment of gains and losses, and it sets different requirements dependent on the economic substance of the transaction.

SORP: OFF-BALANCE SHEET INSTRUMENTS This is the most relevant UK authoritative document on accounting policy currently available to users of derivative products. Issued by the BBA, it is addressed primarily to the banking community, but it nevertheless contains individual guidelines that can be tailored for use by corporates.

The document sets out guidelines for valuation, income recognition, balance sheet recognition and off-balance-sheet disclosure of most types of derivative product. Distinction is made between trading and hedging activities and the general principles of mark-to-market and accrual accounting are made clear. The appendices contain specific paragraphs on forward foreign exchange, futures, options, swaps, FRAs, caps/floors, and so on, as well as other off-balance-sheet commitments such as underwriting commitments and documentary letters of credit.

TR 677: ACCOUNTING FOR COMPLEX CAPITAL ISSUES The purpose of this paper, issued in November 1987, was to 'assist preparers and auditors to improve the communication of financial information in those situations where complex instruments are used'. The principles set out are general in nature, aimed at promoting consistency of treatment among users. They encourage paying regard to the commercial effect of transactions as a whole, and disclosing sufficient information on a given complex transaction for readers to appreciate its impact. Seven examples of these complex instruments are set out in its appendix, including deep discount bonds, variable redemption and convertible bonds, share options issued and interest rate swaps. However, the examples are given for illustrative purposes only, and specific guidance is limited.

TR 773: THE USE OF DISCOUNTING IN FINANCIAL STATEMENTS This paper, issued in December 1989, addresses one of the fundamental principles underlying mark-to-market accounting, namely the impact of the time value of money. To the extent that any derivative product can be analysed as a series of estimated future cash flows, then those cash flows can be discounted back at current rates to give an approximation of the current value of the product. As time and rates change, so does the value of the product.

The paper concedes that, although the technique of discounting future cash flows is not used extensively in the preparation of financial statements, it is accepted in specialised cases. The paper's aim was primarily to provide discussion and encourage wider disclosure by companies using discounting techniques. It addresses the issues of reflecting economic substance rather than legal form, and recognition of unrealised gains as well as losses, that are fundamental to the principles underlying the BBA's SORP issued in November 1991.

Current and Future Developments

The issue of accounting for new financial instruments is not currently on the agenda of the ASB. An ASB project on debt/equity resulted in a Discussion Paper entitled 'Accounting for Capital Instruments' in December 1991, but this paper restricts itself to issues of the distinction between debt and equity and disclosure thereof. Hence 'Capital Instruments' covered broadly those items in the Capital and Reserves section of the balance sheet and other long-term finance such as subordinated debt and convertible bonds.

In a bulletin on its future work programme issued in September 1991, the ASB concedes that while the project on debt/equity was underway, 'there remain many other aspects of financial instruments that it has not sought to address'. The bulletin continues to note that projects underway internationally (see below) 'will eventually lead the Board to undertake a project on new financial instruments' but admits that so far 'there has been surprisingly little pressure on either the ASB or its predecessor to launch a major project on this subject'.

In the meantime, the Institute of Chartered Accountants in England and Wales commissioned a research project on accounting for new financial instruments in 1988. This project focused primarily on funding instruments, i.e. capital instruments of the type covered in the ASB paper, and has not to date resulted in the issuance of any guidance on derivative products.

It is clear that, given the harmonisation of accounting standards worldwide, the extensive work on accounting for new financial instruments being carried out internationally, notably by the Financial Accounting Standards Board in the USA and by the UK-based International Accounting Standards Committee, is being monitored carefully in the UK. As and when internationally acceptable standards are agreed and issued, it appears likely that it will not be a large step towards their formal incorporation into accepted UK accounting standards.

International

Background

The proliferation of new financial products and the need for standardised accounting guidelines is clearly not restricted to the UK. Work has now been under way for some years, notably in the USA, Canada and France, on putting together acceptable accounting standards to cover the variety of new instruments.

It is intended in this section to focus primarily on developments in the USA, where accounting standards for new financial instruments are undoubtedly the furthest advanced among OECD countries. The Financial Accounting Standards Board (FASB), broadly the equivalent of the ASB in the United Kingdom, launched a major project into financial instruments in 1986 known as the Financial Instruments Project, and this has already resulted in two new Statements of Financial Accounting Standards (SFAS).

In addition to the FASB in the United States, the International Accounting Standards Committee (IASC) is also working on issuance of accounting standards for financial instruments. The IASC, set up in 1973, aims to involve experts in accounting and financial reporting throughout the world as well as intergovernmental organisations such as the European Commission and the OECD, in the preparation of International Accounting Standards (IASs). To date there are 31 IASs which mirror in many ways the 26 SSAPs and FRSs issued in the UK, and a number of Exposure Drafts awaiting further discussion and consultation prior to ratification as new accounting standards. The most relevant of these to derivative products is Exposure Draft E40 on Financial Instruments issued in September 1991.

Existing Authoritative Guidance

Listed below are currently available standards and papers issued by the FASB and IASC which have relevance in respect of the accounting and disclosure requirements for derivative products:

SFAS 5	(FASB: March 1975): Accounting for Contingencies
SFAS 52	(FASB: December 1981): Foreign Currency Translation
SFAS 80	(FASB: August 1984): Accounting for Futures Contracts
SFAS 105	(FASB: March 1990): Disclosure of Information about Financial Instruments
SFAS 107	(FASB: December 1991): Disclosures about Fair Value of Financial Instruments
IAS 10	(IASC: January 1980): Contingencies and Events Occurring after the Balance Sheet Date
IAS 21	(IASC: January 1985): Accounting for the Effects of Changes in Foreign Exchange Rates

E40 (IASC: September 1991): Financial Instruments (Exposure Draft)

For the purposes of this chapter there will be no further examination of SFAS 5 and 52 and IAS 10 and 21 as their relevance to derivative products is broadly similar to that of SSAPs 18 and 20 on contingencies and foreign currency translation discussed above. The other four papers cover new ground, however, and as such the salient points from each are summarised below.

SFAS 80: ACCOUNTING FOR FUTURES CONTRACTS This standard, issued in 1984, sets out specific requirements for the accounting for futures contracts, distinguishing between the two fundamental types of activity, namely trading and hedging. Until the issue of SFAS 105 in 1990, SFAS 80 was the only specific authoritative guidance available for users of new financial products. Although applicable only to exchange traded futures contracts (excluding foreign exchange futures), in the absence of any other paper on financial instruments its principles can be and have been extended to many other derivative products, including options, caps and floors.

The standard requires that changes in value of open futures contracts be recognised as a gain or loss in the period of the change unless the contract qualifies as a hedge of certain exposures to price standard interest rate risk. Detailed criteria based on correlation of price sensitivity are given for ascertaining whether a given contract qualifies for hedge accounting treatment, which effectively permits the deferral of gains and losses. Hence the fundamental concepts of trading and hedging are critical in the determination of accounting treatment. The standard allows for hedges of both existing and anticipated transactions.

SFAS 105: DISCLOSURE OF INFORMATION ABOUT FINANCIAL INSTRUMENTS WITH OFF-BALANCE SHEET RISK AND FINANCIAL INSTRUMENTS WITH CONCENTRATION OF CREDIT RISK This was the first accounting standard to be issued as a direct result of work carried out by the FASB Financial Instruments Project. The FASB recognised at the outset the wide extent of its objective to develop broad standards for the accounting and disclosure of financial instruments in general. For this reason, it restricted initial work to improving disclosure requirements deemed to be inadequate on a widespread scale, before attempting to set accounting standards for the recognition and measurement of profit.

SFAS 105 gives specific guidance as to information disclosures for the majority of new financial instruments, mentioning specifically futures, swaps, options and caps/floors. Its requirements apply equally to corporates and financial institutions, although it is recognised that the usage of the instruments may vary significantly. The information disclosures required are aimed to provide the user of the financial statements with an appropriate degree of information to appraise the risk exposures being run by the financial institution/

corporate in question. To this effect they include details of the nature and terms of the financial instruments, including the face or notional amount, an explanation of the market/credit risk being run and details of the accounting policy adopted. Further information is also required on concentrations of credit risk. The appendices show interesting illustrations of disclosures that could be included in a company's financial statements. These illustrations include suggested accounting policies for individual instruments that give a flavour of the probable direction that will be taken by future SFASs to be issued on the subject of income recognition and measurement.

SFAS 107: DISCLOSURES ABOUT FAIR VALUE OF FINANCIAL INSTRUMENTS This standard, the second and most recent to be issued as a result of the Financial Instruments Project, completed the 'disclosure' segment of the project. Whereas SFAS 105 concentrated on disclosure of the existence and nature of financial instruments held, SFAS 107 addresses the issue of 'fair values'. Fair value is a broad term which is essentially equivalent to market value, but covers instruments for which there is no active 'market'. The standard stops short of addressing when and whether 'fair value' accounting is appropriate, but sets out in its appendices methods by which fair value can be calculated for the purposes of disclosure. Hence, in a similar way to SFAS 105 the ground is prepared for the 'Recognition and Measurement' phase of the Financial Instruments Project.

Fair Value is defined as 'the amount at which the instrument could be exchanged in a current transaction between willing parties, other than in a forced or liquidation sale'. The standard recognises that when quoted prices may not be available, i.e. for over the counter products, fair values may be estimated which are based on accepted models (e.g. Black–Scholes for options) or methods (e.g. discounted cash flow techniques). Having defined the concept, the standard goes on to require all entities to disclose in their financial statements the fair value of financial instruments both recognised and not recognised in the financial position.

IASC E40: FINANCIAL INSTRUMENTS This comprehensive exposure draft covers both the disclosure of and the accounting for all types of financial instrument. The disclosure requirements are similar to those set out in SFASs 105 and 107, and it may be assumed that the proposed accounting requirements will be broadly in line with the proposals to be issued in the next phase of the FASB Financial Instruments Project. For today's user of financial instruments, this exposure draft and the BBA SORP on Off-Balance Sheet Instruments offer the most detailed authoritative guidance on appropriate accounting policy.

In a similar way to the BBA SORP, the exposure draft recognises that differing accounting treatments are appropriate based on the economic substance of a given transaction. E40 identifies three main categories of activity, namely investing/financing, hedging and operating, each of which is to be afforded different accounting treatment.

Investing/financing activities are for a long-term acquisition/assumption of assets/liabilities, and the exposure draft recommends a form of lower of cost and market (LOCOM) accounting for instruments falling into this category. However, E40 recognises that this category will not generally be appropriate for derivative financial instruments. Hence for derivative products the decision as to accounting treatment will depend on whether the activity can be classified as 'hedging' or 'operating'.

This IASC definition of 'operating' activity is equivalent to what the BBA calls 'trading', and instruments falling into this category are to be afforded fair value or mark-to-market accounting treatment. For its definition of hedging activity, the IASC draws on SFAS 80 (Accounting for Futures Contracts), requiring relatively stringent criteria to be satisfied before an enterprise is allowed to categorise a transaction as a hedge, and by doing so defer profits/losses for matching with specifically identifiable hedge items.

Current and Future Developments

In the United States, work continues on the second and third initially identified segments of the FASB Financial Instruments Project. With the disclosure segment effectively complete subsequent to the issuance of SFASs 105 and 107, the second segment 'Recognition and Measurement' is now underway, and a Discussion Memorandum on this topic was issued in November 1991. The third segment covers the issue of distinction of financial instruments between liabilities and equity.

Internationally, a Symposium on New Financial Instruments was organised by the OECD Working Group on Accounting Standards in 1988, at which members of OECD pooled resources in identifying the inadequacy of authoritative accounting guidance throughout member countries at that time. The OECD published the main contributions to the Symposium ('New Financial Instruments: Disclosure and Accounting' – OECD 1988) and follow-up meetings have been held. The OECD continues to work on the topic in conjunction with national standard setting boards, encouraging harmonisation of standards worldwide.

The fact remains, however, that no country, including the UK, has yet issued an authoritative accounting standard covering recognition and measurement of income for derivative products. Discussion papers and exposure drafts offer appropriate guidance, but these are not written into law and hence not binding. Companies using derivative products must to a great extent still resort to 'current best practice', formulated well before issuance of the various guidelines listed above. The overriding impression is that the pace of market development will continue to ensure that it is the standard setters who follow in the steps of the users rather than vice versa.

ACCOUNTING POLICY

Swap Products

The detailed accounting policy guidelines presented below are designed to cover as far as possible the full variety of swap products currently available. While an equity swap involves a fundamentally different market from a commodity swap, for example, the accounting principles underlying the recognition of profit are broadly similar. The complexity of such products lies more in the valuation than in the accounting aspects.

For all derivative products it is the economic substance of the individual transaction that must be ascertained prior to formulation of an appropriate accounting policy. Swap products involve changing one risk stream into another and the most important distinction to be made is between the 'hedger', who has an existing or anticipated risk to be covered by the swap, and the 'trader' who is taking an open position by entering into the swap, either in a market-making capacity or as a pure speculator. Traditionally it is the corporate sector who are the 'hedgers' and the financial institutions the market-makers/speculators or 'traders'. However, it is perfectly feasible for a corporate to take open or speculative positions or indeed for a financial institution to take hedging positions to cover existing or anticipated risk. Hence any institution can and will find itself in a position in which it may be appropriate for an identical product to be accounted for in fundamentally different ways.

As the swap markets have developed, so has 'current best practice', this being in line with the authoritative guidance set out in the previous section. It is now generally accepted that swaps entered into for trading purposes should be marked-to-market and that the accounting for hedge swaps should mirror the accounting of the hedged item, i.e. most often some form of accrual or lower of cost and market accounting.

Trading Swaps

The underlying principle of mark-to-market accounting is that at any given moment an instrument has a value for which the holder could relinquish the open position. To the extent that this value can be realised at any moment it is appropriate to carry the instrument at its market or fair value. Reported profits would be capable of distortion should the trading instrument be carried at cost. For swap transactions, termination fees offer an indication of the carrying value. Under mark-to-market accounting, the event of a swap termination fee will involve a transfer from unrealised to realised profit, but no net profit or loss. Similarly interim cash payments/receipts under the swap transaction represent purely the realisation of previously recognised unrealised profits/losses.

At its simplest, mark-to-market accounting for swap transactions involves the following accounting events:

At Inception

- Recognition of notional principal under swap transaction in off-balance-sheet memorandum accounts, and the NPV of future cash flows will clearly take into account the reduced principal value.
- Recognition of net present value (NPV) of all future cash flows as unrealised gain/loss (UGL). This will be a net asset/liability in the balance sheet, representing the carrying value of the swap. On this basis, on-market swaps will have zero carrying value at inception.
- Netting of any up front fees against the carrying value of future cash flows.

Subsequent Reporting Dates

- Interim cash payments/receipts will give rise to movements in the NPV of future cash flows offset by movements in cash (no net profit and loss impact).
- A valuation of future cash flows is to be obtained at each reporting date and the UGL balance in the balance sheet up-dated to reflect current value. Valuation changes will arise due to the impact of time and the impact of market movements, both of which must be recognised currently in profit and loss.
- For amortising swaps, reductions in notional principal are to be reflected in adjustments to memorandum accounts, and the NPV of future cash flows will clearly take into account the reduced principal value.

Termination/Maturity

- At both termination and maturity any off-balance-sheet memorandum balances which were set up at inception are to be reversed.
- As a swap approaches maturity, the value of future cash flows will tend towards the value of any cash receipt/payment at maturity. Hence the maturity itself will not give rise to any profit and loss event.
- Similarly, upon termination/unwind it is assumed that the termination fee will be equivalent to the carrying value of the swap in the balance sheet at that time, and hence the fee received or paid will merely reduce the swap's carrying value on the balance sheet to zero and generate no other profit and loss impact.

Hedging Swaps

The principle of hedge accounting is to match recognition on profit for the hedge transaction with the item being hedged. As such it is critical that the item being hedged is identified at the outset, as this item may be accounted for on either an accruals or a mark-to-market basis. If the hedged item is marked-to-market, it is logical that the hedging transaction should also be marked-to-market, and for swap hedges this would involve the same accounting treatment as detailed for trading swaps above.

More commonly, however, hedge swaps will cover existing risk exposures that are accounted for on an accruals or LOCOM basis. For example, a corporate may have a five-year fixed rate liability which it wishes to convert into floating rate under a swap transaction. It is logical that income recognition on the two legs of the swap should match the recognition of income on the existing liability, regardless of market values in the period to maturity.

Hedging swaps when the hedged item is not marked-to-market should thus be accounted for as follows:

At Inception

- Recognition of notional principal under swap transaction in off-balance sheet memorandum accounts.
- Up front fees other than brokerage to be deferred to income over the period of the swap transaction, generally on a straight line basis.

Subsequent Reporting Dates

- Income on both legs of the swap is to be accounted for on an accruals basis, i.e. any income/expense will be accrued on a straight line basis to the next interim receipt/payment date. The income profile of the swap will thus match that of the hedged item. As and when cash receipts/payments are made these will clear the appropriate receivable/payable balances which have been accumulated as a result of the accruals process.

Termination/Maturity

- Reversal of memorandum account entries.
- At maturity any cash receipts/payments will clear residual receivable/payable balances to zero.
- Upon termination the termination fee should normally be deferred and accrued to income over the residual period of the hedged item. If the hedged item is terminated then the fee should be taken direct to income to match the equivalent profit/loss upon termination of the hedged item.

Valuation Issues

The basic accounting framework set out above assumes simply structured swaps which are easy to value. In practice swaps are increasingly less simple, incorporating option, variable redemption or other features which complicate the accounting treatment and give rise to valuation difficulties. A number of these are detailed below along with potential solutions:

VARIABLE REDEMPTION FEATURES Swaps may feature interim or final payments/receipts determined by reference to future events unknown at inception. For example, an asset swap of a bond with redemption linked to a stock index would normally contain a variable redemption feature to match the bond redemption amount. In order to account for this feature it must effectively be 'stripped out' of the valuation of the rest of the swap, and afforded an individual valuation of its own. This valuation may incorporate option theory should, for example, the reference level of the index at maturity be set between certain levels, or capped. In such cases an equal and opposite value could be obtained for the stock option(s) required to hedge the exposure. This may be easier in theory than in practice due to an illiquid or non-existent option market. In such a case judgement will be required and prudence needs to be exercised. The concept of stripping products down into their constituent parts or 'building blocks' is widely accepted in authoritative accounting guidance for complex financial instruments.

EMBEDDED OPTIONS, CALLABLE SWAPS In similarity to variable redemption features, some swaps may be extended or cancelled at or before maturity. These provisions represent embedded options, which need to be stripped out and separately valued in the same way as variable redemption features. Once the option feature has been stripped out, the residual swap risk can be valued in the same way as a standard interest rate or currency swap.

DIFFERING INDICES Standard interest rate swaps can be valued against market cash and swap rates which are widely available due to the liquidity of the swap market. Longer-term swap legs can be marked against the prevailing swap curve and shorter-term legs against the cash or futures curve. Increasingly, however, one or both legs of swap contracts are against non-standard indices. Examples include the commercial paper, Fed Funds and Prime indices in the USA. In addition to these interest rate indices, swap coupons may also be determined on the basis of an equity or commodity index.

For most non-standard interest rate indices, the yield curve is generally quoted on the basis of a spread against the standard cash/swap curve, and in such cases valuation models can be adapted so that the non-standard legs are marked against an adjusted yield curve. For equity and commodity index linked swaps, the 'building blocks' approach must be adopted to separate out the various components that give the swap value. These components then need to be valued against the appropriate market rate for the purposes of calculating the carrying value of the swap.

Pricing Issues

Having determined a market index against which the swap can be valued, there are other considerations that should be taken into account in determining an appropriate price at which the swap should be recorded in the financial statements. Given that the underlying concept of mark-to-market accounting is to bring forward future potential profits, i.e. to move away from historical cost accounting, any prudent valuation policy should endeavour to estimate potential future costs that may offset the future gains being recognised.

The most important pricing issues to be addressed are as follows:

BID/OFFER The use of a bid or offer price can give rise to significant valuation differences, notably when wide bid/offer spreads are quoted. As an example, consider a 10 year overlent (receiving fixed) US $100 million interest rate swap with an annual coupon of 8.48 per cent. 10 year swap rates are quoted at 8.48–8.52 per cent and this swap was entered into at the bid rate. It may be assumed that to close out the position the holder of the overlent swap would have to pay 8.52 per cent on an identical 10 year overborrowed (paying fixed) deal. The present value of one basis point per annum (US $10,000) received in semi-annual instalments over 10 years is US $66,472, given a discount rate of 8.5 per cent. By closing out the 8.48 per cent overlent swap with an overborrowed swap at 8.52 per cent the holder has locked in a loss of 4 basis points, or US $265,888, which would be taken currently to income under mark-to-market accounting.

The critical issue of bid/offer pricing is whether any given swap position should be marked to the bid, the offer or the mid-market level of the swap curve. The current consensus is broadly in favour of a prudent approach reflecting the circumstances of the swap holder. This implies that open overlent positions should be valued at the offer side of the curve, as it is this price at which it is assumed the swap would need to be closed out, and open overborrowed positions valued at the bid side for the same reason. Using the same logic for a flat position, it would seem appropriate to value swaps at mid-market. Certain users prefer the very prudent approach of valuing all overlent positions at offer and all overborrowed at bid. In the example above, this would imply taking a loss of US $265,888 on both swaps, i.e. a total loss of US $531,776.

The appropriate accounting approach must be based on the user's particular circumstances. For the market-maker, a policy of marking all overlent swaps to offer and all overborrowed to bid is extremely, and probably overly, prudent, and a more appropriate approach would normally be to view the net risk on the portfolio as a whole. But for the corporate or investor with a small portfolio of swaps, this prudent valuation policy may be considered appropriate.

CREDIT One critical influence on the value of any financial instrument is the credit risk of the counterparty. A swap with an AAA-rated counterparty clearly has more value than an identical swap with a BB-rated counterparty. In addition, credit risk is greater on a swap which is heavily in-the-money than on an at market deal. During a swap's life, both the credit rating of the counterparty and the extent to which the swap is in-the-money can change, often dramatically. These two key factors should therefore be taken into account when determining an appropriate valuation. Ideally some form of reserve should be set aside to cover the credit risk, and the reserve adjusted periodically to reflect changes in circumstances, although this reserve should not duplicate any amount set aside to cover the market bid/offer.

OPERATIONAL COSTS In the same way that credit is an additional factor to be built into an appropriate pricing model, so the potential future costs in servicing the swap through its life should also be taken into account. Such costs include the operational cost of arranging coupon receipts/payments through the swap's life and hedging potential future exposures such as floating leg refixes. Any estimation of these costs should be based on current cost levels and the life of the deal in question. For consistency it is appropriate to hold a reserve at a level equivalent to the present value of identified future expected costs. As with a credit reserve, the level should be adjusted periodically to reflect the impact of time and any potential changes in the cost structure.

LIQUIDITY Many of the valuation and pricing guidelines above depend on reliable market information being available. For some of the newer swap products and markets, there are no easily accessible quoted rates against which a particular instrument can be valued. Illiquid markets suggest a cautious approach to the determination of an appropriate valuation policy. The concept of prudence would justify at the very least a reserve to reflect illiquidity, and in more extreme cases a LOCOM policy may be more appropriate. As with any reserve, an illiquidity reserve should normally be able to be analysed on a deal-by-deal basis, and will need to be monitored and adjusted periodically dependent on market circumstances. Even in established markets, illiquidity reserves may be justified for deals which are significantly off-market, for example when deals are heavily in- or out-of-the-money.

Option Products

As with swap products, the accounting policy to be adopted for options is determined by the economic substance of the transaction. Valuation and pricing refinements are similar to those applicable for swaps.

The risk profile for options differs from swaps, however, in that the purchaser of an option has limited downside risk and unlimited upside risk, whereas the risk to the seller, or writer, is limited on the upside but unlimited on the downside. This profile suggests that it is not as straightforward for options as it is for swap products to determine whether a transaction can be described as a hedge. Although the profit/loss on an option 'hedge' may be opposite to the profit/loss on the underlying instrument in terms of direction, the nature of an option is such that when it moves sufficiently far out of the money to have negligible value, little or no protection is provided against the underlying exposure.

It is generally accepted that written options should not be afforded hedge accounting treatment. The premium received on the option is the maximum profit that the writer will ever be able to take on the position. Although it could be argued that a short position in an option heavily in-the-money may follow the profit and loss profile of an underlying instrument relatively closely, it is unlikely that this would be offered as a product given the inevitably high premium that would be required. In addition, the risk profile of written options is such that hedge accounting treatment will normally imply deferral of losses, and this will always be afforded increased scrutiny on the grounds of imprudence.

A written option position can, of course, hedge a bought option position; indeed it is the only effective hedge, given the volatility exposure inherent only in option products. In such circumstances, consistency of accounting treatment should be applied to both the bought and the sold position. Practically speaking, this would normally involve marking both positions to market, and thus effectively treating them as 'trading' transactions.

The accounting position on purchased options is different. With unlimited profit potential, options are often considered by corporates as well as financial institutions to be attractive hedges of underlying instruments. For accountants the concept of deferring gains, which underlies hedge accounting, is much more palatable than deferring losses. As an example, a corporate may have floating rate debt and be concerned about a potential rise in interest rates. By purchasing a cap on a notional amount equal to the outstanding debt, the corporate ensures the cost of the debt cannot exceed a given strike rate. In such circumstances it is entirely appropriate to match the profit and loss on the cap with the cost of the debt and hence adopt a form of hedge accounting treatment.

Once the economic substance of the option transaction has been ascertained, the accounting treatment will normally be the same as for swaps, i.e. mark-to-market for trading positions and accrual or LOCOM for hedging positions.

Trading Options

As for swaps, the principle of mark-to-market accounting for options is that at any given moment positions are held in the balance sheet at their market or fair value. Unrealised gains and losses are recorded currently in trading profits and losses. The following accounting events apply:

At Inception

- Recognition of notional principal under option transaction in off-balance-sheet memorandum accounts.
- Option premiums paid or received are to be set up as trading account assets or liabilities respectively. If the premium is to be settled over a period of time, the current value should still be recorded in trading account assets/liabilities, offset by an equal and opposite payable/receivable for the present value of the future premium instalments.
- Up-front brokerage fees are normally written off to income as incurred.

Subsequent Reporting Dates

- Interim cash payments/receipts under option contracts, typically interest rate caps or floors, will give rise to movements in the value of the option equivalent to the cash paid/received. These movements represent merely a switch from unrealised gains/losses to realised, and hence will have no impact on profits/losses. For example, when an in-the-money cap purchased reaches a refix date, the amount to be received should be set up as a receivable by reducing the value of the cap in the balance sheet, with zero profit and loss impact. After the relevant refix period, when the cash is received, the receivable balance is cleared and again there is no impact on profit and loss.
- At each reporting date, an appropriate valuation needs to be obtained for the open option position, and the value of the option in the balance sheet updated, any movement being taken to profit and loss. Valuation changes will arise due to market movements and time.

Exercise/Expiration

- Upon exercise and/or expiry of an option, any memorandum account entries set up at inception are to be reversed.
- When an option expires without being exercised, its value at expiry is clearly nil. To the extent that the decrease in value to nil has not already been taken to profit and loss, the residual profit/loss since the last mark-to-market date should be taken to income and the balance sheet value reduced to zero.
- When an option is exercised, it has value to the holder at the exercise date. The writer has an equal liability. Under mark-to-market accounting the gain or loss arising on exercise will be equivalent to the value at which the option is held in the balance sheet. Hence the cash gain or loss realised will clear the option value in the balance sheet to zero, the only impact on income being the residual profit and loss since the last mark-to-market date.

Hedging Options

It is assumed here that, for the reasons set out previously, hedge accounting will only ever be applied to purchased options. For the corporate option user, some form of hedge accounting is normally most appropriate, given that speculative or trading use of options is less common. The following accounting events apply:

At Inception

- Recognition of notional principal under option transaction in off-balance-sheet memorandum accounts.

- A hedge option premium purchased is to be set up as an asset in the balance sheet.
- Reflecting the economic substance of the transaction, which could be considered as an insurance premium, the cost should be amortised over the period of the contract.

Subsequent Reporting Dates

- The principle of hedge accounting is that income on the option should match income on the underlying hedged item. In practice this would normally entail deferring any profits/losses arising from revaluation of the option to current market value. The deferred profits/losses would then be taken to income over the same time period as the income on the underlying item. For example, an interim cash receipt on an in-the-money cap purchased would be accrued over the period during which it covers the exposure on the underlying floating rate liability. The premium would be held in the balance sheet on an amortised cost basis, regardless of current market value.
- Amortisation of the option premium over the life of the contract could, however, be regarded as imprudent if the value of the option declines significantly below its carrying value in the balance sheet. Although this unrecognised decline in value would normally be offset by an equivalent unrecognised gain on the hedged item, it could be argued that a LOCOM basis of accounting would be more appropriate on grounds of prudence, in which case decreases in value below cost would be recognised currently in income.
- Certain users have adopted another form of accounting for hedging options, under which the premium paid on purchased hedging options is split at inception between time and intrinsic value. This splitting of the option value is consistent with an Issues Paper on Accounting for Options issued by the US Auditing Board, the AICPA, in 1986. This paper was not widely accepted, however, and is likely to be superseded entirely by the next phase of the FASB Financial Instruments Project. All subsequent guidance on option accounting does not recommend dividing the option value in the way suggested by the Paper. However, users may in certain circumstances wish to identify the time value at the outset, defer this element to income over the period of the option, and then treat the intrinsic value separately for the purposes of income recognition. In practice this treatment may over-complicate the accounting approach and so it is not generally recommended.

Exercise/Expiration

- Reversal of memorandum account entries.
- On expiry of a purchased hedging option, the value of the option will

have been amortised to zero, hence no further accounting entries are required.

— On exercise of the same option, the profit arising is deferred and spread to income over the period of the underlying item. The profit should include any unamortised balance on the (balance sheet) premium account, which should be cleared to nil upon exercise.

Valuation and Pricing Issues

Once the economic substance of the option transaction has been ascertained, the accounting entries to record movements in value at the various stages throughout the option's life are relatively straightforward. The major problems in accounting for options arise in determining the appropriate valuation to be applied to open positions. For exchange traded options, widely available quoted prices provide a reliable benchmark for valuation. However, the valuation of OTC options, for which there is generally no market quote available, can present the user and accountant with significant difficulty. The key pricing issues are the same as those for swap products, namely bid/offer, credit and liquidity.

BID/OFFER Wide bid/offer spreads can be encountered in the option market, notably for more exotic structures. Prices are often quoted in terms of the implied volatility of the option and, if this is the case, the vega of the option, being the price movement implicit in a 1 per cent shift in implied volatility levels, can be quantified. For prudence, it would normally be appropriate to value long, or bought, option positions at bid and short positions at offer. If, for example, volatility on a five-year cap was quoted at 9–11 per cent, it would seem appropriate to value the option assuming 9 per cent implied volatility, i.e. effectively to hold a bid/offer reserve of one vega against mid-market.

CREDIT Problems arise for the market-maker who will generally hold a portfolio of options and open positions with various maturities. As with swaps, it would appear to be overly prudent for a market-maker with offsetting option positions to hold long positions at bid and short at offer, yet potentially imprudent to value all positions at mid, especially if the market is illiquid (see below). Some form of categorisation of positions into appropriate maturity bands may be appropriate. The option user must therefore formulate a valuation strategy which is neither overly prudent nor dangerously imprudent. This is obviously easier said than done, but the proof of the suitability of any strategy will be the extent to which large swings in profit/loss arise which have no basis in market movements.

For the corporate user who may have no access to an option valuation model, and limited access to market volatility data, obtaining reliable valuations for options held may be virtually impossible, and the bid/offer issue may be of little significance when compared with the problem in obtaining a reliable mid-market value. To the extent that bid/offer prices are obtainable, however, a policy of marking long positions to bid and short to offer would seem most appropriate.

The only credit risk in written options lies in the extent to which the premium has not been received, for example in the case of premiums paid over the life of the option. The majority of options have up front premiums, and credit is not an issue for the writer.

The option purchaser, however, is exposed to the risk that the counterparty will default. As with swap products, the two factors determining the level of credit risk are the credit rating of the counterparty and the extent to which the option is in-the-money, i.e. its market value. These two factors can vary enormously throughout the life of the option. Given the potential earnings distortion from default events, it is appropriate to hold a reserve against open purchased option positions that are in-the-money, up-dating the reserve periodically to reflect changes in circumstances.

LIQUIDITY The most substantial problem in obtaining a reliable market value for a given option position is, in most cases, the lack of liquidity of the relevant market. This can be due to the underlying instrument (e.g. a currency which is not widely traded), the strike rate of the option, which may be way out-of-the-money, or the exotic nature of the option itself – for example Asian options, based on average prices, barrier options or look-back options. In such circumstances, prudence would suggest at the very least a reserve for illiquidity and/or a LOCOM policy.

Balance Sheet Issues

The primary focus of the accounting policies set out thus far has been on the timing and recognition of profit and loss, as it is these issues that are generally of most concern to the users of derivative products. This focus is borne out in the authoritative guidance on the subject.

Yet in the early days of the derivative markets, much of the impetus behind developments arose from the fact that users were able not to record risk positions on the balance sheet. 'Off-balance-sheet' finance enabled users to keep the size of balance sheets down and potentially increase the key performance ratio of return on assets. In addition, disclosure requirements for off-balance-sheet instruments were negligible compared with those for balance sheet assets and liabilities. Regulators and accounting standards boards are clearly now more familiar with off-balance-sheet instruments. As has been seen, 'current best practice' has been translated into a variety of authoritative guidance, and there is now little dispute over the appropriate balance sheet reporting for the various types of derivative product.

The products mentioned in this chapter could all be described as off-balance-sheet instruments. For swaps, foreign exchange contracts, options, caps/floors and other similar instruments, the underlying principal of the transaction is not normally recorded on the balance sheet. This is intuitive in most cases, as there is no cash settlement of the principal amount, although there are two notable exceptions, namely currency exchanges and foreign exchange transactions. Most currency exchanges involve an up front exchange of principal and it has been argued as a result that this amount should be recorded on the balance sheet as both an asset and a liability. The opposing argument, that the currency exchange merely changes the features of an existing asset or liability, coupled with the fact that the risk is with the same counterparty, has resulted in the now almost universal acceptance of off-balance-sheet treatment for these instruments. Similarly, foreign exchange swaps, in which a current exchange of two currencies with the same counterparty is matched with an agreed future exchange of the same currencies, are accepted as off-balance-sheet instruments despite the fact that cash is exchanged upon inception.

The current primary accounting issue regarding balance sheet treatment of derivative products is the extent to which balance sheet assets/liabilities and/or amounts receivable/payable in respect of these products can be netted. Any netting of assets and liabilities clearly enables the user to enhance the return on assets ratio by restricting the size of the balance sheet.

For the majority of corporate users of derivative products the issue of netting will not normally be of any major significance. It acquires importance only when the volume and size of deals are sufficiently high to cause a material impact on the balance sheet, as will be the case for most financial institutions.

In the United States this issue was addressed in the FASB Technical Bulletin TB 88-2, 'The Definition of a Right of Setoff'. TB 88-2 required unrealised gains and losses to be recorded gross in the balance sheet unless the asset and liability amounts could be netted by novation. Novation provides the strictest form of netting: a formal agreement under which offsetting legal obligations for the same date and currency are cancelled and replaced with a new legal obligation for the net payment. Hence TB 88-2 provided little scope for netting in the balance sheet, setting the trend firmly towards gross reporting of assets and liabilities.

In March 1992 the FASB issued FASB Interpretation no. 39 entitled 'Offsetting of Amounts Related to Certain Contracts', which effectively supersedes TB 88-2. Under this paper, market value accounts for off-balance-sheet contracts are required to be reported gross for financial statements ending after December 15 1993, unless a 'right of setoff' exists. This is defined as a 'debtor's legal right . . . to discharge all or a portion of the debt owed to another party by applying against the debt an amount that the other party owes to the debtor', and can only exist if four restrictive conditions are met, notably that the right of setoff is enforceable at law.

Hence the FASB paper does not allow netting of amounts across different currencies or counterparties. In practice, market participants wishing to apply netting under the FASB paper will need to maintain a sufficiently detailed database of payment and counterparty information and, even if full benefit is taken of the netting allowed by the FASB, it appears likely that the net impact will be to show assets and liabilities much closer to figures calculated on a fully grossed up basis than those calculated on a fully netted basis.

There is no specific accounting guidance in the UK on the issue of grossing up, but it seems probable that the guidelines set by the FASB would be acceptable to the UK accounting authorities and hence that these provide an appropriate accounting framework for the UK user.

REGULATORY ENVIRONMENT

Introduction

Having covered the accounting aspects of derivative products, attention will now be directed at the implications of the current regulatory environment for the user of these instruments.

In the United Kingdom, all limited companies are effectively 'regulated' by the Companies Acts. It is these Acts which require the annual submission of audited financial statements and hence indirectly require for derivative products that the accounting principles set out in the previous section to be adopted. The term regulation, however, is more commonly applied to the rules and requirements of the various bodies, or regulators, which have been established to control and monitor specific businesses on a more detailed and regular basis than is possible under the Companies Acts. For the UK financial markets, the key regulatory body for banks and credit institutions is the Bank of England (BOE). For the securities and investment businesses, a number of regulatory authorities exist. The umbrella organisation set up by the Financial Services Act is the Securities and Investment Board (SIB), under whom individual regulatory authorities are authorised to monitor market participants, notably, for derivative products, the Securities and Futures Authority (SFA) and the Investment Management Regulatory Organisation (IMRO).

Internationally, the majority of banks are regulated by some form of central bank, and other authorities exist for the investment and securities businesses, for example the Securities and Exchange Commission (SEC) in the USA. Complications can arise for institutions which cannot be clearly categorised as banks or securities businesses, but normally in such circumstances the institution must agree with the various regulatory bodies who is to be the 'lead regulator' so as to avoid either duplication of control or misunderstanding as to who is ultimately responsible. In addition, overseas organisations need to agree upon whether the lead regulator is to be the local regulatory authority or the body based in the institution's country of origin. It is noteworthy that, just as is the case for accounting convergence, much effort is being expended internationally to harmonise regulatory requirements, notably amongst G10 countries.

This section will focus primarily on the implications for the derivative product user of the regulatory environment in the United Kingdom, considering first the regulations for banks and credit institutions, and then those for investment and securities businesses.

Banks and Credit Institutions

The primary role of bank regulators has always been to ensure that banks under their supervision maintain sufficient capital to cover outstanding risk exposure and hence safeguard the value of deposits. It should be stressed at the outset that the focus for bank regulators is on credit risk. Given that the primary activity of banks is the extension of credit, it is logical that the regulators should wish to concentrate most effort on controlling the level of credit risk, to ensure that banks are sufficiently capitalised to cover potential losses due to counterparty default.

Since the 1970s much work has been carried out in developing a framework to be used internationally for monitoring capital adequacy, the result of which is a set of specific guidelines to be applied in determining whether a bank is deemed to have sufficient capital. The principle behind these guidelines is that all exposures can be quantified in terms of 'risk adjusted assets', and the sum of risk adjusted assets can then be expressed as a percentage of a predetermined capital base specific to the institution known as the risk asset ratio. The higher the percentage, the stronger the capital base is deemed to be. A minimum risk asset ratio is specified, and banks need to ensure that this ratio is maintained at all times.

The development of the current framework started in the late 1970s when the G10 countries agreed to establish a committee of bank supervisors from each member country whose aim was to harmonise banking regulation for capital adequacy. This 'Committee on Banking Regulations and Supervisory Practices' became known as the Basle Committee after the location of its patron, the Bank for International Settlements.

The Basle Committee published its final report on capital adequacy in July 1988, entitled the 'International Convergence of Capital Measurements and Capital Standards'. This is the core report for all subsequent authoritative regulatory guidance on this topic. The BOE issued a paper in October 1988 (BSD/1988/3) which broadly required UK banks to adopt the Basle Committee proposals. The EC has subsequently issued two directives on the subject, the

Own Funds Directive and the Solvency Ratio Directive, which pick up the Basle Committee report requirements and apply them to EC member states. In both cases the BOE followed the directives closely with papers detailing how UK regulated banks should conform with the directives' requirements (BSD/1990/2 and BSD/1990/3). Throughout this period the Federal Reserve Board in the USA issued papers on the topic which again follow broadly the guidelines in the original Basle Committee report.

The Basle Committee report sets out a framework for the measurement of risk adjusted assets, and details how the denominator of the risk asset ratio, i.e. the capital base, is to be calculated. It sets the basic minimum requirement for the risk asset ratio at 8 per cent, a percentage now widely accepted internationally, even if certain countries may disagree with individual guidelines on the calculation of either the capital base or risk adjusted assets.

For derivative products the significance of the Basle report is that these instruments are included in the scope of risk adjusted assets, even though the principals are recorded off-balance-sheet. A separate section of the report covers off-balance-sheet instruments, and within this section 'foreign exchange and interest rate related contingencies' are considered. The report states that a 'majority of G10 supervisory authorities are of the view that the best way to assess the credit risk on these items is to ask banks to calculate the current replacement cost by marking contracts to market, . . . and then adding a factor (the 'add-on') to reflect the potential future exposure over the remaining life of the contract'. This method of calculating the credit equivalent amount is known as the 'current exposure method'. An alternative method, known as the 'original exposure method', is also allowed under the Basle agreement, whereby credit weights are applied to notional principal balances regardless of current market value. This latter method is not, however, favoured by the BOE, which, in the guidance notes to both the Basle Committee report (BSD 1988/3) and the EC Solvency Ratio Directive (BSD 1990/3), recommends banks to adopt the 'current exposure' or 'replacement cost' method.

Under the replacement cost method for off-balance-sheet instruments, the current market value of all open contracts with a positive value is added to an amount for potential future credit exposure to give a 'credit equivalent amount'. The amount for future credit exposure is calculated as a percentage of the notional principal amount dependent on maturity as follows:

Residual Maturity	**Interest Rate Contracts (a)**	**Exchange Rate Contracts (b)**
One year or less	Nil	1.0%
Over one year	0.5%	5.0%

(a) Single currency interest rate swaps, basis (floating/floating) swaps, forward rate agreements and products with similar characteristics, interest rate futures and interest rate options purchased.

(b) Cross currency swaps, cross currency interest rate swaps, outright forward foreign exchange contracts, currency futures and currency options purchased. These contracts attract a higher percentage due to the deemed higher volatility of the foreign exchange markets.

Exchange traded contracts subject to daily margining requirements are excluded from the scope, as are foreign exchange contracts with a maturity of 14 calendar days or less. A minor concession is granted for single floating/floating interest rate swaps, whereby no 'add on' is required to be calculated.

Once the credit equivalent amount is calculated for each contract, a credit weighting is applied to this amount dependent on the type of counterparty. The risk weighting percentages range from 0 per cent for government counterparties to 20 per cent for OECD banks and up to a maximum of 50 per cent for other counterparties. This maximum differs from the 100 per cent maximum applied to on-balance-sheet exposures such as loans to reflect that, per the Basle report, 'most counterparties in these markets, particularly for long-term contracts, tend to be first class names'. The amount calculated by applying the credit risk weighting to the credit equivalent amount represents the risk adjusted asset value.

As an example, a five-year US $100 million cap purchased from an OECD bank with a market value of $1,000,000 would have a risk adjusted asset value of $300,000, calculated as follows:

Market Value	1,000,000
'Add on' for future credit exposure	500,000*
Total credit equivalent	$1,500,000

* $100 million × 0.5%

Risk weighting: 20%; hence the risk adjusted asset value is $300,000.

The implication for the holder of such a cap is that capital equivalent to at least 8 per cent of the risk adjusted asset value, i.e. $24,000, must be held to support the credit risk inherent in the position. This capital requirement should normally be factored into the pricing of such products.

While the progress achieved by the Basle Committee and the European Community on harmonisation of capital adequacy guidelines should not be understated, there are widely acknowledged limitations in the conclusions drawn. The primary criticism of the Basle report is that no account is taken of the relative creditworthiness of individual counterparties. Risk weighting percentages divide counterparties between governmental institutions, banks and corporates, but all institutions within any one of these categories are afforded the same weighting. Hence exposures to AAA corporate counterparties attract the same credit weighting as identical exposures to BB corporate counterparties, even though the credit risk of the latter exposure is clearly higher.

The other main shortcoming of the Basle report is that it does not separately identify market risk, restricting itself to credit risk. Increasingly banks are extending their activities to encompass products, notably derivatives, for which potential losses arising due to credit risk are dwarfed by losses that can occur from market movements. The regulation of market risk, or position risk, has to date been covered primarily by regulators of the investment and securities business, but it is recognised by the Basle Committee and the European Commission that market risk must also be incorporated into capital adequacy guidelines for banks and credit institutions. This will ensure a consistency of regulatory approach based on products, rather than on the nature of the institution's business, and minimise the risk of competitive disadvantages arising.

Investment and Securities Business

It is in the securities industry that the development of the derivatives markets has evolved. For this reason, despite the fact that deregulation of the financial markets has opened these markets to banks and credit institutions, it is the regulators of the securities business who have thus far developed the means of identifying and controlling the non-credit related risks inherent in derivative products. Regulators recognise that the shorter-term nature of the securities business requires that close and regular attention be taken by industry participants to market exposures. Hence the focus for the regulators is to ensure the smooth function of the markets and to provide corporates and others wishing to use derivative products with the confidence to deal with firms under their regulation.

In the United Kingdom the majority of market makers in derivative products are regulated either by the Bank of England or by the Securities and Futures Authority (SFA), the body formed from the merger in 1991 of The Securities Association (TSA) and the Association of Futures Brokers and Dealers (AFBD). In certain cases, the BOE may defer the regulation of specific business areas to the SFA's rules, given that these may be more specific than BOE guidelines. While similar institutions exist in other countries, there is as yet little international convergence among securities industry regulators, compared with the degree of harmonisation achieved in the regulation of banks and credit institutions by the Basle Committee. For this reason, this section will focus primarily on existing SFA regulations for derivative products, with an additional discussion of the draft Capital Adequacy Directive for the securities business, recently issued by the European Commission.

SFA Regulations

On 1 October 1992 the Securities and Futures Authority issued its New Financial Rules to be adopted by member firms. The New Rules replace existing regulatory requirements as laid down by TSA and AFBD, but do not adopt a radically different approach and complement the current framework. It is this document which gives the most recent indication of detailed regulatory requirements for the UK securities industry.

At the core of the SFA approach to regulation is the concept of capital adequacy. As is the case for banks, the securities regulators are generally agreed that the most effective manner to control the business is to ensure that regulated firms maintain sufficient capital to cover risk exposures. In the SFA regulations, capital is known as 'financial resources', and early in the Financial Regulations it is stated that 'a firm must, at all times, maintain financial resources in excess of its financial resources requirement'. Financial resources include capital, reserves and eligible capital substitutes, for example subordinated loans and approved bank bonds, less any intangible assets. The 'Financial Resources Requirement' is the SFA's measure of the regulated firm's outstanding risk exposure.

There are three components of the Financial Resources Requirement, known as the primary requirement, the position risk requirement (PRR) and the counterparty risk requirement (CRR). The primary requirement sets *de minimis* amounts for all firms based on the volume of business and/or expenditure. The CRR is the SFA's measure of credit risk, addressing regulated firms' exposures to the potential default of counterparties in a similar way to the capital adequacy requirements for banks and credit institutions. The PRR is the measure of the position or market risk inherent in a firm's outstanding positions, having no equivalent in current regulatory requirements for banks and credit institutions.

Position Risk

The detailed guidelines for the measurement of PRR constitute well over half of the SFA's Financial Regulations, and individual sections cover the calculation of PRR for the wide variety of financial instruments, including derivative products, that regulated firms may hold.

In the field of OTC derivatives, products are divided into three risk categories, namely equity, debt (i.e. interest rate) and foreign currency. For each of these three product types, separate guidelines are included in the Financial Regulations for calculation of PRR, although the principles underlying the calculation are similar.

(i) EQUITY DERIVATIVES The provisions for equity derivatives cover futures and options on equity indices, equity options and equity legs of equity swaps. For each of these products, firms are required to derive 'equity equivalent positions'. A variable percentage, known as the position risk adjuster (PRA) dependent on the country of the risk and status (e.g. listed or unlisted), of the underlying stock, is then applied to the equity equivalent position to arrive at the PRR. The equity equivalent position for an index option or future is the mark-to-market value of the underlying notional equity portfolio. For an individual equity option, it is the mark-to-market value of the underlying equity, and for an equity swap it is the nominal value of the swap. PRAs for individual stock derivatives vary from 10.5 per cent for FT-SE 100 stocks to 30 per cent for non-UK unlisted stocks. For index derivatives the PRAs are lower, reflecting the lower equity risk due to diversification, varying from 6.5–7.5 per cent for UK, Japan and the USA to 20 per cent for countries outside the FT-Actuaries World Indices. The PRR on written options can be reduced by the extent to which the option is out of the money. In addition, the lower risk inherent in purchased option positions is recognised by a further provision, which allows the PRR to be limited to the current mark-to-market value of the option.

The lack of netting provisions in the regulations means that in practice it does not require a very large portfolio of equity derivatives, especially written options, to generate a significant overall PRR. Recognising this, the SFA permits regulated firms to use a 'risk assessment model' in the calculation of their equity equivalent positions. Such a model must be used as part of the day-to-day management supervision of the firm's option business and may only be used to calculate notional positions with the prior written approval of SFA. In practice market makers will have risk assessment models which provide exposure information on volatility and equity risk for their derivative portfolios. The process of obtaining SFA approval for use of the model will depend on the ability of the firm to prove that the model accurately represents outstanding risk positions and the sensitivity of the portfolio to market movements. Without approval, the firm is required to calculate PRR on an individual instrument basis using the guidelines above, and such a method may severely restrict the ability to take on new business.

(ii) DEBT DERIVATIVES This category covers interest rate swaps, OTC forwards, futures and options on debt securities, options on futures, swap options and interest rate caps/floors. The method for calculating the appropriate PRR for these instruments is similar to the method for equity derivatives. For each instrument the notional debt equivalent position must be ascertained, and from this a percentage or PRA, is applied to arrive at the PRR.

For interest rate swaps, each leg is treated separately, such that the overlent leg is considered as a long debt position and the overborrowed a short position. The maturity for a fixed leg is the maturity of the swap, while for a floating leg it is considered to be the next reset date. For purchased interest rate options the PRR is the mark-to-market value of the underlying position multiplied by the appropriate debt PRA, but limited, in the same way as for purchased equity options, to the mark-to-market value of the option itself. The calculation is the same for written options but it is not possible to limit the PRR to the option's market value. Caps, floors and swap options are treated in the same way as interest rate options.

Debt PRAs are generally lower than equity PRAs and are dependent on the maturity and currency of the debt equivalent position. The SFA categorises positions into eight maturity bands, from 0–3 months out to over 20 years, and PRAs are clearly higher the longer the maturity. Positions in adjacent maturity bands are permitted to be matched to a certain degree, to avoid large movements in PRR when exposures move across the designated bands. There is a wide difference in PRAs dependent on the currency of the underlying, and sovereign debt is separately treated, attracting lower PRAs. However, no PRA is over 10 per cent, and percentages range from 0.1 per cent for three-month deutschemark sovereign debt to 9.5 per cent for debt over 20 years in a non-standard currency. The PRAs are clearly judgemental and in some cases may appear inequitable, in that for example all except the major currencies are included in a catch all 'other currency' category which attracts disproportionately high PRAs.

Like equity derivatives, the 'basic method' of PRR calculation set out above will soon absorb a significant amount of capital for firms with significant debt derivative positions, given the limited scope for netting. The SFA permits the use of approved risk assessement models and it is incumbent on the firm to prove the model's ability to reflect outstanding risk exposure accurately. This will necessarily involve some form of procedure to analyse positions into maturity bands, and firms need to decide whether an approach based on delta (i.e. interest rate risk) or vega (i.e. volatility risk) is the more appropriate. The onus sits squarely on the regulated firm for all risk assessment models and little detailed guidance is given by the SFA, other than that the model must be integral to the firm's day-to-day risk management system.

(iii) FOREIGN CURRENCY DERIVATIVES This category covers foreign exchange options and futures, which are afforded the simplest approach of all derivatives for the purposes of calculating PRR. The principles of calculating a currency equivalent position are the same as for the equity and debt derivatives, with the same potential limitations for purchased option positions. The PRA, however, is a flat 5 per cent for all positions. As with equity and debt derivatives, any active market player will need to take advantage of the provision in the regulations which allows PRRs to be calculated using an approved risk assessment model.

While there may be limitations in the various provisions in the SFA's Financial Regulations which deal with the assessment of position, or market risk, and the development of the rules has not been without controversy, the principles are clearly logical, offering a sound basis for monitoring the capital adequacy of regulated firms.

Credit Risk

The other main component of a firm's financial resources requirement is the Counterparty Risk Requirement (CRR). As with the PRR guidelines, separate provisions exist in the Financial Regulations for derivative products. The CRR is calculated for each instrument by applying a credit percentage, dependent on the status of the counterparty, to the credit equivalent amount. The credit equivalent amount is dependent on the mark-to-market value of the instrument and the period to maturity. If the mark-to-market value is negative, the credit equivalent is a simple percentage (from nil to 5 per cent dependent on maturity and type of instrument) of the underlying notional principal. For instruments with positive value, the same calculation applies, except that the mark to market value is added to the percentage of notional to arrive at the total credit equivalent. To derive the CRR one of three credit percentages is applied to the credit equivalent: zero for sovereign exposure, 2 per cent for 'regulated financial institutions', covering most banks, securities houses and brokers, and 5 per cent for all other counterparties. It should be noted that this broadbrush approach is open to the same criticism as has been levelled at the Basle Committee proposals.

EC Capital Adequacy Directive

Having covered existing regulations to cover UK securities houses, attention will now be drawn to the draft Capital Adequacy Directive (CAD) being developed by the European Commission. The draft Directive has been changed many times since its first issue, reflecting the diversity of regulatory approaches in the member states and concern that national interests might be compromised. Yet in June 1992 agreement in principle was reached by EC Finance Ministers on its general terms. Given the wide scope of the provisions, this is not an insignificant achievement, although it is recognised that much detailed work still needs to be done before implementation, not least because implementation is dependent on ratification by all member states of the draft Investment Services Directive (ISD). The ISD is at the core of the EC's drive to create a 'level playing field' for credit institutions and investment firms across the Community, and to date disagreement among member states has dogged its progress. Its aim is to enable securities firms to trade freely within member states, by giving firms an EC-wide 'passport'.

This can clearly only be achieved in the context of a consistent regulatory framework across the EC, and hence the importance of the recent agreement in principle to the terms of the CAD.

The CAD complements the existing Own Funds and Solvency Ratio Directives which are applicable specifically to banks and credit institutions. The concept of the 'trading book' is introduced, whereby regulated institutions are required to separate that part of their portfolio which is actively traded, and hence most subject to position risk, from their longer-term portfolio for which the primary risk is the credit exposure. Regulated institutions include all types of financial institution, so that banks with trading books will find themselves subject to the capital adequacy constraints in the CAD in addition to those specified in the Own Funds and Solvency Ratio Directives. This means that banks will need to split their books for regulatory purposes.

The approach adopted by the CAD for calculation of capital adequacy is broadly similar to that of the SFA, in that separate risk types are identified, and for each of these a capital requirement is calculated for individual financial instruments. The sum of the requirements for each risk type is then compared with a pre-defined capital level to ascertain whether the regulated institution is deemed to have adequate capital to continue in business.

Four separate risks are identified, being position risk, settlement and counterparty risk, foreign exchange risk and other risks. 'Other risks' is a catch-all provision requiring firms to hold capital equivalent to one quarter of the previous year's fixed overheads. Detailed provisions are included in the annexes to the Directive which set out the method by which the capital requirement is to be calculated for each individual risk type. These include specific reference to individual types of financial instrument, including derivative products.

The approach for position risk is to derive an underlying open position for each instrument in a designated set of maturity bands and to apply percentages against these positions to arrive at the capital requirement. There are various provisions for netting long and short positions and positions across maturity bands, these being similar in concept to SFA guidelines. Percentages for individual maturity bands and for matching across bands do, however, differ from SFA guidelines. The concept of disaggregating complex positions into individual component parts ('building blocks') is incorporated into the rules. In addition, the Directive permits use of approved 'sensitivity', i.e. risk assessment, models for the calculation of risk positions for derivative products, enabling active market participants to take greater advantage of netting than is possible under the detailed rules which are on an instrument by instrument basis.

In assessing counterparty risk for derivative products, the Directive lifts the credit risk guidelines directly from the Solvency Ratio Directive. Hence the capital requirement is based on market value plus a percentage of notional principal dependent on maturity and counterparty type, being calculated in a manner identical to the Basle Committee guidelines discussed earlier in this section.

The Directive's approach to foreign exchange risk is as similarly wide-ranging as that adopted by the SFA. Where an institution's overall net foreign exchange position exceeds 2 per cent of capital, the excess is multiplied by 8 per cent to arrive at the capital requirement for this type of business. The net foreign exchange position encompasses spot and forward positions and delta equivalents for options.

The controversy over the CAD lies more in its scope than in the detailed provisions to be found in the annexes for calculation of the capital adequacy requirement. Hence the framework and principles for monitoring the capital adequacy for institutions active in the securities and derivative markets are certainly in place, although it is clear that there is much negotiation and discussion ahead before the Directive is likely to be ratified.

CONCLUSION

As the derivative markets develop and expand, it is clear that the various regulatory authorities will adapt and build on existing rules to ensure institutions maintain sufficient capital to cover the risks inherent in the products. From the user's perspective, the cost of maintaining this capital level should not be underestimated. Much progress has been made in recent years in harmonising regulations worldwide, and it can now be only a matter of time before the consensus on regulation of banks and credit institutions is extended to the investment and securities business. A consistent regulatory framework is critical to the efficiency and long-term effectiveness of the derivative markets and it is in the interests of both the regulators and the participants to ensure that this objective is achieved.

BIBLIOGRAPHY

Accounting Standards 1991–2 (1991), vols 1 and 2 (Financial Accounting Standards Board, USA)

Accounting Standards 1992–3 (1992) (The Institute of Chartered Accountants in England & Wales)

Accounting Standards Harmonization No. 6: New Financial Instruments (1991) (OECD)

Amended Proposal for a Council Directive on Capital Adequacy of Investment Firms and Credit Institutions (June 1992) (The Council of the European Communities)

Andrews, Peter and Brian Smouha (1990) *The Touche Ross Guide to Regulation of Banks in the United Kingdom* (Eurostudy Publishing)

Board Notice No. 71: New Financial Rules (March 1992) (The Securities and Futures Authority)

International Accounting Standards 1991–2 (1991) (International Accounting Standards Committee)

Murray-Jones, A. and A. Gamble (1991) *Managing Capital Adequacy – A Handbook of International Regulations* (Woodhead-Faulkner Ltd)

New Financial Instruments, Disclosure and Accounting (1988) (OECD)

Peerless, Simon and Andrew Boynton (1991) *Taxation and Accounting for Financial Instruments* second edition (IFR)

SORP: Off Balance Sheet Instruments and Other Commitments and Contingent Liabilities (1991) (British Bankers' Association and Irish Bankers' Federation)

Statements of Fundamental Accounting Concepts 1991–2 (1991) (Financial Accounting Standards Board, USA)

Tiner, John I. and Joe M. Conneely (1989) *Accounting for Treasury Products* second edition (Woodhead-Faulkner Ltd)

12: UK Tax Treatment

Leon Cane, Touche Ross & Co.

INTRODUCTION

Taxation of financial instruments in the UK is undergoing review. A Consultative Document published by the Inland Revenue in August 1991 highlights difficulties encountered under current law and practice. The Document makes recommendations for reform and invited representations on the proposals by 31 January 1992.

Many of the difficulties in ascertaining the tax consequences of using derivative instruments stem from the application of fundamental principles of tax law. Therefore, this chapter begins with an overview of these principles, in so far as they have a bearing on financial instruments. A second section reviews the current UK tax treatment of individual instruments, and an explanation of the Revenue's proposals concludes the chapter.

ASPECTS OF THE UK TAX SYSTEM WHICH BEAR ON DERIVATIVE INSTRUMENTS

The Schedular System

A distinction is drawn in the UK tax system between income and capital gains. Calculation of taxable income is undertaken by reference to its source. Sources are identified by the legislation, and a distinct set of rules applied (on issues such as the timing of the recognition of income, the deductibility of expenses and utilisation of losses) to establish taxable income for each. Taxation of capital gains falls under a separate regime.

The rules applicable to tax each source of income are contained in five 'schedules' within the Taxes Act and Schedule D is sub-divided into six 'cases'. The rules of Schedule D Case I (taxation of profits from a trade) are often of concern to users of financial instruments who seek to secure tax relief for payments made or establish the basis of assessment of receipts. Important rules governing the deductibility of expenses of investment companies are contained in a separate statutory tax code outside the schedular system. The principal features of Schedule D Case I which have relevance for users of derivative instruments are reviewed below.

Schedule D Case I

STATUS OF TRANSACTIONS Whether or not a transaction falls to be included within the trading activities of a company is a factual issue. For transactions in financial instruments, the company could either be investing in the instruments, speculating in them, using the instruments to hedge an exposure or trading in the instruments. Considerations such as the motive for entering into transactions and the frequency with which the transactions are undertaken will be relevant in establishing a trade in instruments. However, where the company is undertaking transactions in instruments ancillary to its main trading activities (for example, for hedging purposes), it will be necessary to establish a link between the transaction and the underlying activities if the taxpayer wishes to confer trading status upon the former. This principle has caused some difficulty and is dealt with more fully in a section below ('The distinction between hedging and speculation').

RECOGNITION OF INCOME Assuming that a transaction is correctly identified as on trading account, income generated will be charged under Schedule D Case I on the full amount of profits or gains 'accruing' from the trade. The determination of the profit 'accruing' is undertaken in line with ordinary commercial practice, which will normally involve following principles of commercial accountancy, in so far as they do not conflict with tax law. These principles will be employed to determine when income is taxable as a trading receipt. Thus, for example, a premium received under a financial instrument (such as an option) may be legitimately taxed as a trading receipt and the income spread over several accounting periods, in line with the length of the life of the instrument.

DEDUCTIBILITY OF EXPENSES To qualify for a deduction under Schedule D Case I, an expense must satisfy statutory criteria. It must be incurred wholly and exclusively for the purpose of the trade, be of a 'revenue' and not a 'capital' nature, and must not be specifically disallowed in legislation. The condition that the expense be on revenue account has caused difficulty in relation to financial instruments and is therefore given wider consideration below.

Assuming that the expense will qualify as a revenue item, timing of the deduction must be established. Deduction for a premium paid on an instrument will be legitimately spread over the life of that instrument, in line with ordinary principles of commercial accountancy.

The Capital/Revenue Distinction

When determining the deductibility of an expense against trading income under Schedule D Case I, both general principles and statute law provide that it must be a 'revenue' rather than a 'capital' item. Similarly, receipts taxable under Schedule D Case I have to be of an income, not a capital, nature. The status of a receipt or payment as income or capital is a question of law, and the courts have established criteria which can be applied in determination of the issue.

For expenses, the courts have stated that the character and duration of the benefit sought from the expenditure, the manner in which the benefit or asset is to be used, and the frequency of its occurrence, will help in its classification as capital or revenue. However, above any such evaluation, it is a common-sense appreciation of all the guiding features which must provide the ultimate answer (*BP Australia Ltd* v. *Commissioner of Taxation* [1966] AC 224). No single factor is determinative, but each will be indicative. Thus, a foreign exchange loss on repayment of a currency loan which was determined to be an accretion to the capital of the company was not a revenue expense and was thus disallowed as a trading expense. Likewise, expenditure on financial instruments which are viewed as hedging capital items will not be deductible against trading income.

However, the taxation of receipts from financial instruments as income or capital gains is sometimes simplified by legislation. A transaction in financial futures or options which is not undertaken as a trading transaction in itself, nor referable to a trading transaction on revenue account, is taken into the capital gains tax regime (TA 1988, s.128 and ICGA 1992, s.143). To establish the link between the trading activity and the ancillary transaction in the financial instrument (so that the latter can be accorded 'trading' status), the principles outlined below in the section on hedging and speculation must be applied.

The requirement that an expense be on revenue and not capital account is modified for instruments which hedge interest costs, where the loan is from a UK bank and used for the purpose of the trade. Although such instruments may hedge a loan of a duration which could categorise it as 'capital', profits or losses on the instruments may still qualify for taxation or relief as trading items. This is because of the assimilation of interest to a trading expense in these circumstances.

The Status of Companies

The status of a company will be determined by the nature of its activities. When undertaking an analysis of the tax consequences of transactions in financial instruments, it is helpful to distinguish three categories of company: financial trading companies, other trading companies and investment companies.

A financial trading company will often deal in derivative products as an integral part of its principal trading activity. Thus, profits and losses arising on contracts concluded in the course of this activity will be taxed or relieved under Schedule D Case I. Contracts still open at the year-end will probably be valued on a 'mark-to-market' basis, and any profit or loss arising on these open positions reflected in the taxable results.

A company with a non-financial trade, which uses instruments to hedge trading exposures, may have trading treatment accorded to the results from contracts in financial instruments. This will be so if the contracts in financial instruments are 'ancillary' to the main trading activities.

An investment company is specifically defined in tax legislation as one whose business consists wholly or mainly of the making of investments and the principal part of whose income is derived therefrom (TA 1988, s.130). The holding company of most quoted groups will be an investment company, as it simply holds shares in the trading subsidiaries, receives dividends from them and pays these dividends on to the shareholders.

An investment company is taxable on the income it receives from its investments (other than dividend income from other UK companies, as this is outside the scope of corporation tax) and on gains realised from the sale of investments. Against this income and gains, the legislation permits offset of certain interest costs and 'expenses of management'. The latter category of expenses is restricted to items incurred in managing the business, and foreign exchange losses and payments made under financial instruments are not within the definition. Thus, utilisation of losses incurred by an investment company under a financial instrument is restricted to offset against capital gains. For this reason, groups often prefer to locate transactions in financial instruments in trading companies rather than investment companies.

The Distinction Between Hedging and Speculation

A taxpayer which is not trading in derivatives will often prefer to have a contract in derivative instruments taxed as an activity ancillary to a main trading activity (i.e. under Schedule D Case I). This is because more use can be made of any losses. It will therefore be necessary to establish the connection between the contract and the underlying trading transaction. There is case law authority which confirms the legitimacy of taxing a derivative contract by reference to its underlying purpose (for example, *Van den Berghs Ltd* v. *Clark* [1935] AC 431). However, it may not always be straightforward to link a hedge with the underlying asset or transaction hedged.

It is possible for a contract in futures or options to be a trading transaction in its own right. The intention of the parties and the frequency with which such contracts are undertaken are important considerations in the identification of an activity of trading. The Revenue have published a Statement of Practice

(SP14/91), which sets out their criteria for identifying transactions in financial futures and options which can be linked with trading activities. Whilst this Statement of Practice refers only to financial futures and options, the principles applied to link a contract with an underlying asset or transaction to which it is 'ancillary' can be applied generally in the context of financial instruments. Nowhere in the Statement of Practice is the term 'hedging' mentioned, but a contract in futures or options which is 'ancillary' to a main contract can be taken to include a hedging activity.

The Statement of Practice explains that a financial futures or options contract clearly ancillary to a trading transaction on 'current account' (i.e. of a revenue nature) will satisfy the qualifying criteria of Schedule D Case I and thus will give rise to a profit or loss which can be taxed or relieved within the trading results. A contract which is not a trading transaction on current account will be taxed under the capital gains regime.

In determining whether a financial futures or options transaction is ancillary to another transaction, factors identified by the Statement of Practice as relevant are an intention to eliminate risk and the economic appropriateness of the proposed hedge to that transaction.

The Statement explains that the financial futures or options contract may be ancillary to more than one transaction and that more than one financial futures or options transaction may be ancillary to a particular transaction. The Statement accepts that it may be necessary to enter into new financial futures or options transactions, or to terminate existing ones, to reflect changes in the value of the assets or liabilities resulting from the underlying transaction.

It may therefore be necessary to determine whether the financial futures or options contract is 'economically appropriate' to the elimination or reduction of risk. The Statement sets out considerations used by the Revenue in making this judgement. These are:

- the contract is one which, by virtue of the relationship between fluctuations in its own price and the value of the transaction to which it is ancillary, may reasonably be regarded as appropriate to be used in order to eliminate or reduce risk;
- the use of a financial futures or options contract based on an index is not regarded as precluding the existence of the expectation that the above relationship exists;
- the principal on which the financial futures or options contract is based should not exceed significantly the principal of the transaction to which it is ancillary;
- where the main transaction falls away or the intention to enter into it is abandoned, the financial futures or options contract will still be regarded as ancillary to this transaction, if it closed out within as short a period as is practicable.

The burden of proof is upon the taxpayer to show that a derivative instrument should be linked to a trading transaction on revenue account and thus secure a trading deduction for any expense. The timing of the deduction must be determined by reference to the general principles of Schedule D. The taxpayer will address whatever evidence is available to secure trading treatment, amongst which may be the criteria set out in the Revenue's Statement of Practice.

Interest

The UK tax treatment of interest is notoriously complex. This complexity is compounded when the principles are extended to the tax treatment of financial instruments. This section provides an overview of the relevant principles, in so far as they are especially relevant to users of derivative instruments.

Definition of Interest
Case law has established that, to qualify as interest, as payment must satisfy two conditions. First, there must be a sum of money by reference to which the payment is to be ascertained. Second, this money must be owed to the person to whom the 'interest' is paid.

Short Interest
It is necessary to draw a distinction between short interest and annual interest. Where the borrowing is for a term of less than one year and is not intended to continue for more than a year, any interest paid will be 'short'. This distinction is important because deductibility is determined under the general principles of Schedule D Case I (for trading companies) and the regime applicable to expenses of management (for investment companies). Furthermore, no withholding tax arises on short interest. Short interest paid by non-trading companies may be relieved as a charge on income (see below) if paid to a UK bank.

Annual Interest
Annual interest paid by companies is specifically disallowed as a *trading* expense, other than when payable in the UK for the purposes of a trade to a bank carrying on a bona fide banking business in the UK. However, a deduction against total profits (i.e. all income and gains) is available for annual interest paid, and relief is granted under the rules of deduction applicable to 'charges on income'. Payments which may qualify as charges on income include annual interest, certain discounts and other 'annual payments'. The term 'annual payment' takes its definition from Case III of Schedule D. Where the annual payment has a UK source, a company making such a payment is required to withhold tax at the basic rate of income tax and account

to the UK Revenue for the tax withheld. Companies receive tax relief for charges on income on a 'paid' (not accruals) basis and such income is assessed strictly on a 'received' basis.

Annual interest outside these rules (i.e. paid to a UK bank) is relieved on an accruals basis, and assessed on the bank as trading income on the same basis. No withholding tax is applied to such payments.

Discounts

The UK tax system treats discounts, other than 'deep discounts', differently from interest. Investment companies will obtain no tax deduction for discounts, as they fall outside the definition of 'expenses of management', and trading companies must rely on the general principles of Schedule D for a deduction. Thus, in the latter case, any discounted security would have to be short-term (i.e. on revenue account) and the borrowing undertaken to finance trading activities. There is no withholding tax on discounts.

The 'deep discount security' was defined by the 1984 Finance Act. A deep discount is one which exceeds either 15 per cent overall or 0.5 per cent per annum. The legislation identifies a deep discount security as a redeemable security which yields a deep discount. Tax relief is granted to issuers of deep discounted securities on an accruals basis over the life of the security. The holders of the securities are not taxed on the discount until they either dispose of the security (in which case they are taxed on the proportion of discount which has accrued to the date of the disposal) or until the security is redeemed. This tax asymmetry does not apply to deep discount securities held by companies associated with the issuer or within the same 51 per cent group.

Tax relief on the discount is given as if the discount allocated to each accounting period were a charge on income. The legislation defining a deep discount security is complex. Among the qualifying conditions are requirements that the security should not be convertible into shares and that there should be only one redemption facility (which precludes an 'investor put' back to the issuer). Deep discount securities are very widely used for bond issues, because of the tax asymmetry between deduction and assessment, the fact that deduction is guaranteed as a charge on income, and the absence of withholding tax.

Foreign Exchange and Foreign Currency

Foreign exchange gains and losses may fall either within the scope of Schedule D Case I or within the capital gains tax regime.

Trading Activities

Currency gains and losses which arise in the course of trading activities and which are on revenue account (for example, in respect of trade receivables or payables) will fall within Schedule D Case I. It may also be possible to include profits or losses on currency hedging techniques within the Schedule D Case I rules, if the necessary link between the hedge and an underlying trading activitiy can be established. Only realised currency gains can be brought into charge. However, unrealised gains and losses on trading items can be brought within the trading results for tax purposes, provided this is done on a consistent basis.

Where an exchange loss arises on long-term borrowing, difficulties will arise in securing a deduction under Schedule D Case I, on the grounds that the currency loss is not a 'revenue' deduction. On the other hand, gains on repayments of long-term loans are similarly outside the scope of Schedule D Case I. The rules are more complex with regard to 'matched positions' i.e. where long-term (capital) loans in a foreign currency finance trading assets in the same currency. As a result of the judgement in favour of the taxpayer in a landmark tax case in which this situation arose (*Pattison* v. *Marine Midland Ltd* [1984] STC 10), a 'matching principle' can be applied. This principle operates so that, to the extent that foreign currency denominated monetary assets are matched by liabilities in the same currency (i.e. any translation adjustments would be equal and opposite), no overall effect need be recognised for tax purposes. The rule applies only in relation to trading companies and is explained in an Inland Revenue Statement of Practice (SP1/84). The Statement of Practice extends the rule to unmatched positions and provides a regime for partial offset in these circumstances. A currency position which is not actually matched by an asset or liability in the same currency, but which is hedged by a currency forward or futures contract (but *not* an option contract), is treated under the Statement of Practice as matched for these purposes.

Foreign Currency and Capital Gains Tax

Foreign currency is a chargeable asset for capital gains tax purposes. Hence transactions by companies in currency which are outside a trading activity (i.e. not taxed under Schedule D Case I) will be taxable or relievable as a chargeable gain or loss. For capital gains tax purposes, currency is disposed of either by conversion into sterling or upon its being spent (for example, its application in repayment of a foreign currency loan). The date of acquisition or disposal of an asset under the capital gains regime is generally the contract date. Where the contract is conditional, the date of acquisition or disposal is the date the contract becomes unconditional. Thus, currency sold under a forward contract is treated as disposed of at the date the forward contract is entered into, and not at the date of maturity of the contract (i.e. the delivery date).

For calculation of the gain and loss on disposal of an asset denominated in a foreign currency, it is necessary to establish the sterling equivalent of the acquisition cost at the date of acquisition and the sterling equivalent of the disposal proceeds at the date of disposal. The gain or loss is then the difference between the two sterling amounts, as adjusted for indexation.

A gain or loss on repayment of foreign currency borrowings is outside the scope of capital gains tax. This is because the loss arises on the extinction of a liability and not the disposal of an asset. To qualify for tax relief on such losses, it is necessary to pull the borrowings into 'revenue' account of a trading company, i.e. they must be taken out to finance a trade and be of a short-term nature.

TREATMENT OF SPECIFIC INSTRUMENTS

Options (Including Warrants)

The tax treatment of options will depend upon the circumstances in which they are granted (written) or acquired, as well as upon the nature of the options. It is necessary to examine the general principles of tax law which apply to options before proceeding to a more detailed consideration of financial options, traders and the use of options as hedging instruments.

General Principles

Under the capital gains regime, the sale of an option is treated as a disposal of an asset (the option itself) by the writer. This produces a gain equal to the premium received, less any incidental costs of wrting the option. If the option is never exercised, no further tax consequences arise for the writer.

If the option is exercised, the exercise and the sale must be combined for tax purposes, and any tax paid by the writer on the sale of the option can be recovered. Thus, if the option conferred a right upon the buyer to buy an asset from the writer (a call option), the premium received for the option will be added to the consideration received for the sale of the asset on exercise, and the two events will be treated as a single disposal by the writer. The tax base cost of the asset to the purchaser will be both the cost of the option and the price paid on exercise (subject to the respective indexation allowances).

If the option conferred a right upon the buyer to sell an asset to the writer (a put option), the premiums received for the option will reduce the tax base cost of the asset for the writer, on exercise, and reduce the consideration received for the asset by the purchaser.

In the hands of the buyer, the option represents an asset. Since almost invariably options have a life of less than 50 years, an option will constitute a 'wasting asset'. Under UK tax law, the tax base cost of this asset will be progressively reduced day by day as the option's term approaches expiry.

However, the wasting asset rules do not apply to 'qualifying' 'traded' and 'financial' options (see below), nor do they apply to options to acquire assets which, if acquired, will be used by the buyer for the purposes of a trade. Abandonment of a wasting-asset option by a grantee does not usually constitute a disposal of the asset, and thus no capital loss will arise. Again, this rule does not apply in the case of 'qualifying', 'traded' and 'financial' options, nor in the case of options to acquire assets which, if acquired, will be used by the buyer for the purposes of a trade.

Qualifying Traded and Financial Options

Special rules apply to 'traded options' and 'financial options' as defined in the tax legislation. These two classes are collectively called 'qualifying options'. The term 'traded option' covers any option which, at the date of its disposal, is quoted on a 'recognised stock exchange' or a 'recognised futures exchange' (as explained below). Thus, as well as traded options in the usual sense, the term covers listed warrants.

The term 'financial option' itself covers two classes of option, which are broadly as follows:

(i) options dealt in (but not quoted) on a 'recognised stock exchange', e.g. London Stock Exchange traditional options;
(ii) OTC options granted by an authorised or exempt person as defined under the Financial Services Act 1986 (and concurrent cross options).

The advantages of these 'qualifying' categories of option are threefold. The first is that they are specifically excluded from the wasting asset rules, and so their expiry will constitute a disposal for capital gains purposes. The second is that they are excluded from the scope of Schedule D Case VI, which taxes incidental gains from options in a fashion which is not favourable. The third advantage (which does not extend to 'financial options') is that the cost of closing out a 'traded option' by buying an identical option will be treated as part of the cost of writing the first option, under the capital gains rules. This leaves open the potential difficulty of obtaining tax relief under the capital gains rules for the cost of closing out options which are not 'traded', i.e. OTC positions.

For tax purposes, the terms 'recognised stock exchange' and 'recognised futures exchange' mean exchanges which have been designated by the Inland Revenue. Designation orders are not retrospective. At the time of writing, there are recognised stock exchanges in twenty-five (predominantly developed) countries; and recognised futures exchanges in six: Australia; Canada; Hong Kong; Sweden; the UK; and the US.

The Inland Revenue has been known to question whether a cash settled option subject to automatic exercise (such as a cap) can qualify as an option for tax purposes, as the ordinary use of the term 'option' implies the need to exercise a choice. The wasting asset consequences of the treatment of an option contract as a future for tax purposes, are explained under the section below on forward rate agreements. A similar wasting asset problem can arise if an option on a future is exercised, because the premium paid for the option is now deemed to be an upfront payment for the futures contract.

Exemptions from Tax

Options on gilts and qualifying corporate bonds are outside the scope of tax on capital gains. Pension funds and authorised unit trusts are exempt from tax on both capital gains and income from transactions in options (except that authorised unit trusts might be taxed under Schedule D Case VI on dealings in options which are not 'qualifying'). Investment trusts are exempt from tax on capital gains from transactions in options.

Options Traders

Banks and financial traders dealing in options will be taxed on their dealing profits or losses as a Schedule D Case I activity. The open positions at the year-end will commonly be marked-to-market in the financial accounts, and this treatment is acceptable for tax purposes. Where, exceptionally, such persons write options other than in the course of their trade, the capital gains rules will apply.

Options as Hedging Instruments

It is necessary to establish whether an option contract is ancillary to a trading activity, which may therefore accord the transaction treatment under Schedule D Case I in line with the principles set out earlier. If this is the case, any premium paid would constitute an expense deductible under Schedule D Case I, and sums received would be Schedule D Case I receipts. The relevant principles for timing of deduction of expenses and recognition of income would then have to be applied. Where, however, such contracts are not referable to trading activities, the capital gains regime will apply.

Forward Foreign Exchange Contracts

A forward foreign exchange contract executed by a financial trader in the course of a trade will produce a profit or loss for Schedule D Case I purposes. If the open year-end positions are valued on a mark-to-market basis, any resultant unrealised gains or losses can be included in the taxable results, provided that this policy is followed consistently. If forward contracts by entities other than financial traders can be linked to an underlying trading activity, profits or losses will, again, be dealt with under the rules of Schedule D Case I. In the latter circumstances, however, a mark-to-market year-end valuation would not be acceptable for tax purposes.

Forward foreign exchange contracts concluded outside a trading activity will fall within the capital gains regime, as foreign currency is a chargeable asset. A forward sale of currency will constitute a disposal at the date the forward contract is made. However, while the disposal proceeds will be fixed under the contract, the acquisition cost of the currency will not be known until later. Thus the taxable gain or allowable loss may not be known until the maturity of the contract. It is possible to delay the disposal date (for tax purposes) by the use of cross options.

Financial Futures

Dealers in financial futures will be taxed on the resultant profits or losses under the general principles of Schedule D Case I. For other parties, financial futures which are referable to a trading activity may fall to be taxed in accordance with the Schedule D Case I rules, if the criteria set out earlier are satisfied.

Contracts in financial futures which are not entered into during the course of a trade and which are not referable to an underlying trading activity fall generally within the capital gains regime. The capital gains legislation treats the closing out of a futures position, by matching or by cash settlement, as a disposal of a notional asset (the obligations under the original contract).

Thus, if a futures contract is closed out by a reciprocal contract, the capital gain or loss will be equal to the actual profit or loss (there is no indexation allowance). A cash settlement will similarly be treated as producing a capital gain or loss equal to the cash received or paid on settlement.

A futures contract which runs to delivery is treated simply as a purchase or sale of the underlying asset for capital gains purposes.

Qualifying 'Financial Futures'

Protection from assessment under Schedule D Case VI is given for 'financial futures'. For convenience, these specially protected futures contracts are referred to below as 'qualifying futures'. A corollary of their protection from Case VI is, reasonably enough, that losses on such contracts cannot qualify as Case VI losses. 'Qualifying futures' comprise two classes of contract, which are broadly as follows:

(i) futures dealt in on a 'recognised futures exchange' (as discussed above);
(ii) futures bought from or sold to an authorised or exempt person as defined under the Financial Services Act 1986.

A catch is that there is no protection from Case VI assessment on profits from futures contracts dealt in on 'recognised stock exchanges' outside the UK (e.g. futures contracts traded on the Tokyo Stock Exchange).

Exemptions from Tax

Futures which relate to gilts and qualifying corporate bonds are outside the scope of tax on capital gains. Pension funds and authorised unit trusts are exempt from tax on both capital gains and income from transactions in futures (except that authorised unit trusts could be taxed under Schedule D Case VI on dealings which are not classed as qualifying futures).

Forward Rate Agreements (FRAs)

Banks and financial institutions will generally be taxed or relieved on FRA contracts as trading receipts or expenses, provided the contract is executed in the course of the trade. An FRA which is used to hedge a liability incurrred for trading purposes will also give rise to a trading receipt or payment. A receipt or payment other than in these circumstances will generally be treated as a capital gain (receipt) or a capital loss (payment), as an FRA is treated as a financial future. If, however, the FRA involves payment of an upfront premium, the wasting asset rules will be applied to this amount, as the FRA is not a qualifying option. Thus, by the expiry of the contract, the premium will be exhausted in tax terms.

Interest Rate Swaps

The tax treatment of swap payments will depend upon the status of the user and the purpose for which the swap is undertaken. Again, for the purpose of this analysis, it is helpful to distinguish swaps traders from other users of swap instruments.

Recurrent swap payments made by banks and other financial institutions actively engaged in a swaps business will normally be deductible as a trading expense on an accruals basis. Payments made by banks acting as principal in the ordinary course of their banking business, or by UK swaps dealers acting as principals in the ordinary course of their business, will not be subject to a withholding tax obligation. Payments to such entities will be recognised for tax on an accruals basis and are not subject to withholding tax in the UK. Payments and receipts for early termination of the agreement will be included in the trading results of such entities.

In the case of other corporate users of swaps, Revenue practice is to allow tax deductions for recurrent swap payments as charges, on a 'paid' basis, except where they are paid gross to a UK bank by a trading company (for trading purposes). In the latter case, the payments are deductible as a trading expense, on an accruals basis.

For swap payments deductible as charges, income tax must be deducted, except when made to a UK bank or swaps dealer or to a counterparty resident in a country with which the UK has an appropriate double tax agreement. Swap fees are covered by the 'business profits' article of tax treaties.

Initial fees for entering into a swap are not tax deductible. For this reason, these fees are often factored into the recurrent payment schedule. Payments made for early termination of a swap agreement by corporates (other than swaps dealers) will not qualify for tax relief, unless they can be brought within the qualifying conditions of Schedule D Case I. Receipts for early termination will be taxed as trading receipts or under Schedule D Case VI.

Currency Swaps

Recurrent payments and receipts, payments on receipts for early termination and initial fees are dealt with in the same way as for interest rate swaps (above). Currency gains or losses on the principal sum will be trading gains or losses for traders in swaps and for other trading companies, where the swap transaction can be correctly treated as on revenue account. A particular difficulty with currency swaps (for users other than swap dealers) is that foreign currency is itself a chargeable asset for capital gains purposes. Thus, if the swap is not regarded as a Schedule D Case I item, the exchange of currency for sterling at a predetermined rate on the unwinding of the swap will rise to a chargeable disposal. However, as with forward foreign exchange contracts, the date of the disposal is at the inception of the swap. As the capital gains tax cost of the currency sold will not usually be known until the date of unwinding, it will not be possible to calculate the chargeable gain. This problem can be dealt with through the use of cross options, so that recognition of the disposal can be delayed until the termination date.

PROPOSED REFORM

Introduction

It should be apparent from the preceding sections that the taxation of foreign exchange differences and transactions in derivative instruments produces uncertainty for UK companies. This uncertainty has led to much dissatisfaction, and two recent Consultative Documents have sought to introduce reform which will ameliorate the position. Both Documents move towards assimilation to income of foreign exchange differences and profits or losses from use of financial instruments. The Documents herald important changes to the UK tax system and are therefore summarised in this section.

Foreign Exchange

Reform of the taxation of foreign exchange differences has been under review for some time. The Consultative Document published in March 1991 is the second on this subject and has generated much debate.

The proposals in the Document would apply to companies. They would not apply to certain institutions which are exempt from taxation on capital gains, such as unit and investment trusts. The Document recommends that exchange differences on 'monetary' items be recognised as part of the Schedule D Case I trading results (if the difference arises from a transaction, asset or liability referable to a trade) or as a Schedule D Case III receipt or expense. These differences would be recognised for tax purposes on a translation basis, i.e. as they accrue. The definition of 'monetary' asset or liability would follow that provided under the accounting rules of SSAP 20. Thus, cash, debts and advances are monetary assets; and loans, creditors and deposits held are monetary liabilities. The status of monetary assets denominated in foreign currency as chargeable assets for capital gains purposes would be withdrawn.

The potential difficulties which could arise from taxation of unrealised exchange gains are mitigated in the proposals. This is achieved by restricting recognition of net unrealised gains on long-term capital borrowings to 10 per cent of the taxable profit (including exchange differences) for the year. The excess of any unrealised gains would be carried forward to subsequent years, and the same test applied again.

The use of a foreign currency as a 'functional' currency for tax purposes is considered in the Document. Transitional rules are proposed for the introduction of the new regime whereby foreign currency assets and liabilities are revalued at the date of introduction of the proposals, with foreign exchange differences accruing after the date being taxed under the new rules.

A significant problem with these proposals is that the matching of exchange differences on monetary liabilities (currency loans) with non-monetary assets (particularly shares in subsidiaries) is rejected. Thus, unrealised gains on the loans will be subect to tax. The proposals introduce a facility for matching in such circumstances to avoid the possible disadvantages of recognising such 'profits' on an asymmetric basis. Allied to this issue is the rejection of share capital as a monetary liability, which is not considered.

Financial Instruments

A Consultative Document entitled 'The Tax Treatment of Financial Instruments for Managing Interest Rate Risk' was published in August 1991. The instruments covered by the proposals are therefore restricted, but currency swaps are specifically included. The new rules would apply to all corporate users, but not unit trusts, investment trusts or offshore funds.

The development of a revised system is undertaken in two stages. The first stage deals with the most satisfactory basis for taxing the results, the second deals with recognition of profits or losses. Three alternative bases for taxation are set out. The first is a 'hedging' approach, which assimilates the tax treatment of the instrument to that of any underlying asset or transaction, where this identification can be made. The second is an 'analytic' approach, which breaks the instrument into component parts and applies the correct tax treatment to each. The third basis is the 'income' approach, which taxes all payments and receipts under these instruments as income or expenses.

The Document identifies the 'income' approach as the most satisfactory and recommends its adoption. For trading companies, results from the use of instruments for the purposes of the trade would form part of the trading results. For transactions in instruments by investment companies or by trading companies other than for the purpose of their trade, receipts and payments will be treated as interest. The same treatment would be accorded to lump sums paid or received to terminate an instrument before its maturity date.

The timing of recognition of receipts and payments is then examined by the Document. Three alternative bases are considered. The first is a 'payments' basis, under which receipts and payments are recognised for tax as and when received and paid. The second basis is an accruals method, which spreads the payments or receipts over the life of the instrument. The final basis is termed 'mark-to-market', which brings into tax both payments and receipts made in each accounting period and also shifts in the value of the underlying instrument over its life. The Document expresses preference for the 'mark-to-market' approach. The basis would always be accepted by the Revenue where it is adopted by the user of the instrument for accounting purposes. However, the suggestion is made that the taxpayer should be given the alternative of adopting an 'acceptable accruals' basis to calculate the tax effect of using the instruments.

The failure of the Document to permit a 'hedging' approach introduces a major problem. This is the possibility that hedging transactions which are effective on a pre-tax basis will not be effective post-tax; and the tax treatment of the instrument may have to be taken into account independently of the underlying asset or transaction. This will prove unsatisfactory to many corporates which use derivatives solely for the purposes of hedging. As with the foreign exchange proposals, the apparent introduction of clarity may actually result in a reduction of the ability of companies to provide for commercial uncertainties by tax efficient methods.

Note The views expressed in this chapter are the author's and do not necessarily reflect those of Touche Ross & Co.

Appendix

ISDA MASTER AGREEMENT (JUNE 1992)

The ISDA multi-currency cross border Master Agreement contained in this appendix was issued in June 1992 and represents a revised version of the 1987 agreement. Separately, ISDA has issued a single jurisdiction document which can be used by counterparties domiciled in the same country and a series of booklets and confirmations for particular classes of instrument. The latter underlie the Master Agreement and provide the legal details for individual transactions. The Master Agreement may be restricted or tailored by counterparties to reflect the nature of the relationship and specific transactions and instruments. It has been designed to admit as many of the standard types of instrument as possible in order to increase the scope of cross-product netting provisions. In the absence of specific agreement to the contrary, the documentation provides for two-way payments to be enforced in the event of default.

ISDA®

International Swap Dealers Association, Inc.

MASTER AGREEMENT

dated as of ....

.... and ....

have entered and/or anticipate entering into one or more transactions (each a 'Transaction') that are or will be governed by this Master Agreement, which includes the schedule (the 'Schedule'), and the documents and other confirming evidence (each a 'Confirmation') exchanged between the parties confirming those Transactions.

Accordingly, the parties agree as follows:–

1. Interpretation

(a) ***Definitions*** The terms defined in Section 14 and in the Schedule will have the meanings therein specified for the purpose of this Master Agreement.

(b) ***Inconsistency*** In the event of any inconsistency between the provisions of the Schedule and the other provisions of this Master Agreement, the Schedule will prevail. In the event of any inconsistency between the provisions of any Confirmation and this Master Agreement (including the Schedule), such Confirmation will prevail for the purpose of the relevant Transaction.

(c) ***Single Agreement*** All Transactions are entered into in reliance on the fact that this Master Agreement and all Confirmations form a single agreement between the parties (collectively referred to as this 'Agreement'), and the parties would not otherwise enter into any Transactions.

2. Obligations

(a) ***General Conditions***

(i) Each party will make each payment or delivery specified in each Confirmation to be made by it, subject to the other provisions of this Agreement.

(ii) Payments under this Agreement will be made on the due date for value on that date in the place of the account specified in the relevant Confirmation or otherwise pursuant to this Agreement, in freely transferable funds and in the manner customary for payments in the required currency. Where settlement is by delivery (that is, other than by payment), such delivery will be made for receipt on the due date in the manner customary for the relevant obligation unless otherwise specified in the relevant Confirmation or elsewhere in this Agreement.

(iii) Each obligation of each party under Section 2(a)(i) is subject to (1) the condition precedent that no Event of Default or Potential Event of Default with respect to the other party has occurred and is continuing, (2) the condition precedent that no Early Termination Date in respect of the relevant Transaction has occurred or been effectively designated and (3) each other applicable condition precedent specified in this Agreement.

(b) ***Change of Account*** Either party may change its account for receiving a payment or delivery by giving notice to the other party at least five Local Business Days prior to the scheduled date for the payment or delivery to which such change applies unless such other party gives timely notice of a reasonable objection to such change.

(c) ***Netting*** If on any date amounts would otherwise be payable:–

(i) in the same currency; and

(ii) in respect of the same Transaction,

by each party to the other, then, on such date, each party's obligation to make payment of any such amount will be automatically satisfied and discharged and, if the aggregate amount that would otherwise have been payable by one party exceeds the aggregate amount that would otherwise have been payable by the other party, replaced by an obligation upon the party by whom the larger aggregate amount would have been payable to pay to the other party the excess of the larger aggregate amount over the smaller aggregate amount.

The parties may elect in respect of two or more Transactions that a net amount will be determined in respect of all amounts payable on the same date in the same currency in respect of such Transactions, regardless of whether such amounts are payable in respect of the same Transaction. The election may be made in the Schedule or a Confirmation by specifying that subparagraph (ii) above will not apply to the Transactions identified as being subject to the election, together with the starting date (in which case subparagraph (ii) above will not, or will cease to, apply to such Transactions from such date). This election may be made separately for different groups of Transactions and will apply separately to each pairing of Offices through which the parties make and receive payments or deliveries.

(d) ***Deduction or Withholding for Tax***

(i) ***Gross-Up*** All payments under this Agreement will be made without any deduction or withholding for or on account of any Tax unless such deduction or withholding is required by any applicable law, as modified by the practice of any relevant governmental revenue authority, then in effect. If a party is so required to deduct or withhold, then that party ('X') will:–

(1) promptly notify the other party ('Y') of such requirement;

(2) pay to the relevant authorities the full amount required to be deducted or withheld (including the full amount required to be deducted or withheld from any additional amount paid by X to Y under this Section 2(d)) promptly upon the earlier of determining that such deduction or withholding is required or receiving notice that such amount has been assessed against Y;

(3) promptly forward to Y an official receipt (or a certified copy), or other documentation reasonably acceptable to Y, evidencing such payment to such authorities, and

(4) if such Tax is an Indemnifiable Tax, pay to Y, in addition to the payment to which Y is otherwise entitled under this Agreement, such additional amount as is necessary to ensure that the net amount actually received by Y (free and clear of Indemnifiable Taxes, whether assessed against X or Y) will equal the full amount Y would have received had such deduction or withholding been required. However, X will not be required to pay any additional amount to Y to the extent that it would not be required to be paid but for:–

(A) the failure by Y to comply with or perform any agreement contained in Section 4(a)(i), 4(a)(iii) or 4(d); or

(B) the failure of a representation made by Y pursuant to Section 3(f) to be accurate and true unless such failure would not have occurred but for (I) any action taken by a taxing authority, or brought in a court of competent jurisdiction, on or after the date on which a Transaction is entered into (regardless of whether such action is taken or brought with respect to a party to this Agreement) or (II) a Change in Tax Law.

(ii) *Liability*. If:–

(1) X is required by any applicable law, as modified by the practice of any relevant governmental revenue authority, to make any deduction or withholding in respect of which X would not be required to pay any additional amount to Y under Section 2(d)(i)4;

(2) X does not so deduct or withhold; and

(3) a liability resulting from such Tax is assessed directly against X,

then, except to the extent Y has satisfied or then satisfies the liability resulting from such Tax, Y will promptly pay to X the amount of such liability (including any related liability for interest, but including any related liability for penalties only if Y has failed to comply with or perform any agreement contained in Section 4(a)(i), 4(a)(iii) or 4(d)).

(e) ***Default Interest; Other Amounts*** Prior to the occurrence or effective designation of an Early Termination Date in respect of the relevant Transaction, a party that defaults in the performance of any payment obligation will, to the extent permitted by law and subject to Section 6(c), be required to pay interest (before as well as after judgement) on the overdue amount to the other party on demand in the same currency as such overdue amount, for the period from (and including) the original due date for payment to (but excluding) the date of actual payment, at the Default Rate. Such interest will be calculated on the basis of daily compounding and the actual number of days elapsed. If, prior to the occurrence or effective designation of an Early Termination Date in respect of the relevant Transaction, a party defaults in the performance of any obligation required to be settled by delivery, it will compensate the other party on demand if and to the extent provided for in the relevant Confirmation or elsewhere in this Agreement.

3. Representations

Each party represents to the other party (which representations will be deemed to be repeated by each party on each date on which a Transaction is entered into and, in the case of the representations in Section 3(f), at all times until the termination of this Agreement) that:–

(a) ***Basic Representations***

(i) ***Status*** It is duly organised and validly existing under the laws of the jurisdiction of its organisation or incorporation and, if relevant under such laws, in good standing;

(ii) ***Powers*** It has the power to execute this Agreement and any other documentation relating to this Agreement to which it is a party, to deliver this Agreement and any other documentation relating to this Agreement that it is required by this Agreement to deliver and to perform its obligations under this Agreement and any obligations it has under any Credit Support Document to which it is a party and has taken all necessary action to authorise such execution, delivery and performance;

(iii) ***No Violation or Conflict*** Such execution, delivery and performance do not violate or conflict with any law applicable to it, any provision of its constitutional documents, any order or judgement of any court or other agency of government applicable to it or any of its assets or any contractual restriction binding on or affecting it or any of its assets;

(iv) ***Consents*** All governmental and other consents that are required to have been obtained by it with respect to this Agreement or any Credit Support Document to which it is a party have been obtained and are in full force and effect and all conditions of any such consents have been complied with; and

(v) ***Obligations Binding*** Its obligations under this Agreement and any Credit Support Document to which it is a party constitute its legal, valid and binding obligations, enforceable in accordance with their respective terms (subject to applicable bankruptcy, reorganisation, insolvency, moratorium or similar laws affecting creditors' rights generally and subject, as to enforceability, to equitable principles of general application (regardless of whether enforcement is sought in a proceeding in equity or at law)).

(b) ***Absence of Certain Events*** No Event of Default or Potential Event of Default or, to its knowledge, Termination Event with respect to it has occurred and is continuing and no such event or circumstance would occur as a result of its entering into or performing its obligations under this Agreement or any Credit Support Document to which it is a party.

(c) ***Absence of Litigation*** There is not pending or, to its knowledge, threatened against it or any of its Affiliates any action, suit or proceeding at law or in equity or before any court, tribunal, governmental body, agency or official or any arbitrator that is likely to affect the legality, validity or enforceability against it of this Agreement or any Credit Support Document to which it is a party or its ability to perform its obligations under this Agreement or such Credit Support Document.

(d) ***Accuracy of Specified Information*** All applicable information that is furnished in writing by or on behalf of it to the other party and is identified for the purpose of this Section 3(d) in the Schedule is, as of the date of the information, true, accurate and complete in every material respect.

(e) ***Payer Tax Representation*** Each representation specified in the Schedule as being made by it for the purpose of this Section 3(e) is accurate and true.

(f) ***Payee Tax Representations*** Each representation specified in the Schedule as being made by it for the purpose of this Section 3(f) is accurate and true.

4. Agreements

Each party agrees with the other that, so long as either party has or may have any obligation under this Agreement or under any Credit Support Document to which it is a party:–

(a) ***Furnish Specified Information*** It will deliver to the other party or, in certain cases under subparagraph (iii) below, to such government or taxing authority as the other party reasonably directs:–

(i) any forms, documents or certificates relating to taxation specified in the Schedule or any Confirmation;

(ii) any other documents specified in the Schedule or any Confirmation; and

(iii) upon reasonable demand by such other party, any form or document that may be required or reasonably requested in writing in order to allow such other party or its Credit Support Provider to make a payment under this Agreement or any applicable Credit Support Document without any deduction or withholding for or on account of any Tax or with such deduction or withholding at a reduced rate (so long as the completion, execution or submission of such form or document would not materially prejudice the legal or commercial position of the party in receipt of such demand), with any such form or document to be accurate and completed in a manner reasonably satisfactory to such other party and to be executed and to be delivered with any reasonably required certification,

in each case by the date specified in the Schedule or such Confirmation or, if none is specified, as soon as reasonably practicable.

(b) ***Maintain Authorisation*** It will use all reasonable efforts to maintain in full force and effect all consents of any governmental or other authority that are required to be obtained by it with respect to this Agreement or any Credit Support Document to which it is a party and will use all reasonable efforts to obtain any that may become necessary in the future.

(c) ***Comply with Laws*** It will comply in all material respects with all applicable laws and orders to which it may be subject if failure so to comply would materially impair its ability to perform its obligations under this Agreement or any Credit Support Document to which it is a party.

(d) ***Tax Agreement*** It will give notice of any failure of a representation made by it under Section 3(f) to be accurate and true promptly upon learning of such failure.

(e) ***Payment of Stamp Tax*** Subject to Section 11, it will pay any Stamp Tax levied or imposed upon it or in respect of its execution or performance of this Agreement by a jurisdiction in which it is incorporated, organised, managed and controlled, or considered to have its seat, or in which a branch or office through which it is acting for the purpose of this Agreement is located ('Stamp Tax Jurisdiction') and will indemnify the other party against any Stamp Tax levied or imposed upon the other party or in respect of the other party's execution or performance of this Agreement by any such Stamp Tax Jurisdiction which is not also a Stamp Tax Jurisdiction with respect to the other party.

5. Events of Default and Termination Events

(a) ***Events of Default*** The occurrence at any time with respect to a party or, if applicable, any Credit Support Provider of such party or any Specified Entity of such party of any of the following events constitutes an event of default (an 'Event of Default') with respect to such party:–

(i) ***Failure to Pay or Deliver*** Failure by the party to make, when due, any payment under this Agreement or delivery under Section 2(a)(i) or 2(e) required to be made by it if such failure is not remedied on or before the third Local Business Day after notice of such failure is given to the party;

(ii) ***Breach of Agreement*** Failure by the party to comply with or perform any agreement or obligation (other than an obligation to make any payment under this Agreement or delivery under Section 2(a)(i) or 2(e) or to give notice of a Termination Event or any agreement or obligation under Section 4(a)(i), 4(a)(iii) or 4(d)) to be complied with or peformed by the party in accordance with this Agreement if such failure is not remedied on or before the thirtieth day after notice of such failure is given to the party;

(iii) ***Credit Support Default***

(1) Failure by the party or any Credit Support Provider of such party to comply with or perform any agreement or obligation to be complied with or performed by it in accordance with any Credit Support Document if such failure is continuing after any applicable grace period has elapsed;

(2) the expiration or termination of such Credit Support Document or the failing or ceasing of such Credit Support Document to be in full force and effect for the purpose of this Agreement (in either case other than in accordance with its terms) prior to the satisfaction of all obligations of such party under each Transaction to which such Credit Support Document relates without the written consent of the other party; or

(3) the party or such Credit Support Provider disaffirms, disclaims, repudiates or rejects, in whole or in part, or challenges the validity of, such Credit Support Document;

(iv) ***Misrepresentation*** A representation (other than a representation under Section 3(e) or (f)) made or repeated or deemed to have been made or repeated by the party or any Credit Support Provider of such party in this Agreement or any Credit Support Document proves to have been incorrect or misleading in any material respect when made or repeated or deemed to have been made or repeated;

(v) ***Default under Specified Transaction*** The party, any Credit Support Provider of such party or any applicable Specified Entity of such party (1) defaults under a Specified Transaction and, after giving effect to any applicable notice requirement or grace period, there occurs a liquidation of, an acceleration of obligations under, or an early termination of, that Specified Transaction, (2) defaults, after giving effect to any applicable notice requirement or grace period, in making any payment or delivery due on the last payment, delivery or exchange date of, or any payment on early termination of, a Specified Transaction (or such default continues for at least three Local Business Days if there is no applicable requirement or grace period) or (3) disaffirms, disclaims, repudiates or rejects, in whole or in part, a Specified Transaction (or such action is taken by any person or entity appointed or empowered to operate it or act on its behalf);

(vi) ***Cross Default*** If 'Cross Default' is specified in the Schedule as applying to the party, the occurrence or existence of (1) a default, event of default or other similar condition or event (however described) in respect of such party, any Credit Support Provider of such party or any applicable Specified Entity of such party under one or more agreements or instruments relating to Specified Indebtedness of any of them (individually or collectively) in an aggregate amount of not less than the applicable Threshold Amount (as specified in the Schedule) which has resulted in such Specified Indebtedness becoming, or becoming capable at such time of being declared, due and payable under such agreements or instruments, before it would otherwise have been due and payable or (2) a default by such party, such Credit Support Provider or such Specified Entity (individually or collectively) in making one or more payments on the due date thereof in an aggregate amount of not less than the applicable Threshold Amount under such agreements or instruments (after giving effect to any applicable notice requirement or grace period);

(vii) ***Bankruptcy*** The party, any Credit Support Provider of such party or any applicable Specified Entity of such party:–

(1) is dissolved (other than pursuant to a consolidation, amalgamation or merger); (2) becomes insolvent or is unable to pay its debts or fails or admits in writing its inability generally to pay its debts as they become due; (3) makes a general assignment, arrangement or composition with or for the benefit of its creditors; (4) institutes or has instituted against it a proceeding seeking a judgement of insolvency or bankrupty or any other relief under any bankruptcy or insolvency law or other similar law affecting creditors' rights, or a petition is presented for its winding-up or liquidation, and, in the case of any

such proceeding or petition instituted or presented against it, such proceeding or petition (A) results in a judgement of insolvency or bankruptcy or the entry of an order for relief or the making of an order for its winding-up or liquidation or (B) is not dismissed, discharged, stayed or restrained in each case within 30 days of the institution or presentation thereof; (5) has a resolution passed for its winding-up, official management or liquidation (other than pursuant to a consolidation, amalgamation or merger); (6) seeks or becomes subject to the appointment of an administrator, provisional liquidator, conservator, receiver, trustee, custodian or other similar official for it or for all or substantially all its assets; (7) has a secured party take possession of all or substantially all its assets or has a distress, execution, attachment, sequestration or other legal process levied, enforced or sued on or against all or substantially all its assets and such secured party maintains possession, or any such process is not dismissed, discharged, stayed or restrained, in each case within 30 days thereafter; (8) causes or is subject to any event with respect to it which, under the applicable laws of any jurisdiction, has an analogous effect to any of the events specified in clauses (1) to (7) (inclusive); or (9) takes any action in furtherance of, or indicating its consent to, approval of, or acquiescence in, any of the foregoing acts; or

(viii) ***Merger Without Assumption*** The party or any Credit Support Provider of such party consolidates or amalgamates with, or merges with or into, or transfers all or substantially all its assets to, another entity and, at the time of such consolidation, amalgamation, merger or transfer:–

(1) the resulting, surviving or transferee entity fails to assume all the obligations of such party or such Credit Support Provider under this Agreement or any Credit Support Document to which it or its predecessor was a party by operation of law or pursuant to an agreement reasonably satisfactory to the other party to this Agreement; or

(2) the benefits of any Credit Support Document fail to extend (without the consent of the other party) to the performance by such resulting, surviving or transferee entity of its obligations under this Agreement.

(b) ***Termination Events*** The occurrence at any time with respect to a party or, if applicable, any Credit Support Provider of such party or any Specified Entity of such party of any event specified below constitutes an Illegality if the event is specified in (i) below, a Tax Event if the event is specified in (ii) below or a Tax Event Upon Merger if the event is specified in (iii) below, and, if specified to be applicable, a Credit Event Upon Merger if the event is specified pursuant to (iv) below or an Additional Termination Event if the event is specified pursuant to (v) below:–

(i) ***Illegality*** Due to the adoption of, or any change in, any applicable law after the date on which a Transaction is entered into, or due to the promulgation of, or any change in, the interpretation by any court, tribunal or regulatory authority with competent jurisdiction of any applicable law after such date, it becomes unlawful (other than as a result of a breach by the party of Section 4(b)) for such party (which will be the Affected Party):–

(1) to peform any absolute or contingent obligation to make a payment or delivery or to receive a payment or delivery in respect of such Transaction or to comply with any other material provision of this Agreement relating to such Transaction; or

(2) to perform, or for any Credit Support Provider of such party to perform, any contingent or other obligation which the party (or such Credit Support Provider) has under any Credit Support Document relating to such Transaction;

(ii) ***Tax Event*** Due to (x) any action taken by a taxing authority, or brought in a court of competent jurisdiction, on or after the date on which a Transaction is entered into (regardless of whether such action is taken or brought with respect to a party to this Agreement) or (y) a Change in Tax Law, the party (which will be the Affected Party) will, or there is a substantial likelihood that it will, on the next succeeding Scheduled Payment Date (1) be required to pay to the other party an additional amount in respect of an Indemnifiable Tax under Section 2(d)(i)(4) (except in respect of interest under Section 2(e), 6(d)(ii) or (2) receive a payment from which an amount is required to be deducted or withheld for or on account of a Tax (except in respect of interest under Section 2(e), 6(d)(ii) or 6(e)) and no additional amount is required to be paid in respect of such Tax under Section 2(d)(i)(4) (other than by reason of Section 2(d)(i)(4)(A) or (B));

(iii) ***Tax Event Upon Merger*** The party (the 'Burdened Party') on the next succeeding Scheduled Payment Date will either (1) be required to pay an additional amount in respect of an Indemnifiable Tax under Section 2(d)(1)(4) (except in respect of interest under Section 2(e), 6(d)(ii) or 6(e)) or (2) receive a payment from which an amount has been deducted or withheld for or on account of any Indemnifiable Tax in respect of which the other party is not required to pay an additional amount (other than by reason of Section 2(d)(i)(4)(A) or (B)), in either case as a result of a party consolidating or amalgamating with, or merging with or into, or transferring all or substantially all its assets to, another entity (which will be the Affected Party) where such action does not constitute an event described in Section 5(a)(viii);

(iv) ***Credit Event Upon Merger*** If 'Credit Event Upon Merger' is specified in the Schedule as applying to the party, such party ('X'), any

Credit Support Provider of X or any applicable Specified Entity of X consolidates or amalgamates with, or merges with or into, or transfers all or substantially all its assets to, another entity and such action does not constitute an event described in Section 5(a)(viii) but the creditworthiness of the resulting, surviving or transferee entity is materially weaker than that of X, such Credit Support Provider or such Specified Entity, as the case may be, immediately prior to such action (and, in such event, X or its successor or transferee, as appropriate, will be the Affected Party); or

(v) ***Additional Termination Event*** If any 'Additional Termination Event' is specified in the Schedule or any Confirmation as applying, the occurrence of such event (and, in such event, the Affected Party or Affected Parties shall be as specified for such Additional Termination Event in the Schedule or such Confirmation).

(c) ***Event of Default and Illegality*** If an event or circumstance which would otherwise constitute or give rise to an Event of Default also constitutes an Illegality, it will be treated as an Illegality and will not constitute an Event of Default.

6. Early Termination

(a) ***Right to Terminate Following Event of Default*** If at any time an Event of Default with respect to a party (the 'Defaulting Party') has occurred and is then continuing, the other party (the 'Non-defaulting Party') may, by not more than 20 days notice to the Defaulting Party specifying the relevant Event of Default, designate a day not earlier than the day such notice is effective an Early Termination Date in respect of all outstanding Transactions. if, however, 'Automatic Early Termination' is specified in the Schedule as applying to a party, then an Early Termination Date in respect of all outstanding Transactions will occur immediately upon the occurrence with respect to such party of an Event of Default specified in Section 5(a)(vii)(1), (3), (5), (6) or, to the extent analogous thereto, (8), and as of the time immediately preceding the institution of the relevant proceeding or the presentation of the relevant petition upon the occurrence with respect to such party of an Event of Default specified in Section 5(a)(vii)(4) or, to the extent analogous thereto, (8).

(b) ***Right to Terminate Following Termination Event***

(i) ***Notice*** If a Termination Event occurs, an Affected Party will, promptly upon becoming aware of it, notify the other party, specifying the nature of that Termination Event and each Affected Transaction and will also give such other information about that Termination Event as the other party may reasonably require.

(ii) ***Transfer to Avoid Termination Event*** If either an Illegality under Section 5(b)(i)(1) or a Tax Event occurs and there is only one Affected Party, or if a Tax Event Upon Merger occurs and the Burdened Party is the Affected Party, the Affected Party will, as a condition to its right to designate an Early Termination Date under Section 6(b)(iv), use all reasonable efforts (which will not require such party to incur a loss, excluding immaterial, incidental expenses) to transfer within 20 days after it gives notice under Section 6(b)(i) all its rights and obligations under this Agreement in respect of the Affected Transactions to another of its Offices or Affiliates so that such Termination Event ceases to exist.

If the Affected Party is not able to make such a transfer it will give notice to the other party to that effect within such 20 day period, whereupon the other party may effect such a transfer within 30 days after the notice is given under Section 6(b)(i).

Any such transfer by a party under this Section 6(b)(ii) will be subject to and conditional upon the prior written consent of the other party, which consent will not be withheld if such other party's policies in effect at such time would permit it to enter into transactions with the transferee on the terms proposed.

(iii) ***Two Affected Parties*** If an Illegality under Section 5(b)(i)(1) or a Tax Event occurs and there are two Affected Parties, each party will use all reasonable efforts to reach agreement within 30 days after notice thereof is given under Section 6(b)(i) on action to avoid that Termination Event.

(iv) ***Right to Terminate*** If:–

(1) a transfer under Section 6(b)(ii) or an agreement under Section 6(b)(iii), as the case may be, has not been effected with respect to all Affected Transactions within 30 days after an Affected Party gives notice under Section 6(b)(i); or

(2) an Illegality under Section 5(b)(i)(2), a Credit Event Upon Merger or an Additional Termination Event occurs, or a Tax Event Upon Merger occurs and the Burdened Party is not the Affected Party,

either party in the case of an Illegality, the Burdened Party in the case of a Tax Event Upon Merger, any Affected Party in the case of a Tax Event or an Additional Termination Event if there is more than one Affected Party, or the party which is not the Affected Party in the case of a Credit Event Upon Merger or an Additional Termination Event if there is only one Affected Party may, by not more than 20 days notice to the other party and provided that the relevant Termination Event is then continuing, designate a day not earlier than the day such notice is effective as an Early Termination Date in respect of all Affected Transactions.

(c) ***Effect of Designation***

(i) If notice designating an Early Termination Date is given under Section 6(a) or (b), the Early Termination Date will occur on the date so designated, whether or not the relevant Event of Default or Termination Event is then continuing.

(ii) Upon the occurrence or effective designation of an Early Termination Date, no further payments or deliveries under Section 2(a)(i) or 2(e) in respect of the Terminated Transactions will be required to be made, but without prejudice to the other provisions of this Agreement. The amount, if any, payable in respect of an Early Termination Date shall be determined pursuant to Section 6(e).

(d) ***Calculations***

(i) ***Statement*** On or as soon as reasonably practicable following the occurrence of an Early Termination Date, each party will make the calculations on its part, if any, contemplated by Section 6(e) and will provide to the other party a statement (1) showing, in reasonable detail, such calculations (including all relevant quotations and specifying any amount payable under Section 6(e)) and (2) giving details of the relevant account to which any amount payable to it is to be paid. In the absence of written confirmation from the source of a quotation obtained in determining a Market Quotation, the records of the party obtaining such quotation will be conclusive evidence of the existence and accuracy of such quotation.

(ii) ***Payment Date*** An amount calculated as being due in respect of any Early Termination Date under Section 6(e) will be payable on the day that notice of the amount payable is effective (in the case of an Early Termination Date which is designated or occurs as a result of an Event of Default) and on the day which is two Local Business Days after the day on which notice of the amount payable is effective (in the case of an Early Termination Date which is designated as a result of a Termination Event). Such amount will be paid together with (to the extent permitted under applicable law) interest thereon (before as well as after judgement) in the Termination Currency, from (and including) the relevant Early Termination Date to (but excluding) the date such amount is paid, at the Applicable Rate. Such interest will be calculated on the basis of daily compounding and the actual number of days elapsed.

(e) ***Payments on Early Termination*** If an Early Termination Date occurs, the following provisions shall apply based on the parties' election in the Schedule of a payment measure, either 'Market Quotation or 'Loss', and a payment method, either the 'First Method' or the 'Second Method'. If the parties fail to designate a payment measure or payment method in the Schedule, it will be deemed that 'Market Quotation' or the 'Second Method', as the case may be, shall apply. The amount, if any, payable in respect of an Early Termination Date and determined pursuant to this Section will be subject to any Set-off.

(i) ***Events of Default*** If the Early Terminate Date results from an Event of Default:–

(1) *First Method and Market Quotation* If the First Method and Market Quotation apply, the Defaulting Party will pay to the Non-defaulting Party the excess, if a positive number, of (A) the sum of the Settlement Amount (determined by the Non-defaulting Party) in

respect of the Terminated Transactions and the Termination Currency Equivalent of the Unpaid Amounts owing to the Non-defaulting Party over (B) the Termination Currency Equivalent of the Unpaid Amounts owing to the Defaulting Party.

(2) *First Method and Loss* If the First Method and Loss apply, the Defaulting Party will pay to the Non-defaulting Party, if a positive number, the Non-defaulting Party's Loss in respect of this Agreement.

(3) *Second Method and Market Quotation* If the Second Method and Market Quotation apply, an amount will be payable equal to (A) the sum of the Settlement Amount (determined by the Non-defaulting Party) in respect of the Terminated Transactions and the Termination Currency Equivalent of the Unpaid Amounts owing to the Non-defaulting Party less (B) the Termination Currency Equivalent of the Unpaid Amounts owing to the Defaulting Party. If that amount is a positive number, the Defaulting Party will pay it to the Non-defaulting Party; if it is a negative number, the Non-defaulting Party will pay the absolute value of that amount to the Defaulting Party.

(4) *Second Method and Loss* If the Second Method and Loss apply, an amount will be payable equal to the Non-defaulting Party's Loss in respect of this Agreement. If that amount is a positive number, the Defaulting Party will pay it to the Non-defaulting Party; if it is a negative number, the Non-defaulting Party will pay the absolute value of that amount to the Defaulting Party.

(ii) ***Termination Events*** If the Early Termination Date results from a Termination Event:–

(1) *One Affected Party* If there is one Affected Party, the amount payable will be determined in accordance with Section 6(e)(i)(3), if Market Quotation applies, or Section 6(e)(i)(4), if Loss applies, except that, in either case, references to the Defaulting Party and to the Non-defaulting Party will be deemed to be references to the Affected Party and the party which is not the Affected Party, respectively, and, if Loss applies and fewer than all the Transactions are being terminated, Loss shall be calculated in respect of all Terminated Transactions.

(2) *Two Affected Parties* If there are two Affected Parties:–

(A) if Market Quotation applies, each party will determine a Settlement Amount in respect of the Terminated Transactions, and an amount will be payable equal to (I) the sum of (a) one-half of the difference between the Settlement Amount of the party with the higher Settlement Amount ('X') and the Settlement Amount of the party with the lower Settlement Amount ('Y') and (b) the Termination Currency Equivalent of the Unpaid Amounts owing to X less (II) the Termination Currency Equivalent of the Unpaid Amounts owing to Y; and

(B) If Loss applies, each party will determine its Loss in respect of this Agreement (or, if fewer than all the Transactions are being terminated, in respect of all Terminated Transactions) and an amount will be payable equal to one-half of the difference between the Loss of the party with the higher Loss ('X') and the Loss of the party with the lower Loss ('Y').

If the amount payable is a positive number, Y will pay it to X; if it is a negative number, X will pay the absolute value of that amount to Y.

(iii) ***Adjustment for Bankruptcy*** In circumstances where an Early Termination Date occurs because 'Automatic Early Termination' applies in respect of a party, the amount determined under this Section 6(e) will be subject to such adjustments as are appropriate and permitted by law to reflect any payments or deliveries made by one party to the other under this Agreement (and retained by such other party) during the period from the relevant Early Termination Date to the date for payment determined under Section 6(d)(ii).

(iv) ***Pre-Estimate*** The parties agree that if Market Quotation applies an amount recoverable under this Section 6(e) is a reasonable pre-estimate of loss and not a penalty. Such amount is payable for the loss of bargain and the loss of protection against future risks and except as otherwise provided in the Agreement neither party will be entitled to recover any additional damages as a consequence of such losses.

7. Transfer

Subject to Section 6(b)(ii), neither this Agreement nor any interest or obligation in or under this Agreement may be transferred (whether by way of security or otherwise) by either party without the prior written consent of the other party, except that:–

(a) a party may make such a transfer of this Agreement pursuant to a consolidation or amalgamation with, or merger with or into, or transfer of all or substantially all its assets to, another entity (but without prejudice to any other right or remedy under this Agreement); and

(b) a party may make such a transfer of all or any part of its interest in any amount payable to it from a Defaulting Party under Section 6(e).

Any purported transfer that is not in compliance with this Section will be void.

8. Contractual Currency

(a) ***Payment in the Contractual Currency*** Each payment under this Agreement will be made in the relevant currency specified in this Agreement for that payment (the 'Contractual Currency'). To the extent permitted by applicable law, any obligation to make payments under this Agreement in the Contractual Currency will not be discharged or satisfied by any tender in any currency other than the Contractual Currency, except to the extent such tender results in the actual receipt by the party to which payment is owed, acting in a reasonable manner and in good faith in converting the currency so tendered into the Contractual Currency, of the full amount in the Contractual Currency of all amounts payable in respect of this Agreement. If for any reason the amount in the Contractual Currency so received falls short of the amount in the Contractual Currency payable in respect of this Agreement, the party required to make the payment will, to the extent permitted by applicable law, immediately pay such additional amount in the Contractual Currency as may be necessary to compensate for the shortfall. If for any reason the amount in the Contractual Currency so received exceeds the amount in the Contractual Currency payable in respect of this Agreement, the party receiving the payment will refund promptly the amount of such excess.

(b) ***Judgements*** To the extent permitted by applicable law, if any judgement or order expressed in a currency other than the Contractual Currency is rendered (i) for the payment of any amount owing in respect of this Agreement, (ii) for the payment of any amount relating to any early termination in respect of this Agreement or (iii) in respect of a judgement or order of another court for the payment of any amount described in (i) or (ii) above, the party seeking recovery, after recovery in full of the aggregate amount to which such party is entitled pursuant to the judgement or order, will be entitled to receive immediately from the other party the amount of any shortfall of the Contractual Currency received by such party as a consequence of sums paid in such other currency and will refund promptly to the other party any excess of the Contractual Currency received by such party as a consequence of sums paid in such other currency if such shortfall or such excess arises or results from any variation between the rate of exchange at which the Contractual Currency is converted into the currency of the judgement or order for the purposes of such judgement or order and the rate of exchange at which such party is able, acting in a reasonable manner and in good faith in converting the currency received into the Contractual Currency, to purchase the Contractual Currency with the amount of the currency of the judgement or order actually received by such party. The term 'rate of exchange' includes, without limitation, any premiums and costs of exchange payable in connection with the purchase of or conversion into the Contractual Currency.

(c) ***Separate Indemnities*** To the extent permitted by applicable law, these indemnities constitute separate and independent obligations from the other obligations in this Agreement, will be enforceable as separate and independent causes of action, will apply notwithstanding any indulgence granted by the party to which any payment is owed and will not be affected by judgement being obtained or claim or proof being made for any other sums payable in respect of this Agreement.

(d) ***Evidence of Loss*** For the purpose of this Section 8, it will be sufficient for a party to demonstrate that it would have suffered a loss had an actual exchange or purchase been made.

9. Miscellaneous

(a) ***Entire Agreement*** This Agreement constitutes the entire agreement and understanding of the parties with respect to its subject matter and supersedes all oral communication and prior writings with respect thereto.

(b) ***Amendments*** No amendment, modification or waiver in respect of this Agreement will be effective unless in writing (including a writing evidenced by a facsimile transmission) and executed by each of the parties or confirmed by an exchange of telexes or electronic messages on an electronic messaging system.

(c) ***Survival of Obligations*** Without prejudice to Sections 2(a)(iii) and 6(c)(ii), the obligations of the parties under this Agreement will survive the termination of any Transaction.

(d) ***Remedies Cumulative*** Except as provided in this Agreement, the rights, powers, remedies and privileges provided in this Agreement are cumulative and not exclusive of any rights, powers, remedies and privileges provided by law.

(e) ***Counterparts and Confirmations***

(i) This Agreement (and each amendment, modification and waiver in respect of it) may be executed and delivered in counterparts (including by facsimile transmission), each of which will be deemed an original.

(ii) The parties intend that they are legally bound by the terms of each Transaction from the moment they agree to those terms (whether orally or otherwise). A Confirmation shall be entered into as soon as practicable and may be executed and delivered in counterparts (including by facsimile transmission) or be created by an exchange of telexes or by an exchange of electronic messages on an electronic messaging system, which in each case will be sufficient for all purposes to evidence a binding supplement to this Agreement. The parties will specify therein or through another effective means that any such counterpart, telex or electronic message constitutes a Confirmation.

(f) ***No Waiver of Rights*** A failure or delay in exercising any right, power or privilege in respect of this Agreement will not be presumed to operate as a waiver, and a single or partial exercise of any right, power or privilege will not be presumed to preclude any subsequent or further exercise, of that right, power or privilege or the exercise of any right, power or privilege.

(g) ***Headings*** The headings used in this Agreement are for convenience of reference only and are not to affect the construction of or to be taken into consideration in interpreting this Agreement.

10. Offices; Multibranch Parties

(a) If Section 10(a) is specified in the Schedule as applying, each party that into a Transaction through an Office other than its head or home office represents to the other party that, notwithstanding the place of booking office or jurisdiction of incorporation or organisation of such party, the obligations of such party are the same as if it had entered into the Transaction through its head or home office. This representation will be deemed to be repeated by such party on each date on which a Transaction is entered into.

(b) Neither party may change the Office through which it makes and receives payments or deliveries for the purpose of a Transaction without the prior written consent of the other party.

(c) If a party is specified as a Multibranch Party in the Schedule, such Multibranch Party may make and receive payments or deliveries under any Transaction through any Office listed in the Schedule, and the Office through which it makes and receives payments or deliveries with respect to a Transaction will be specified in the relevant Confirmation.

11. Expenses

A Defaulting Party will, on demand, indemnify and hold harmless the other party for and against all reasonable out-of-pocket expenses, including legal fees and Stamp Tax, incurred by such other party by reason of the enforcement and protection of its rights under this Agreement or any Credit Support Document to which the Defaulting Party is a party or by reason of the early termination of any Transaction, including, but not limited to, costs of collection.

12. Notices

(a) ***Effectiveness*** Any notice or other communication in respect of this Agreement may be given in any manner set forth below (except that a notice or other communication under Section 5 or 6 may not be given by facsimile transmission or electronic messaging system) to the address or number or in accordance with the electronic messaging system details provided (see the Schedule) and will be deemed effective as indicated:–

(i) if in writing and delivered in person or by courier, on the date it is delivered;

(ii) if sent by telex, on the date the recipent's answerback is received;

(iii) if sent by facsimile transmission, on the date that transmission is received by a responsible employee of the recipient in legible form (it being agreed that the burden of proving receipt will be on the sender and will not be met by a transmission report generated by the sender's facsimile machine);

(iv) if sent by certified or registered mail (airmail, if overseas) or the equivalent (return receipt requested), on the date that mail is delivered or its delivery is attempted; or

(v) if sent by electronic messaging system, on the date that electronic message is received,

unless the date of that delivery (or attempted delivery) or that receipt, as applicable, is not a Local Business Day or that communication is delivered (or attempted) or received, as applicable, after the close of business on a Local Business Day, in which case that communication shall be deemed given and effective on the first following day that is a Local Business Day.
(b) ***Change of Address*** Either party may by notice to the other change the address, telex or facsimile number or electronic messaging system details at which notices or other communications are to be given to it.

13. Governing Law and Jurisdiction
(a) ***Governing Law*** This Agreement will be governed by and construed in accordance with the law specified in the Schedule.
(b) ***Jurisdiction*** With respect to any suit, action or proceedings relating to this Agreement ('Proceedings'), each party irrevocably:–

(i) submits to the jurisdiction of the English courts, if this Agreement is expressed to be governed by English law, or to the non-exclusive jurisdiction of the courts of the State of New York and the United States District Court located in the Borough of Manhattan in New York City, if this Agreement is expressed to be governed by the laws of the State of New York; and

(ii) waives any objection which it may have at any time to the laying of venue of any Proceedings brought in any such court, waives any claim that such Proceedings have been brought in an inconvenient forum and further waives the right to object, with respect to such Proceedings, that such court does not have any jurisdiction over such party.

Nothing in this Agreement precludes either party from bringing Proceedings in any other jurisdiction (outside, if this Agreement is expressed to be governed by English law, the Contracting States, as defined in Section 1(3) of the Civil Jurisdiction and Judgements Act 1982 or any modification, extension or re-enactment thereof for the time being in force) nor will the bringing of Proceedings in any one or more jurisdictions preclude the bringing of Proceedings in any other jurisdiction.
(c) ***Service of Process*** Each party irrevocably appoints the Process Agent (if any) specified opposite its name in the Schedule to receive, for it and on its behalf, service of process in any Proceedings. If for any reason any party's Process Agent is unable to act as such, such party will promptly notify the other party and within 30 days appoint a substitute process agent acceptable to the other party. The parties irrevocably consent to service of process given in the manner provided for notices in Section 12. Nothing in this Agreement will affect the right of either party to serve process in any other manner permitted by law.
(d) ***Waiver of Immunities*** Each party irrevocably waives, to the fullest extent permitted by applicable law, with respect to itself and its revenues and assets

(irrespective of their use or intended use), all immunity on the grounds of sovereignty or other similar grounds from (i) suit, (ii) jurisdiction of any court, (iii) relief by way of injunction, order for specific performance or for recovery of property, (iv) attachment of its assets (whether before or after judgement) and (v) execution or enforcement of any judgement to which it or its revenues or assets might otherwise be entitled in any Proceedings in the courts of any jurisdiction and irrevocably agrees, to the extent permitted by applicable law, that it will not claim any such immunity in any Proceedings.

14. Definitions

As used in this Agreement:–

'Additional Termination Event' has the meaning specified in Section 5(b).

'Affected Party' has the meaning specified in Section 5(b).

'Affected Transactions' means (a) with respect to any Termination Event consisting of an Illegality, Tax Event or Tax Event Upon Merger, all Transactions affected by the occurrence of Such Termination Event and (b) with respect to any other Termination Event, all Transactions.

'Affiliate' means, subject to the Schedule, in relation to any person, any entity controlled, directly or indirectly, by the person, any entity that controls, directly or indirectly, the person or any entity directly or indirectly under common control with the person. For this purpose, 'control' of any entity or person means ownership of a majority of the voting power of the entity or person.

'Applicable Rate' means:–

(a) in respect of obligations payable or deliverable (or which would have been but for Section 2(a)(iii)) by a Defaulting Party, the Default Rate;

(b) in respect of an obligation to pay an amount under Section 6(e) of either party from and after the date (determined in accordance with Section 6(d)(ii) on which that amount is payable, the Default Rate;

(c) in respect of all other obligations payable or deliverable (or which would have been but for Section 2(a)(iii)) by a Non-defaulting Party, the Non-default Rate; and

(d) in all other cases, the Termination Rate.

'Burdened Party' has the meaning specified in Section 5(b).

'Change in Tax Law' means the enactment, promulgation, execution or ratification of, or any change in or amendment to, any law (or in the application or official interpretation of any law) that occurs on or after the date on which the relevant Transaction is entered into.

'Consent' includes a consent, approval, action, authorisation, exemption, notice, filing, registration or exchange control consent.

'Credit Event Upon Merger' has the meaning specified in Section 5(b).

'Credit Support Document' means any agreement or instrument that is specified as such in this Agreement.

'Credit Support Provider' has the meaning specified in the Schedule.

'Default Rate' means a rate per annum equal to the cost (without proof or evidence of any actual cost) to the relevant payee (as certified by it) if it were to fund or of funding the relevant amount plus 1 per cent per annum.

'Defaulting Party' has the meaning specified in Section 6(a).

'Early Termination Date' means the date determined in accordance with Section 6(a) or 6(b)(iv).

'Event of Default' has the meaning specified in Section 5(a), if applicable, in the Schedule.

'Illegality' has the meaning specified in Section 5(b).

'Indemnifiable Tax' means any Tax other than a Tax that would not be imposed in respect of a payment under this Agreement but for a present or former connection between the jurisdiction of the government or taxation authority imposing such Tax and the recipient of such payment or a person related to such recipient (including, without limitation, a connection arising from such recipient or related person being or having been a citizen or resident of such jurisdiction, or being or having been organised, present or engaged in a trade or business in such jurisdiction, or having or having had a permanent establishment or fixed place of business in such jurisdiction, but excluding a connection arising solely from such recipient or related person having executed, delivered, performed its obligations or received a payment under, or enforced, this Agreement or a Credit Support Document).

'law' includes any treaty, law, rule or regulation (as modified, in the case of tax matters, by the practice of any relevant governmental revenue authority) and ***'lawful'*** and ***'unlawful'*** will be construed accordingly.

'Local Business Day' means subject to the Schedule, a day on which commercial banks are open for business (including dealings in foreign exchange and foreign currency deposits) (a) in relation to any obligation under Section 2(a)(i), in the place(s) specified in the relevant Confirmation or, if not so specified, as otherwise agreed by the parties in writing or determined pursuant to provisions contained, or incorporated by references, in this Agreement, (b) in relation to any other payment, in the place where the relevant account is located and, if different, in the principal financial centre, if any, of the currency of such payment, (c) in relation to any notice or other communication, including notice contemplated under Section 5(a)(i), in the city specified in the address for notice provided by the recipient and, in the case of a notice contemplated by Section 2(b), in the place where the relevant new account is to be located and (d) in relation to Section 5(a)(v)(2), in the relevant locations for performance with respect to such Specified Transaction.

'Loss' means, with respect to this Agreement or one or more Terminated Transactions, as the case may be, and a party, the Termination Currency Equivalent of an amount that party reasonably determines in good faith to be its total losses and costs (or gain, in which case expressed as a negative number) in connection with this Agreement or that Terminated Transaction or group of Terminated Transactions, as the case may be, including any loss of bargain, cost of funding or, at the election of such party but without duplication, loss or cost incurred as a result of its terminating, liquidating, obtaining or reestablishing any hedge or related trading position (or any gain resulting from any of them). Loss includes losses and costs (or gains) in respect of any payment or delivery required to have been made (assuming satisfaction of each applicable condition precedent) on or before the relevant Early Termination Date and not made, except, so as to avoid duplication, if Section 6(e)(i)(1) or (3) or 6(e)(ii)(2)(A) applies. Loss does not include a party's legal fees and out-of-pocket expenses referred to under Section 11. A party will determine its Loss as of the relevant Early Termination Date, or, if that is not reasonably practicable, as of the earliest date thereafter as is reasonably practicable. A party may (but need not) determine its Loss by reference to quotations of relevant rates or prices from one or more leading dealers in the relevant markets.

'Market Quotation' means, with respect to one or more Terminated Transactions and a party making the determination, an amount determined on the basis of quotations from Reference Market-makers. Each quotation will be for an amount, if any, that would be paid to such party (expressed as a negative number) or by such party (expressed as a positive number) in consideration of an agreement between such party (taking into account any existing Credit Support Document with respect to the obligations of such party) and the quoting Reference Market-maker to enter into a transaction ('the Replacement Transaction') that would have the effect of preserving for such party the economic equivalent of any payment or delivery (whether the underlying obligation was absolute or contingent and assuming the satisfaction of each applicable condition precedent) by the parties under Section 2(a)(i) in respect of such Terminated Transaction or group of Terminated Transactions that would, but for the occurrence of the relevant Early Termination Date, have been required after that date. For this purpose, Unpaid Amounts in respect of the Terminated Transaction or group of Terminated Transactions are to be excluded but, without limitation, any payment or delivery that would, but for the relevant Early Termination Date, have been required (assuming satisfaction of each applicable condition precedent) after that Early Termination Date is to be included. The Replacement Transaction would be subject to such documentation as such party and the Reference Market-maker may, in good faith, agree. The party making the determination (or its agent) will request each Reference Market-maker to provide its quotation to the extent reasonably practicable as of the same day and time (without regard to different time zones) on or as soon as reasonably practicable after the relevant Early Termination Date. The day and time as of which those quotations are to be obtained will be selected in good faith by the party obliged to make a determination under Section 6(e), and, if each party is so obliged, after consultation with the other. If more than three quotations are provided, the Market Quotation will be the arithmetic mean of the quotations, without regard to the quotations having the highest and lowest values. If exactly three such quotations are provided, the Market Quotation will be the quotation remaining after disregarding in the highest and lowest quotations. For this purpose, if more than one quotation has the same highest value or lowest value, then one of such quotations shall be disregarded. If fewer than three quotations are provided, it will be deemed that the Market Quotation in respect of such Terminated Transaction or group of Terminated Transactions cannot be determined.

'Non-default Rate' means a rate per annum equal to the cost (without proof or evidence of any actual cost) to the Non-defaulting Party (as certified by it) if it were to fund the relevant amount.

'Non-defaulting Party' has the meaning specified in Section 6(a).

'Office' means a branch or office of a party, which may be such party's head or home office.

'Potential Event of Default' means any event which, with the giving of notice or the lapse of time or both, would constitute an Event of Default.

'Reference Market-makers' means four leading dealers in the relevant market selected by the party determining a Market Quotation in good faith (a) from among dealers of the highest credit standing which satisfy all the criteria that such party applies generally at the time in deciding whether to offer or to make an extension of credit and (b) to the extent practicable, from among such dealers having an office in the same city.

'Relevant Jurisdiction' means, with respect to a party, the jurisdictions (a) in which the party is incorporated, organised, managed and controlled or considered to have its seat, (b) where an Office through which the party is acting for purposes of this Agreement is located, (c) in which the party executes this Agreement and (d) in relation to any payment, from or through which such payment is made.

'Scheduled Payment Date' means a date on which a payment or delivery is to be made under Section 2(a)(i) with respect to a Transaction.

'Set-off' means set-off, offset, combination of accounts, right of retention or withholding or similar right or requirement to which the payer of an amount under Section 6 is entitled or subject (whether arising under this Agreement, another contract, applicable law or otherwise) that is exercised by, or imposed on, such payer.

'Settlement Amount' means, with respect to a party and any Early Termination Date, the sum of:–

(a) the Termination Currency Equivalent of the Market Quotations (whether positive or negative) for each Terminated Transaction or group of Terminated Transactions for which a Market Quotation is determined; and

(b) such party's Loss (whether positive or negative and without reference to any Unpaid Amounts) for each Terminated Transaction or group of Terminated Transactions for which a Market Quotation cannot be determined or would not (in the reasonable belief of the party making the determination) produce a commercially reasonable result.

'Specified Entity' has the meaning specified in the Schedule.

'Special Indebtedness' means, subject to the Schedule, any obligation (whether present or future, contingent or otherwise, as principal or surety or otherwise) in respect of borrowed money.

'Specified Transaction' means, subject to the Schedule, (a) any transaction (including an agreement with respect thereto) now existing or hereafter entered into between one party to this Agreement (or any Credit Support Provider of such party or any applicable Specified Entity of such party) and the other party to this Agreement (or any Credit Support Provider of such other party or any applicable Specified Entity of such other party) which is a rate swap transaction, basis swap, forward rate transaction, commodity swap, commodity option, equity or equity index swap, equity or equity index option, bond option, interest rate option, foreign exchange transaction, cap transaction, floor transaction, collar transaction, currency swap transaction, cross-currency rate swap transaction, currency option or any other similar transaction (including any option with respect to any of these transactions), (b) any combination of these transactions and (c) any other transaction identified as a Specified Transaction in this Agreement or the relevant confirmation.

'Stamp Tax' means any stamp, registration, documentation or similar tax.

'Tax' means any present or future tax, levy, impost, duty, charge, assessment or fee of any nature (including interest, penalties and additions thereto) that is imposed by any government or other taxing authority in respect of any payment under this Agreement other than a stamp, registration, documentation or similar tax.

'Tax Event' has the meaning specified in Section 5(b).

'Tax Event Upon Merger' has the meaning specified in Section 5(b).

'Terminated Transactions' means with respect to any Early Termination Date (a) if resulting from a Termination Event, all Affected Transactions and (b) if resulting from and Event of Default, all Transactions (in either case) in effect immediately before the effectiveness of the notice designating that Early Termination Date (or, if 'Automatic Early Termination' applies, immediately before that Early Termination Date).

'Termination Currency' has the meaning specified in the Schedule.

'Termination Currency Equivalent' means, in respect of any amount denominated in the Termination Currency, such Termination Currency amount and, in respect of any amount denominated in a currency other than the Termination Currency (the 'Other Currency'), the amount in the Termination Currency determined by the party making the relevant determination as being required to purchase such amount of such Other Currency as at the relevant Early Termination Date, or, if the relevant Market Quotation or Loss (as the case may be), is determined as of a later date, that later date, with the Termination Currency at the rate equal to the spot exchange of the foreign exchange agent (selected as provided below) for the purchase of such Other Currency with the Termination Currency at or about 11:00 a.m. (in the city in which such foreign exchange agent is located) on such date as would be customary for the determination of such a rate for the purchase of such Other Currency for value on the relevant Early Termination Date or that later date. The foreign exchange agent will, if only one party is obliged to make a determination under Section 6(e), be selected in good faith by that party and otherwise will be agreed by the parties.

'Termination Event' means an Illegality, A Tax Event or a Tax Event Upon Merger or, if specified to be applicable, a Credit Event Upon Merger or an Additional Termination Event.

'Termination Rate' means a rate per annum equal to the arithmetic mean of the cost (without proof or evidence of any actual cost) to each party (as certified by such party) if it were to fund or of funding such amounts.

'Unpaid Amounts' owing to any party means, with respect to an Early Termination Date, the aggregate of (a) in respect of all Terminated Transactions, the amounts that become payable (or that would have become payable but for Section 2(a)(iii) to such party under Section 2(a)(i) on or prior to such Early Termination Date and which remain unpaid as at such Early Termination Date and (b) in respect of each Terminated Transaction, for each obligation under Section 2(a)(i) which was (or would have been but for Section 2(a)(iii)) required to be settled by delivery to such party on or prior to such Early Termination Date and which has not been so settled as at such Early Termination Date, an amount equal to the fair market value of that which was (or would have been) required to be delivered as of the originally scheduled date for delivery, in each case together with (to the extent permitted under applicable law) interest, in the currency of such amounts, from (and including) the date such amounts or obligations were or would have been required to have been paid or performed to (but excluding) such Early Termination Date, at the Applicable Rate. Such amounts of interest will be calculated on the basis of daily compounding and the actual number of days elapsed. The fair market value of any obligation referred to in clause (b) above shall be reasonably determined by the party obliged to make the determination under Section 6(e) or, if each party is so obliged, it shall be the average of the Termination Currency Equivalents of the fair market values reasonably determined by both parties.

IN WITNESS WHEREOF the parties have executed this document on the respective dates specified below with effect from the date specified on the first page of this document.

....	....
(Name of Party)	(Name of Party)
By:	By: ....
Name:	Name:
Title:	Title:
Date:	Date:

ISDA®

International Swap Dealers Association, Inc.

SCHEDULE
to the
Master Agreement

dated as of..

between .... and ....
('Party A') ('Party B')

Part 1. **Terminal Provisions**

(a) ***'Specified Entity'*** means in relation to Party A for the purpose of:–

Section 5(a)(v), ...

Section 5(a)(vi), ...

Section 5(a)(vii), ...

Section 5(b)(iv), ...

and in relation to Party B for the purpose of:–

Section 5(a)(v), ...

Section 5(a)(vi), ...

Section 5(a)(vii), ...

Section 5(b)(iv), ...

(b) ***'Specified Transaction'*** will have the meaning specified in Section 14 of this Agreement unless another meaning is specified here ....

....

....

(c) The ***'Cross Default'*** provisions of Section 5(a)(vi)
will/will not* apply to Party A
will/will not* apply to Party B

If such provisions apply:–

'Specified Indebtedness' will have the meaning specified in Section 14 of this Agreement unless another meaning is specified here ....

....

'Threshold Amount' means ....

....

(d) The ***'Credit Event Upon Merger'*** provisions of Section 5(b)(iv)
will/will not* apply to Party A
will/will not* apply to Party B

(e) The ***'Automatic Early Termination'*** provision of Section 6(a)
will/will not* apply to Party A
will/will not* apply to Party B

(f) ***'Payments on Early Termination'.*** For the purpose of Section 6(e) of this Agreement:–

(i) Market Quotation/Loss* will apply.

(ii) The First Method/The Second Method* will apply.

(g) ***'Termination Currency'*** means ...., if such currency is specified and freely available, and otherwise United States Dollars.

(h) ***Additional Termination Event*** will/will not apply*. The following shall constitute an Additional Termination Event:– ....

....

....

....

....

....

For the purpose of the foregoing Termination Event, the Affected Party or Affected Parties shall be:– ....

....

Part 2. **Tax Representations**

(a) ***Payer Representations.*** For the purpose of Section 3(e) of this Agreement, Party A will/will not* make the following representation and Party B will/will not* make the following representation:–

It is not required by any applicable law, as modified by the practice of any relevant governmental revenue authority, of any Relevant Jurisdiction to make any deduction or withholding for or on account of any Tax from any payment (other than interest under Section 2(e), 6(d)(ii) or 6(e) of this Agreement) to be made by it to the other party under this Agreement. In making this representation, it may rely on (i) the accuracy of any representations made by the other party pursuant to Section 3(f) of this Agreement, (ii) the satisfaction of the agreement contained in Section 4(a)(i) or 4(a)(ii) of this Agreement and the accuracy and effectiveness of any document provided by the other party pursuant to Section 4(a)(i) or 4(a)(iii) of this Agreement and (iii) the satisfaction of the agreement of the other party contained in Section 4(d) of this Agreement, *provided* that it shall not be a breach of this representation where reliance is placed on clause (ii) and the other party does not deliver a form or document under Section 4(a)(iii) by reason of material prejudice to its legal or commercial position.

(b) ***Payee Representations.*** For the purpose of Section 3(f) of this Agreement, Party A and Party B make the representations specified below, if any:

(i) The following representation will/will not* apply to Party A and will/will not* apply to Party B:–

It is fully eligible for the benefits of the 'Business Profits' or 'Industrial and Commercial Profits' provision, as the case may be, the 'Interest' provision or the 'Other Income' provision (if any) of the Specified Treaty with respect to any payment described in such provisions and received or to be received by it in connection with this Agreement and no such payment is attributable to a trade or business carried on by it through a permanent establishment in the Specified Jurisdiction.

If such representation applies, then:–

'Specified Treaty' means with respect to Party A ....

'Specified Jurisdiction' means with respect to Party A ....

'Specified Treaty' means with respect to Party B ....

'Specified Jurisdiction' means with respect to Party B ....

(ii) The following representation will/will not* apply to Party A and will/will not* apply to Party B:–

Each payment received or to be received by it in connection with this Agreement will be effectively connected with its conduct of a trade or business in the Specified Jurisdiction.

If such representation applies, then:–

'Specified Jurisdiction' means with respect to Party A ....

'Specified Jurisdiction' means with respect to Party B ....

(iii) The following representation will/will not* apply to Party A and will/will not* apply to Party B:–

(A) It is entering into each Transaction in the ordinary course of its trade as, and is, either (1) a recognised U.K. bank or (2) a recognised U.K. swaps dealer (in either case (1) or (2), for purposes of the United Kingdom Inland Revenue extra statutory concession C17 on interest and currency swaps dated March 14, 1989), and (B) it will bring into account payments made and received in respect of each Transaction in computing its income for United Kingdom tax purposes.

(iv) Other Payee Representations:– ....

....

....

....

N.B. The above representations may need modification if either party is a Multibranch Party.

Part 3. **Agreement to Deliver Documents**

For the purpose of Sections 4(a)(i) and (ii) of this Agreement, each party agrees to deliver the following documents, as applicable:–

(a) Tax forms, documents or certificates to be delivered are:–

Party required to deliver document	Form/Document/ Certificate	Date by which to be delivered
....	....	....
....	....	....
....	....	....
....	....	....
....	....	....

(b) Other documents to be delivered are:–

Party required to deliver document	Form/Document/ Certificate	Date by which to be delivered	Covered by Section 3(d) Representation
....	....	....	Yes/No*
....	....	....	Yes/No*
....	....	....	Yes/No*
....	....	....	Yes/No*
....	....	....	Yes/No*

Part 4. **Miscellaneous**

(a) ***Addresses for Notices.*** For the purpose of Section 12(a) of this Agreement:–

Address for notices or communications to Party A:–

Address: ....

Attention: ....

Telex No.: .... Answerback: ....

Facsimile No.: .... Telephone No.: ....

Electronic Messaging System Details: ....

Address for notices or communications to Party B:–

Address: ....

Attention: ....

Telex No.: .... Answerback: ....

Facsimile No.: .... Telephone No.: ....

Electronic Messaging System Details: ....

(b) ***Process Agent.*** For the purpose of Section 13(c) of this Agreement:–

Part A appoints as its Process Agent ....

Part B appoints as its Process Agent ....

(c) ***Offices.*** The provisions of Section 10(a) will/will not* apply to this Agreement.

(d) ***Multibranch Party.*** For the purpose of Section 10(c) of this Agreement:–

Part A is/is not* a Multibranch Party and, if so, may act through the following Offices:–

....

....

Part B is/is not* a Multibranch Party and, if so, may act through the following Offices:–

....

....

(e) ***Calculation Agent.*** The Calculation Agent is ...., unless otherwise specified in a Confirmation in relation to the relevant Transaction.

(f) ***Credit Support Document.*** Details of any Credit Support Document:– ....

....

....

....

(g) ***Credit Support Provider.*** Credit Support Provider means in relation to

Party A, ...

....

....

Credit Support Provider means in relation to Party B, ...

....

....

(h) ***Governing Law.*** This Agreement will be governed by and construed in accordance with English law/the laws of the State of New York (without reference to choice of law doctrine)*.

(i) ***Netting of Payments.*** Subparagraph (ii) Section 2(c) of this Agreement will not apply to the following Transactions or groups of Transactions (in each case starting from the date of this Agreement/in each case starting

from ....

....

....

(j) ***'Affiliate'*** will have the meaning specified in Section 14 of this Agreement unless another meaning is specified here ....

....

Part 5. **Other Provisions**

Index